introduction to
music theory

ALLEN WINOLD
School of Music
Indiana University

JOHN REHM
Department of Music
Illinois State University

introduction to music theory

second edition

prentice-hall, inc., englewood cliffs, new jersey 07632

Library of Congress Cataloging in Publication Data

Winold, Allen.
    Introduction to music theory.

    Includes index.
    1. Music—Theory.   I. Rehm, John, joint author.
II. Title.
MT6.W6I6 1979   781   78-17257
ISBN 0-13-489666-1

Printed in the United States of America

10 9 8 7 6 5 4 3

Editorial/production supervision by Teru Uyeyama
Page layout by Terry Reid
Cover design by Jayne Conte
Manufacturing buyer: Phil Galea

PRENTICE-HALL INTERNATIONAL, INC., *London*
PRENTICE-HALL OF AUSTRALIA PTY. LIMITED, *Sydney*
PRENTICE-HALL OF CANADA, LTD., *Toronto*
PRENTICE-HALL OF INDIA PRIVATE LIMITED, *New Delhi*
PRENTICE-HALL OF JAPAN, INC., *Tokyo*
PRENTICE-HALL OF SOUTHEAST ASIA PTE. LTD., *Singapore*
WHITEHALL BOOKS LIMITED, *Wellington, New Zealand*

contents

preface to the revised edition

This revised edition of *Introduction to Music Theory* has the same basic objective as the original edition—to provide a solid foundation in the fundamental skills and concepts of music. It differs from the original edition in two important ways—the inclusion of examples from music literature and the incorporation of concepts of integer notation in the discussions of pitch aspects. We include examples from the literature in response to the requests of teachers for ready access to materials from music literature that will augment and enrich the drill material in the text.

Information on integer notation is included at the end of Chapters 7, 8, 11, 14, 19, and 20. Integer notation has shown itself to be highly effective in the treatment of music from a variety of periods and styles, and it has found increasing currency in music textbooks and curriculums. Furthermore, the study of integer notation has proved a valuable aid in understanding traditional pitch notation.

Introduction to Music Theory has been developed for use in college freshman courses, but it may also be used at the high school level. It presents a comprehensive program that includes coordinated work in written concepts, terminology, and notation; exercises in music reading and sight singing; and practice in ear training. In addition, it provides suggestions for work in analysis and composition.

There are several advantages to such a coordinated approach. The various facets of the program complement and reinforce one another. There is no conflict in terminology and approach, as would result from the combined use of several different texts. The student's level of interest is held high because of the constantly changing nature of the activities presented.

Though we use a "semiprogrammed" format in parts of the text, we do not intend that the materials in this book be entirely self-instructional. In particular, it would be impossible to present in this format adequate material on longer melodies, ensemble composition, analysis of music, and original composition—all essential parts of any solid program in music. These topics must be presented by the teacher working directly with the students in the classroom, in small-group sessions, or on an individual basis.

Classroom presentation can also provide an effective balance to this text in terms of approach. The approach used in the written and aural exercises is basically that of working from small parts toward a larger whole. We suggest that in classroom presentations, the teacher work with the opposite approach—beginning with examples from the literature and then deriving principles and illustrations from them.

More specifically, it will be seen that our approach to durational or rhythmic aspects begins with pulse groups and then works progressively toward larger concepts of organization, such as meter. Our approach to pitch aspects begins with pitch sets and then works progressively toward larger concepts, such as tonality and modality.

One advantage of this approach is that it begins with aspects of music that are common to a wide body of music. It avoids the fallacy of treating contemporary music as a "distortion" of earlier music. A further advantage of this approach is that it will be new for all students, including those with little or no previous knowledge as well as those with knowledge and skills in some areas but deficiencies in others. A more traditional approach can be boring for some, bewildering for others.

The authors wish to acknowledge their indebtedness to two groups of people for their contribution to this text: first, to their colleagues at Indiana University, Illinois State University, and other schools, whose suggestions have helped to shape and refine the content of the text; second, and above all, to the thousands of students who have not only tried out the material but have also in a very real sense taught their teachers.

ALLEN WINOLD
JOHN REHM

introduction

Before you begin, you should consider the objectives of this book and the methods to be used for accomplishing them. Simply stated, the three principal objectives of the text are:

1. to understand the meaning of music notation and music terms;
2. to be able to translate music notation and terms into musical sounds;
3. to be able to translate musical sounds into musical notation and terms.

The first objective is a prerequisite to the last two rather than an end in itself. It is of little value for you as a musician to know that the pitch f is a minor second above the pitch e if you are not able to produce or perceive this relationship.

The second objective, that of translating musical notation and terms into musical sounds, is usually called music reading or sight reading. There are some obvious and specific reasons for developing this skill. Often, singers or instrumentalists are called upon to read music at sight in rehearsals or auditions with no opportunity for previous study. Granting this, however, you may question the need for developing this skill to the extent required in this book. If you are an instrumentalist, you may wonder why you need to learn to sing pitches, since you can produce the correct pitch on your instrument merely by pressing the proper key or string. If you are a singer, you may wonder why you need to learn to read music at sight when you have already learned many songs by hearing them sung or played for you by a teacher or coach.

The answer to these questions and the real reason for developing the ability to read music at sight is that it develops *musical independence*. If you have to rely on the sounds your fingers produce on an instrument or on the sounds that your teacher produces, you can never fully develop your own aural concepts about music. If, on the other hand, you do develop facility in reading music at sight, you will find this skill helps your private practice, ensemble performance, and performance in general.

The third objective, that of translating musical sounds into musical notation and terms, is usually called ear training. This skill follows from and complements that of music reading, and progress made in one skill is usually reflected in the other. Some students will find ear training more difficult than music reading, perhaps because it involves the memory. Others will find music reading more difficult, perhaps because of vocal problems.

Ear training has some obvious, specific, and practical applications for the conductor, the composer, the jazz performer, and the music teacher. More important, however, is the contribution it makes to developing musical independence. If you develop your ability to hear and understand music, you will find that it will not only heighten your comprehension and enjoyment as a listener, but it will also lead to your improvement as a performer. In ensemble playing, it is particularly important to be able to hear and understand what others are performing so that your part can be effectively integrated in the whole musical texture.

Let us turn now to methods for achieving these objectives. The most important single general principle is this: *Concepts and skills must be applied immediately and continually to your own musical experiences as a performer and listener.*

Your study of the material in this book can be easily and effectively coordinated with your own practice and listening. If, for example, you are studying major and minor seconds, you could:

1. study your own music and find examples of major and minor seconds;
2. perform these intervals on various instruments, or sing them;
3. perform them on different pitch levels;
4. listen for major and minor seconds used prominently in music you hear in concert or on records, and then check the score to see if your identification was correct;
5. meet with classmates or friends, have them play examples from their literature for you, and listen for the use of major and minor seconds.

Practice done in this manner takes only a small amount of time and will improve your own applied music performance and your work in theory class.

The second general principle is: *Divide your study and practice into short, concentrated periods on a regularly scheduled basis.* It is far more effective to study these materials every day for two or three periods of less than an hour than to cram your work into one marathon session each week.

The third general principle you should bear in mind is this: *Do not be discouraged if your progress is not uniform in all aspects.* Percussion players will probably find the material on rhythm easier than the material on pitch. Sopranos will probably find melodies in treble clef easier than melodies in bass clef. You should expect to work harder and longer on some parts of the book than on others. You may find it necessary to review some sections several times before you master them.

Finally, your work with the materials in this book is intended as preparation for advanced study in music theory. If you master the concepts and skills outlined here, you will have a solid foundation for future study, especially if that study is devoted to working with actual materials drawn from the literature of music rather than to mechanical exercises in part writing. In this book, we emphasize skills and encourage you to use literature you know and can perform to complement your work in acquiring these skills. In more advanced study, the emphasis will shift more to the study of literature and you will be applying skills you have learned in this book.

HOW TO USE THE WRITTEN AND AURAL EXERCISES

Let us now consider the specific methods of using this text. Notice that each chapter contains written sections, music-reading exercises, ear-training exercises, examples from literature, supplementary exercises, and, in some chapters, optional material.

The written sections contain explanatory text and programmed exercises. Read the explanatory text carefully, just as you would any book. When you see a page that is divided into two columns, you have come to the beginning of a programmed exercise. Before you work these exercises, cover the right-hand column (the answer column) with a masking card. Then, read the instructions at the top of the left-hand column; read the first question, and write your answer in the space provided. Next, slide your masking card down until the answer to the first question is exposed. Compare your answer to this answer. If you were correct, proceed to the next question. If you were incorrect, cross out or erase your original answer and write the correct answer. Mark an X in the left-hand margin so that you can review this question later if needed. Then proceed to the next question. Always write down your answer or correction. Merely saying or thinking the answer is not sufficient. Work as quickly as you can with accuracy. (In a few instances, the answers appear below the exercises.)

The music-reading exercises may be done in class with the teacher or with a drill partner. The instructions that follow are written for a teacher and a student. If you work with a partner, one of you should take the teacher's role, and one the student's role. The music-reading exercises can and should be performed in a variety of ways to develop various skills. Here are some possibilities.

1. Teacher sings or plays the example; student sings back immediately, looking at the music. Teacher indicates whether the singing was correct. The purpose of this exercise is to develop skill in singing accurately and to begin to associate printed symbols and musical sounds. Though not actual sight singing, this is a valuable preliminary exercise. It is useless to try to learn to sing at sight until you have developed the ability to sing a passage you have just heard with accuracy and good musicianship.

2. Teacher drills on patterns similar to those in the exercise. Student

then sings the exercise. Again, this exercise is not as challenging as singing at sight without preparation, but it is a valuable preliminary exercise.

3. Teacher sounds opening pitch and sets a tempo, and student sings at sight. The student may sing with a neutral syllable, such as "dah"; on letter names, such as c, d, and e; or on scale number or solfege syllables.

4. Occasionally, exercises should be read at sight on the piano or on another instrument.

Many of the chapters include music-reading and ear-training exercises in duet form. The music-reading exercises may be performed by two voices or instruments, or they may be performed by one person singing one part and playing the other part on a keyboard instrument. In listening to the duet ear-training exercises, you may begin by listening to one part at a time, but you should work toward developing the ability to hear both parts together.

One of the reasons we have included duet exercises is to emphasize the value of practicing with a partner. Practice with a partner has proved not only far more effective but also more enjoyable for students. We urge you to form such a partnership and establish regular working periods as you study the materials in this book.

The ear-training exercises may be performed by the teacher or played on tapes. The number of hearings for each example will have to be decided by each teacher or student. We would recommend, however, that you constantly work towards reducing the number of hearings necessary, always bearing in mind that in terms of practical value, what really counts is how much you are able to comprehend and recall after one hearing only.

The examples from the literature may be used as additional exercises for music reading, ear training, or analysis, or simply as a change of pace from the discipline of the exercises. Although these examples are meant to emphasize the main points of the chapter in which they appear, they occasionally contain material that is beyond the level reached in the chapter. The purpose of this advanced material is not only to provide an interesting challenge but also to "preview" coming material.

The supplementary exercises approach from a more creative viewpoint the problems considered in the text. They emphasize composition and study of the literature, and they briefly introduce matters not treated in the main body of the text, such as musical form, improvisation, counterpoint, and orchestration.

chapter 1

Felix Mendelssohn once said, "If I could express myself completely with words, I would not need music." We could reverse Mendelssohn's idea and say that if it were somehow possible for us to communicate with you through music, we would have no need for words.

Your own musical experiences have probably shown you how difficult it is to discuss music with words alone. No matter how carefully your instrumental or vocal teachers may explain a point, it is difficult to understand that point until they demonstrate it and allow you to try it yourself. No matter how well written the program notes for a symphony concert or a recording may be, they can never substitute for the actual experience of hearing the music. And so, no matter how clearly we try in this text to explain the theoretical principles of music, you will not understand them fully until you have experienced them in music through performance, writing, or listening.

Let us begin, then, with music. Stop reading at the end of this paragraph, and perform or listen to two different pieces of music. Then, in your own words, list some ways in which the two pieces are similar and some ways in which they are different. Finally, try to write a short definition of music. When you have finished, continue with the text.

Write your comments on the music here:

Write your definition of music in the space below, and then compare it with the three definitions that follow.

René Descartes: "The basis of music is sound; its aim is to please and to arouse various emotions in us."
Edward Hanslick: "Music is form moving in sound."
George Bernard Shaw: "Music is the brandy of the damned."

Look up definitions of music in your dictionary. Which of the above definitions is the correct one? The answer can only be that any of them, including yours and the one we are about to suggest, be regarded as correct, according to the *purpose* behind the definition. Linguists and semanticists have suggested that meaning is not something we get from words, but rather something we give to them. They have also suggested that we assign these meanings with a particular (though perhaps not clearly realized) purpose in mind. We propose the following definition of music:

Music is a form of human behavior in which sound events are intentionally organized for intrinsic aesthetic effect.

This definition is no more "correct" than any of the definitions presented above, but it does reflect the purposes we have in mind. To say that music is a form of behavior is to emphasize something we have already mentioned—that the study of music should be an active study in which you listen, perform, or write, rather than a passive study in which you merely read what we have to say. Our purpose in using the expression "sound event" is to be sure that we include in our study not only tones, but also such things as noise, electronic sounds, and silence. Composers, especially those writing today, may use all of these materials in their music. A sound event is anything we hear—a click, a single tone, a measured silence, or a long, complex combination of sounds, such as a symphony or an opera.

To say that sound events are intentionally organized for intrinsic aesthetic effects is to point out one of the principal ways in which music differs from other types of human behavior involving sound. The driver honking her automobile horn or the fishmonger hawking his wares are making sounds, but they are not making music. They are not producing sounds for their *intrinsic* value—that is, for their value in themselves. Rather, they are producing sounds for their *extrinsic* value, for the sake of what the sounds refer to. A composer could, however, take the same sounds and use them in music. George Gershwin has done just that: he uses the sound of automobile horns in his *An American in Paris,* and the cry of a fishmonger in his opera *Porgy and Bess.*

Now let us return to the differences and similarities you found in the two musical compositions. You probably mentioned differences in rhythm, melody, harmony, orchestration, and form, depending upon your previous experience and knowledge of music terminology. These are sometimes called the elements or the basic aspects of music. But are they really elemental or basic? In the sections that follow, we suggest a structural outline for music that differs from the traditional categories mentioned above and yet includes them within it. We do not present this classification of musical processes as being necessarily superior to the traditional classification. Rather, as with our definition, we present it with some specific purposes in mind. First, we are concerned that you, as a musician of today, be involved with the music of today. The proposed structure represents some of the thinking of present-day composers and theorists. Second, we are concerned that you develop certain basic attitudes and behavior patterns in dealing with music. These are implied in our structure. Finally, we would hope that our attempt at creating a structure for music would encourage you to think about creating your own structure or classification system for music. In other words, we would encourage you to be at least a part-time music theorist as well as a performer, conductor, composer, teacher, or listener.

You may resist this last idea. For you, music may be so marvelous or mysterious that you just want to work with it and enjoy it; you do not wish to analyze it for fear that some of the beauty and mystery may disappear. If this is indeed your attitude, then your work with this book and your work in advanced theoretical studies will appear to you as a meaningless if not a harmful chore.

It is true that music theory does concern itself, at least in part, with the intellectual aspects of music. But it is just as true that the musical experience involves some combination of emotional, physical, and intellectual elements. The three reinforce and complement one another. To neglect or overemphasize one of them is to make the musical experience less complete and less effective.

PARAMETERS OF SOUND

Compare the two rectangles below:

We could say that the first rectangle is higher and narrower than the second. In mathematical terms, we could refer to these aspects or dimensions as *parameters*.

Modern music theorists have borrowed the term *parameter* to refer to various aspects or dimensions of sound. Compare any two sounds, and you will realize that there are at least four basic parameters involved: *duration, pitch, loudness,* and *timbre.* Let us look more closely at each of these.

Duration refers to the length of sounds or silences. Beethoven's Fifth Symphony, for example, opens with a pattern of three short notes and one long note (Ex. 1-1).

Ex. 1-1*

The parameter of duration is one of the main components of the musical element of rhythm. We shall discover, however, that other parameters also contribute to rhythm.

Pitch refers to the highness or lowness of sound. In Ex. 1-1, the three short notes are higher than the long note that follows. The parameter of pitch is often equated with the musical element of melody, but melody always involves the duration parameter—and, indeed, the other parameters—as well as the pitch parameter.

Loudness is easily understood and perceived. If we listen to the opening of the Fifth Symphony, we hear that the first eight notes are all loud and that the following notes begin softly and then grow louder. The traditional term for levels of loudness in music is *dynamics.*

Timbre refers to the tone quality or "tone color" of sound. The powerful timbre of the opening of the Fifth Symphony is created not by the full orchestra, as many people believe, but by two clarinets with the full string section. The parameter of timbre is one of the main considerations in the musical element of orchestration.

*We shall use standard notation for musical examples, even though some of you may not be familiar with all the symbols used. Your teacher can play the examples for you. At this point, our main concern is with the sound of music rather than with its written representation.

For the purposes of study and discussion, it is possible to analyze musical sound into these four parameters; in practice, it is impossible to isolate a single parameter. We cannot have a pitch without having a duration, a degree of loudness, and a particular timbre associated with it.

OPERATIONS

The four basic operations that can be performed with musical sounds are *presentation, repetition, change,* and *return.* These can be performed upon a single sound or upon groups of sounds; upon successive sounds or simultaneous sounds. To illustrate this, let us take only the pitch parameter of the first six sounds of "America." These sounds could be outlined as follows:

Ex. 1–2

We can label the first presentation of a single sound or group of sounds with the letter "A," and we can label subsequent changes with succeeding letters of the alphabet. To illustrate the application of this principle to groups of sounds, we can use the first four groups of the folk song "Hot Cross Buns." These would be outlined as follows:

Ex. 1–3

With groups of notes, the operation of change becomes somewhat more complex. Extensive change between groups is called *contrast;* slight change between groups is called *variation.* The dividing line between contrast and variation is not always clear-cut. Usually, extensive change in both the duration and pitch parameters is necessary to produce contrast. Slight change in just one of these parameters will usually result in variation.

Contrast is indicated with the next consecutive letter of the alphabet (A, B, C, D, etc.); variation is indicated with the same letter, but the appropriate superscript is added (A, A^1, A^2, A^3, etc.). The first four groups of "Silent Night" can be used to illustrate the two principles of contrast and variation:

From group A to group B there are changes in both the duration and pitch parameters. From group B to group B¹ there is no change in the duration parameter and only a slight change in the pitch parameter. (Pitches in both groups have the same approximate contour, but on different pitch levels.)

TEXTURE

When we speak of the texture of cloth, we are referring to the relationships and characteristics of the fibers in the cloth. When we speak of the texture of music, we are referring to the relationships and characteristics of the simultaneously sounding events in a composition. Texture is one of the most fascinating aspects of music. For a vivid demonstration, listen to the quartet from the opera *Rigoletto:* you can hear four different individuals singing at once and still be aware of the characteristics of each voice. We could compare this musical texture to a cloth texture woven with threads of many colors and weights. In contrast, the music of a Catholic priest intoning the Mass without any accompaniment is like a single thread.

We shall be concerned with three basic aspects of musical texture: the *vertical,* the *linear,* and the *spatial.** By vertical aspects, we mean the relations existing between simultaneous sounds at any given moment in time. Traditionally, we think in terms of vertical relations in the pitch parameter, and this is an important part of the study of harmony. We say, for example, that if we simultaneously sound the three tones C–E–G, we produce the vertical sonority commonly called the C-major triad. It is also possible to consider the vertical aspect of the parameters of timbre and loudness, and this is part of the study of orchestration.

By linear aspects, we mean the relations existing between two or more simultaneously sounded musical lines. These relationships, especially in the pitch and rhythm parameters, are important considerations in the study of counterpoint. For instance, we say that in Ex. 1–5 the two lines move independently in terms of the pitch parameter; that is, they often move in opposite directions. In terms of the duration parameter, the two lines do not move independently; that is, they both move in identical durations.

---

*The horizontal aspects of music consist of the relationships between successive sounds. We shall not include these in a discussion of texture, for to do so would be to equate the study of texture with the entire study of music. Although this is possible, we shall find it more helpful to limit texture to the definition above.

Ex. 1-5

Vertical and linear aspects always work in association with each other. Ex. 1-5 could also have been analyzed as a series of vertical sonorities —unison, major third, minor sixth, and so forth. Play or sing Ex. 1-5, or have your teacher play it; try to listen to it vertically, then try to listen to it linearly, and then try to be aware of both aspects at once.

The last aspect of texture to be considered is the spatial aspect. This refers to the location of the musical sound source in relation to the listener. This aspect was important in isolated instances of early music, such as the polychoral works in St. Mark's Cathedral in Venice in the sixteenth and seventeenth centuries. Part of the magnificent effect of these compositions was achieved by placing choral and instrumental groups in widely separated parts of the church. However, the spatial aspect of music was largely ignored in subsequent centuries until some contemporary composers began incorporating it in their works. A popular manifestation of interest in this aspect is the stereophonic record player.

UNITS

In any form of human behavior, there is a tendency to break up large events into smaller units so that they can be dealt with more effectively. To use language as an analogy, we can take a complete speech such as the Gettysburg Address and break it down into paragraphs, sentences, words, or phonemes (individual speech sounds). In music, we can follow a similar procedure and consider larger musical units, smaller musical units, and single sound events. In this section, we shall also consider the subject of sound sets.

It is difficult to set precise limits and to give precise definitions of musical units. Unlike pictures, music compositions do not have definite frames around them, unless we regard the silence before and after as an acoustical frame. Perhaps this is one reason why we applaud at the end of a composition—to give a clearer sense of framing. With smaller units, it is even more difficult to say where one unit ends and the next begins. Actually, the same difficulty holds in language, but we are seldom aware of it. For example, we are sure that the expression "streetcar company" is two words, but the Germans are just as sure that the same expression, *Strassenbahngesellschaft,* is one word.

To give some general notion, however, of the structure and characteristics of musical units, let us begin with the smallest. A single sound event can be a noise with no definite pitch, a tone with a definite pitch, a simultaneous combination of several sounds (that is, a vertical sonority, as discussed above), or a measured period of silence.

Two or more single sound events can be combined successively to form a short, unified, self-contained musical unit. These short units are variously called motives, figures, germs, cells, gestalts, patterns, clichés, idioms, formulas, and so on. The precise name given to the units is not as important as developing the ability to perceive and perform these units. Sometimes it is easy to discover these short units in a composition, especially if they end with a long duration or if they are separated from other material by a period of silence. In other cases it is difficult to identify these units, and an analysis of the interaction of various parameters and textural factors is needed to define the extent of the unit.

Often, two performers will organize the same piece of music in different units, and this analysis will influence their musical interpretation. To see what a difference the choice of unit size can make, try singing the first line of "America" in the following versions:

Version 1 (as five short units):
   My country / 'tis of thee / sweet land of / liberty / of thee I sing.

Version 2 (as three symmetrical units):
   My country 'tis of thee / sweet land of liberty / of thee I sing.

Version 3 (as three asymmetrical units):
   My country / 'tis of thee sweet land of liberty / of thee I sing.

Shorter units in music may be combined into longer units, which are usually called phrases, periods, double periods, phrase groups, sections, or movements. Again, the important thing is not what name we give to the unit, but rather what length we choose for the unit and the relationship that we find among the units in the piece. This is a significant part of the traditional study of form and analysis in music.

Sound sets are the raw materials from which a musical composition is created. Again, music theorists have borrowed a term from mathematics, and, again, the meaning of the term is easy to understand. A set is simply a collection or group of objects. In music, for example, the pitches C, D, and E form the pitch set for the beginning of "Hot Cross Buns" (Ex. 1–3). Other examples of pitch sets are scales, modes, and tone rows. It is also possible to have duration sets, loudness sets, and timbre sets. We shall use the concept of sets for the simplest beginning materials presented in this book, so that you will be familiar with the term when you encounter it in more advanced formal study.

CHARACTERISTICS

Any sound unit may be described or analyzed according to such characteristics as number and density, interval and range, complexity, and conformity.

To find the number of sounds in a sound unit, we could simply count each sound. The first and second sound groups of "Silent Night" (Ex. 1–4), for example, each have four sounds; the third and fourth sound groups each have three sounds. We could also count the number of different sounds in a sound group. In the first sound group of "Silent Night," for example, there are four sounds but only three different pitches—the first and third pitches are the same.

8

Density refers to the number of sounds per given amount of time. There are two ways in which we can make a sound unit more dense. The first is simply to present the single sounds more rapidly in succession. For example, in "Hot Cross Buns" (Ex. 1–3), all four sound groups are equal in length of time. However, the third sound group is more dense because more tones are sounded in it:

Ex. 1–6

	⊢—— one unit of time ——⊣	
first sound group:	Hot cross buns	has three sounds
second sound group:	Hot cross buns	has three sounds
third sound group:	One a-penny two a-penny	has eight sounds
fourth sound group:	Hot cross buns	has three sounds

The second method of making a sound group more dense is to sound more tones simultaneously. Listen again to the opening of Beethoven's Fifth Symphony. The first two sound groups are stated by the orchestra in unison: the instruments play the same tones together. Immediately thereafter, the music becomes more dense as several sections of the orchestra play different tones at different levels.

The concepts of interval and range are usually applied only to the pitch parameter. *Interval* refers to the distance between two pitches. The opening interval of "Somewhere Over the Rainbow" is wider than the opening interval of "Silent Night."

Range refers to the interval between the lowest and highest pitches in a sound unit. The range of "The Star-Spangled Banner" is wider than the range of "Hot Cross Buns."

The terms *interval* and *range* could also be applied to the duration and loudness parameters. We could say, for example, that the range of loudness is narrower in a simple folk song than in a Beethoven symphony.

Complexity refers to the number of different relationships between sounds in a sound unit. We can illustrate this characteristic by considering the pitch parameter only of the two melodies in Ex. 1–7. Both are relatively simple melodies, but it should be obvious from listening to them that "Joy to the World," which consists only of descending pitches with close intervals, is less complex in its pitch motion than "The Swan," which includes various kinds of intervals, both descending and ascending.

Ex. 1–7

Saint-Saëns: "Joy to the World"

Saint-Saëns: "The Swan"

In our discussion of music, we shall use the term *conformity* in much the same way that it is used in everyday language. There are certain traditions or norms that are associated with particular styles, periods, or types of music. We are interested in seeing how a given composition or a given unit from a composition conforms to these traditions or norms. For example, there are certain types of durational patterns, pitch inflections, and vertical sonorities that are traditionally associated with a blues song. We might listen to a particular blues and see how closely it follows traditional practices. One of the main reasons for studying theory and music literature is to learn the norms and traditions of particular periods and composers and to understand how a given composition either conforms to or departs from these norms and traditions.

EFFECTS

We have outlined a broad general basis for a theory of music, a foundation consisting of the parameters of sound, the operations that can be performed upon them, the units into which they may be formed, the textures in which they may appear, and the characteristics of the unit. We could stop here and not say anything at all about the effects that music can have upon us. A discussion of effects can easily become subjective, sentimental, or even senseless. Yet we cannot deny that music does have an effect on us; this is confirmed by a significant body of research on the psychological and physiological effects of music.

To avoid the pitfalls of overromanticizing the effects of music on the one hand or ignoring them completely on the other, we shall attempt to establish some general objective criteria concerning them. These criteria are *cessation* and *continuity, unity* and *variety, excitement* (*tension*) and *calm* (*release*), and *pleasantness* and *unpleasantness*. Each of these pairs represents the poles of continuum.

For example, complete cessation may be achieved at the end of a composition by ending on a long sound. Partial cessation or continuity may be achieved in a variety of ways.* Extreme unity can be achieved by using very few sounds within a very narrow range, with very simple relationships, and with a high degree of conformity to a style that is familiar to the listener. We move toward variety as we increase the number of sounds, extend the range, make the relationships more complex, and conform less to a given style. Rarely will an entire composition create the effect of extreme unity or extreme variety—indeed, one of the generally accepted principles of aesthetics is that any work of art should strike a balance between unity and variety.

Each of the effects of music may vary from individual to individual, but this variation is especially true of the last two pairs of effects we shall mention. The same piece of music may convey excitement or tension to one person and repose or release to another. Again, a composition may seem pleasant to a person on one day and unpleasant on another. Cultural, environmental, and personal factors, therefore, can sometimes play a greater role than purely musical factors in determining the effects music has on us.

*Two other terms that may be used to express the cessation-continuity continuum are *stability* and *instability*.

We include this discussion of the effects of music for another reason. Far too often, students assume that theory courses, theory texts, and theory teachers consider music only in an abstract, analytical, apathetic manner. It is true that very little will be said in this text about the loveliness, brilliance, or excitement of music, and it is true that much will be said about such technical matters as scales, meters, and chords. This does not imply that the authors or your teachers have no interest in the appreciation or performance of music. Ultimately, the only reason for learning anything about the theory of music is to gain a richer understanding and appreciation of music and to enhance one's musical abilities.

In this chapter, we have covered many complex topics in a short space of time. We do not expect you to master all of these concepts before proceeding to the next chapter. Rather, you should return throughout the course to the ideas expressed here in order to increase your understanding of these general ideas and to take a break from the intensive concentration on detail that is characteristic of later chapters.

EAR-TRAINING EXERCISES 1

Here and in each subsequent programmed exercise, cover the answer column before proceeding.

A. You will hear two sounds in each of the following ten exercises. In the first six exercises, indicate which parameter (duration, pitch, loudness, or timbre) has been changed in the second sound.

1. _____

2. _____

3. _____

4. _____

5. _____

6. _____

1. duration

2. loudness

3. timbre

4. pitch

5. duration

6. pitch

In the next four exercises, the second sound differs in two or more parameters. Indicate which parameters have been changed.

7. _____

8. _____

9. _____

10. _____

7. pitch and duration

8. duration and loudness

9. timbre, loudness, and duration

10. duration, pitch, loudness, and timbre

B. Listen to the following pairs of sound groups and indicate which parameter(s) have been changed in the second group.

1. _____

2. _____

3. _____

4. _____

5. _____

C. Each of the following exercises consists of three to five tones. In each exercise, the changes are limited to one parameter. Indicate which parameter is changed, and then underline the letter scheme that applies to the tones of the exercise.

1. The parameter changed is _____.
   (underline one) AAB AAA ABA ABB

2. Parameter: _____
   AAA ABA ABC ABB AAB

3. Parameter: _____
   AABA ABBC ABAB ABCA

4. Parameter: _____
   ABAAC AABBC ABCBA

5. Parameter: _____
   AABAB AABBC AABAC

D. Each of the following exercises consists of two note groups separated by a short silence. Indicate whether the second note group represents a repetition, a variation, or a contrast.

1. _____

2. _____

3. _____

4. _____

5. _____

E. Underline the letter scheme that represents the note group heard in each of the following exercises. Remember to use the same letter for repetitions (AAA), the same letter with a superscript for vari-

12

ations (AA^{1}A^2), a new letter for contrasts (ABC), and a previous letter for a return (ABA).

1. ABA ABA^1 ABCDE AA^{1}B
2. AABB^1 ABCA AA^{1}BA ABCD
3. ABCD ABAB AA^{1}A^{2}A^3 AA^{1}BB^1
4. ABBA ABCB ABA AAB
5. AA^{1}A^{2}A^3 ABCD AABB ABCA

F. Each of the following exercises consists of a short note group followed by three sound sets in one of the parameters. Underline the sound set used for the given note group.

1. (Pitch) Set I Set II Set III
2. (Duration) Set I Set II Set III
3. (Timbre) Set I Set II Set III
4. (Pitch) Set I Set II Set III

G. Listen to the following pairs of musical excerpts and answer each question by underlining the proper answer.

1. Which of the following excerpts has the greater total number of sounds?
   Excerpt A Excerpt B
2. Which of the following excerpts has the greater number of different pitches?
   Excerpt A Excerpt B
3. Which of the following excerpts has the greater number of different durations?
   Excerpt A Excerpt B
4. Which excerpt is more dense?
   Excerpt A Excerpt B
5. Which excerpt has the greater range of pitches?
   Excerpt A Excerpt B
6. Which excerpt has the greater range of loudness?
   Excerpt A Excerpt B
7. Which excerpt is more complex in terms of pitch relations?
   Excerpt A Excerpt B
8. Gregorian chant usually has relatively small intervals between adjacent pitches. Now listen to two excerpts, and indicate which one of them shows greater conformity to characteristic aspects of Gregorian chant.
   Excerpt A Excerpt B

1. Listen to the following examples in recorded or live performance, and discuss them in terms of continuity and closure, unity and variety, excitement and calm, pleasantness and unpleasantness, and other characteristics. Discuss the textures used in each example.

J.S. Bach; Sonata No. 1 in G Minor for Violin Alone, Presto
Beethoven; Symphony No. 7, second movement
Brahms; Symphony No. 2, fourth movement
Bartók; Concerto for Orchestra, second movement
Stockhausen; *Zyklus*
Ives; *The Unanswered Question*

2. Select three or four compositions you know well from playing or listening, and analyze them aurally, using letter schemes such as were used in the ear-training exercises.

3. Practice rote singing in class or with your partner. See how accurately you can sing back short melodies on first hearing. Work on extending the amount of material you can remember on one hearing.

4. Experiment with creating longer melodies from short note groups from several different sources. For example, sing the following words, using the familiar melodies associated with them; then sing the melodies on a neutral syllable.

Three blind mice, frère Jacques, see how they run, dormez-vous, they all ran after the farmer's wife, sonnez les matines, merrily, merrily, merrily, merrily, life is but a dream.

5. Experiment with free improvisation, using note groups of your own creation in various formal patterns. Sing or play them for your partner, and see if he or she can repeat them and analyze them.

6. For students interested in a fuller treatment of the concepts discussed in this chapter, the following books are recommended:

Leonard Meyer, *Emotion and Meaning in Music* (Chicago, University of Chicago Press, 1956)
Edward Cone, *Musical Form and Musical Performance* (New York, W.W. Norton, 1968)
Aaron Copland, *What to Listen for in Music* (New York, McGraw Hill, 1939)

chapter 2

In this chapter, we shall concentrate on the parameters of timbre and loudness and discuss such topics as instruments, voices, and dynamics. Although we present many facts in this chapter, some of them, such as the foreign-language terms, are included for reference, not for memorization. It is far more important that you develop your aural perception of these parameters. We recommend that students bring their instruments to class and play them so that the whole class can hear their capabilities and characteristics.

INSTRUMENTS

All musical sounds are produced by some type of periodically vibrating body, whether it be a drumhead, a violin string, or the vocal cords. Instruments and voices may be categorized according to the source of vibration:

Type	Source of Vibration	Examples
aerophones	column of air	flute, trombone
chordophones	stretched string	violin, piano, voice
electrophones	electronic generator	electronic organ
membranophones	stretched membrane	timpani, snare drum
idiophones	the instrument itself	cymbals, bells

Usually, however, instruments are divided according to the sections of the modern orchestra: woodwinds, brass, percussion, special instruments, and strings. Such a classification appears below. The instruments are listed in four languages in the order in which they normally appear in a full conducting score. Those marked with an asterisk (*) are used more frequently than the others.

The roman numerals following certain instruments indicate the number of different parts usually assigned to those instruments. *Flute I, II,* for example, indicates a part for first flute and a different part for second flute. In the woodwind and brass sections there is usually one player for each part. In the percussion section, one player will often play several different parts or instruments. In the string section of a large orchestra, there will normally be many players on each part. A typical distribution would be twenty first violins, eighteen second violins, sixteen violas, fourteen cellos, and twelve basses.

English	*Italian*	*German*	*French*
WOODWIND INSTRUMENTS			
*piccolo	flauto piccolo or ottavino	kleine Flöte	petite flûte
*flute I, II	flauto	Flöte	flûte
alto flute	flautone	Altoflöte	flûte alto
*oboe I, II	oboe	Oboe	hautbois
*English horn	corno inglese	Englisch Horn	cor anglais
*clarinet (in B♭ or A) I, II	clarinetto	Klarinette	clarinette
alto clarinet in E♭	clarinetto alto	Altklarinette	clarinette alto
bass clarinet in B♭	clarone	Bassklarinette	clarinette basse
contrabass clarinet in B♭	clarino contrabasso	Kontrabass-klarinette	clarinette contrebasse
*bassoon I, II	fagotto	Fagott	basson
*contrabassoon	contrafagotto	Kontrafagott	contrebasson
BRASS INSTRUMENTS			
*French horn I, II, III, IV	corno or corno ventile	Horn or Ventilhorn	cor à pistons
*trumpet I, II, III	tromba	Trompete	trompette
cornet	cornetto	Kornett	cornet-à-pistons
*trombone I, II, III	trombone	Posaune	trombone
baritone	flicorno tenore	Tenorhorn	bugle tenor
*tuba	tuba	Tuba	tuba
PERCUSSION INSTRUMENTS (Only four of many possible instruments are listed.)			
*kettledrums or timpani	timpani	Pauken	timbale
*snare drum	tamburo militare	kleine Trommel	petite caisse
*bass drum	gran cassa	grosse Trommel	grosse caisse
*cymbals	piatti	Becken	cymbales
SPECIAL INSTRUMENTS			
piano or pianoforte	pianoforte	Klavier or Pianoforte	piano
harpsichord	clavicembalo	Cembalo	clavecin
clavichord	clavicordo	Klavichord	clavichord
organ	organo	Orgel	orgue
harp	arpa	Harfe	harpe

English	Italian	German	French

STRINGED INSTRUMENTS

English	Italian	German	French
*violin I, II	violino	Violine or Geige	violon
*viola	viola	Bratsche	alto
*cello or violoncello	violoncello	Violoncell	violoncelle
*bass or string bass	contrabasso	Kontrabass	contrebasse

Ex. 2–1 depicts the ranges of the commonly used instruments in comparison with the piano keyboard.

Ex. 2–1

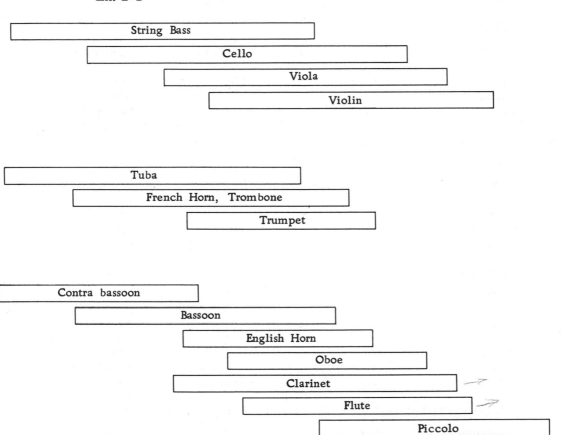

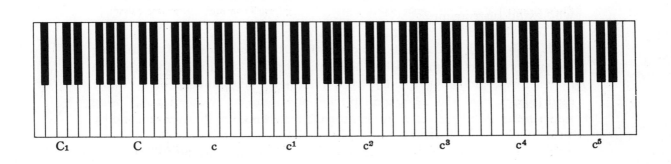

A. Fill in the blanks in the following exercise to see if you are completely familiar with standard score order.

piccolo
flute

1. _____   1. oboe
English horn
clarinet
bass clarinet

2. _____   2. bassoon

3. _____   3. contrabassoon

4. _____   4. French horn
trumpet
trombone
bass trombone

5. _____   5. tuba
percussion

6. _____   6. timpani
violin I, II

7. _____   7. viola

8. _____   8. cello
bass

B. Check your knowledge of instrumental ranges by marking the highest instrument *1,* the next highest *2,* and the lowest *3.*

oboe ( )   piccolo ( )   trombone ( )   oboe (2) piccolo (1) trombone (3)

bassoon ( )   viola ( )   violin ( )   bassoon (3) viola (2) violin (1)

trumpet ( )   string bass ( )   French horn ( )   trumpet (1) string bass (3) French horn (2)

clarinet ( )   cello ( )   flute ( )   clarinet (2) cello (3) flute (1)

Woodwind Instruments

All woodwind instruments produce their tone by means of a vibrating column of air set in motion by the player's breath blowing against a mouth hole (flutes, piccolos), a single reed (clarinets, saxophones), or a double reed (oboes, bassoons). Different pitches are obtained by opening or closing finger holes (which shortens or lengthens the column of vibrating air) and by "overblowing" the instrument (blowing with more force).

Solo passages for all of the woodwind instruments may be found in the standard orchestral repertoire. Generally, the higher-pitched woodwinds, which are somewhat more agile, are used for solo passages. The lower-pitched woodwinds, less agile, are used primarily in ensemble passages or with the other wind instruments in *tutti* (full orchestral) sections.

Brass Instruments

The mechanism that sets the air column in motion in brass instruments is the "buzzing" of the player's lips in the mouthpiece. The early "natural," or valveless, instruments can produce only the tones of the overtone series.* Successive tones of the overtone series are obtained by decreasing the size of the opening between the lips and by increasing the speed at which air is blown into the instrument.

A valve mechanism added to modern trumpets, horns, and tubas makes it possible to increase the column of air by various lengths by depressing the proper valves, and thereby create a new overtone series. In the trombone, the length of the air column is adjusted by a slide mechanism.

The brass instruments are frequently used to provide a harmonic foundation over which the strings and woodwinds play melodic material. Their use as solo instruments in the orchestral repertoire, although limited, has produced some of the most stirring passages in all of Western music.

Stringed Instruments

Sounds are produced on stringed instruments by setting the strings in vibration, either by plucking them with a finger or by bowing them with a horsehair bow. Modern string instruments—the violin, viola, cello, and string bass—have four strings made by gut or wire. Three factors determine the pitch of a string:

1. *Thickness.* The thicker a string, the lower its pitch. The four strings on stringed instruments are of varying thickness.
2. *Tension.* The lower the tension of the string, the lower its pitch. Tension is adjusted by means of tuning pegs.
3. *Length.* The longer the string, the lower its pitch. The length of a string is determined by the instrument's construction, but this length may be changed by placing a finger on the string (*stopping* the string), which shortens the vibrating length of the string.

The string section is the backbone of the orchestra, playing more or less continuously in the majority of standard orchestral works. Although it occasionally provides a harmonic foil against which solo winds carry the melody, it is more frequently the principal vehicle of melodic or thematic exposition. The violin is one of the most versatile and flexible of all the instruments; it is capable of executing all styles of music, from rapid, difficult passages to sustained lyrical melodies. The viola and cello are exploited somewhat less frequently as solo instruments, and the string bass is rarely used in this way.

*see pp. 275–276.

VOICES

The six standard categories of voices, from the highest female voice to the lowest male voice, are as follows:

$$
\text{Female} \begin{cases} \text{Soprano} \\ \text{Mezzo-soprano} \\ \text{Contralto (or alto)} \end{cases}
$$

$$
\text{Male} \begin{cases} \text{Tenor} \\ \text{Baritone} \\ \text{Bass} \end{cases}
$$

Four-part settings for mixed voices are usually written for soprano, alto, tenor, and bass.

Instrumentalists often overlook the importance of developing their singing voice. Yet many instrumental teachers will recommend that a student try to play a phrase as though it were sung. We strongly recommend that you incorporate some rudimentary instruction in singing into your study at this point.

DYNAMICS

We could indicate loudness in music with great precision by specifying the exact decibel level. One decibel is the smallest degree of change in loudness perceivable by the normal human ear. Music ranges in decibel level from about 25 to about 100 decibels. Usually, however, loudness is indicated by special words or symbols called *dynamics.* These are presented in the following table. The Italian terms are used more frequently than the English, French, or German.

English	Italian	Italian Abbreviation	German	French
very soft	*pianissimo*	*pp*	*sehr leise*	*très doux*
soft	*piano*	*p*	*leise*	*doux*
moderately soft	*mezzo-piano*	*mp*	*mässig leise*	*modéré*
moderately loud	*mezzo-forte*	*mf*	*mässig laut*	*modéré*
loud	*forte*	*f*	*laut*	*fort*
very loud	*fortissimo*	*ff*	*sehr laut*	*très fort*

Occasionally *ppp, pppp, fff,* and *ffff* are used for extremes of softness or loudness.

Changes in dynamics are indicated by the following terms or symbols:

English	Symbol	Italian	Italian Abbreviation	German	French
growing softer	——	*decrescendo, diminuendo*	*decres.* or *dim.*	*leiser werden*	*diminuer*
growing louder	——	*crescendo*	*cres.*	*lauter werden*	*augmenter*

Check your understanding of dynamic terms by filling in the blanks below. Check your answers by referring to the previous material.

English	Italian	Italian Abbreviations	Symbol (when used)
soft	_____	_____	_____
moderately loud	_____	_____	_____
moderately soft	_____	_____	_____
loud	_____	_____	_____
very soft	_____	_____	_____
very loud	_____	_____	_____
growing softer	_____	_____	_____
growing louder	_____	_____	_____

The exercises that follow begin with the identification of instruments. Before you proceed to these, we suggest that you study a record such as Benjamin Britten's *The Young Person's Guide to the Orchestra* in order to gain familiarity with the sounds of the various instruments.

EAR-TRAINING EXERCISES 2

A. Underline the instrument playing the solo part in the following excerpts.

1. trumpet, violin, bassoon
2. French horn, oboe, viola
3. tuba, trumpet, clarinet
4. cello, string bass, violin
5. harp, timpani, piano
6. clarinet, flute, oboe

1. violin
2. oboe
3. clarinet
4. string bass
5. piano
6. flute

B. Fill in the blanks.

1. The first instrument was a _____ .

   The second instrument was a _____ .

   The range of the first excerpt is _____ than the range of the second.
   (narrower/wider)

2. The first instrument was a _____ .

   The second instrument was a _____ .

1. trumpet

   trombone

   narrower

2. clarinet

   bassoon

The second excerpt represents a

_____ the first.
   (repetition of, variation of, contrast with)

3. The excerpt is performed by a _____ .

   accompanied by the _____ section.
             (string, woodwind, brass)

4. The excerpt is performed by the _____

   section. It ends with a _____ .
          (crescendo, decrescendo)

> contrast with
>
> 3. piccolo
>
> brass
>
> 4. string
>
> crescendo

SUPPLEMENTARY EXERCISES 2

1. Listen to various orchestral works, especially from the nineteenth and twentieth centuries, and try to identify as many instruments as you can.

2. Try to gain some experience on an instrument you have never played.

3. Sing various excerpts of three sound units each to your drill partner, using one of the following patterns of dynamics. See if your partner can write down the dynamic plan you used.

   a. *ppp, fff, ppp*
   b. *f*, decrescendo to *pp, ff*
   c. *p*, crescendo to *ff*, decrescendo to *p*

4. Study your own music for its use of dynamics. Pay particular attention to these dynamics as you practice.

chapter 3

In the preceding chapter we studied the timbre and loudness parameters of music. In this chapter we shall focus on the duration parameter. It is well to remember that music always involves the interaction of all the parameters of sound. However, it is helpful to isolate a single parameter, as we shall do in this chapter, so that we can develop skill in hearing and performing.

Some simple folk songs are made up of only two or three types of duration. Their durations can be represented simply in terms of long and short tones (Ex. 3–1).

Ex. 3–1

Twink	le,	Twink	le,	Litt	le,	Star
—	—	—	—	—	—	—

We	are	clim	bing	Jac	ob's	lad	der
—	—	—	—	—	—	—	—

It is obvious, however, that such a simple system of long and short designations would be inadequate for the bulk of music literature, which uses a larger variety of durations. To represent the durations used in music, we must somehow divide the even flow of time into units, just as we divide space into units with the markings on a ruler. Then we can express the durations in music in terms of these units, just as we express visual length in terms of inches, feet, or meters.

It might seem possible to use the established units of time, such as seconds and minutes, to measure duration in music. Indeed, some contemporary composers use seconds and microseconds to indicate duration. For most music, however, such a system would be too cumbersome. Instead, we shall use the concept of *pulse* in our consideration of duration.

PULSE

For our purposes, we shall consider a pulse to be one of a series of relatively short, recurring stimuli that divide the flow of time at regular intervals. A pulse can be sounded by claps, ticks, taps, tones, or any other sound. Just as we can feel the pulse in our wrist, so we can feel a pulse in music. It is also possible simply to imagine a pulse without any external stimulus.

Pulse Rate

Pulses occur at various rates. For example, the human pulse can fluctuate from approximately 60 beats per minute to 90 per minute. In music, there is a much wider range of possible pulse rates. Musicians customarily measure pulse rate in terms of the metronome, an instrument that can be set to produce a certain number of sounds (usually short clicks) per minute. For example, if the metronome is set for 60, it will produce 60 clicks per minute, or 1 click per second. Most metronomes have a range of approximately 30 to 200 pulses per minute. It is helpful for musicians to develop the ability to recognize and produce various pulse rates. If they can learn to hear pulse rates of 60, 90, 120, and 150, they can estimate others from these.

In most of the music we shall be dealing with in this text, the pulse rate will be regular and continuous. It is possible, however, to have irregular or changing pulse rates. For example, a piece might begin with a pulse rate of 80 and then in the middle change suddenly to a pulse rate of 100. Another piece might begin at 80, and then speed up gradually to 120 or slow down gradually to 60.

Pulse Span

We shall use the term *pulse span* to refer to the length of time from one pulse to the next. We shall represent pulses with vertical lines and duration with arched horizontal lines. In Ex. 3-2, the first two sounds each have a duration of one pulse span; the third sound has a duration of two pulse spans. Perform this well-known folk tune by singing it and clapping its pulse.

Ex. 3-2

Notice that it is essential to indicate the pulse in writing and in sound. For example, a note lasting two pulse spans involves a total of three pulses, or three vertical lines. Without the concluding pulse (or vertical line), it would be unclear where the sound should end (Ex. 3-3).

Ex. 3-3

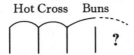

Hot Cross Buns

We have used the terms pulse, pulse rate, and pulse span rather than more traditional terms, such as beat and tempo, in order to avoid the oversimplification and misunderstanding that is too often associated with the latter terms.

Pulse Groups

Listen to a series of pulses, and you will find that you tend to organize them into groups of twos or possibly threes. We shall refer to these as *pulse groups*. If we accompany the pulses with music, this tendency to group pulses becomes even stronger. The two-pulse groupings of a march and the three-pulse groupings of a waltz are clear examples.

The first pulse of a group is called the *strong* or *accented pulse*. Accent can be achieved in many ways. Perhaps the most obvious is to sound one pulse louder than the others. It is also possible to achieve accent through pitch or timbre, or through more subtle musical means, such as changes of harmony or texture. The remaining one or two pulses in a pulse group are called *weak pulses*. We can represent strong and weak pulses by the relative length of the vertical lines, as shown in Ex. 3-4.

Ex. 3-4

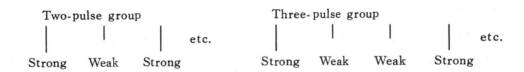

Two-pulse group   Three-pulse group

Strong   Weak   Strong   etc.   Strong   Weak   Weak   Strong   etc.

We can now represent the duration parameter of a melody with more accuracy and completeness than we could with the simple system we used at the beginning of the chapter. We shall represent sounds with arching lines; silence is represented by the absence of those lines (Ex. 3-5).

Ex. 3-5

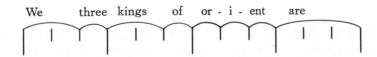

We   three kings   of   or - i - ent   are

PATTERNS

To this point, we have discussed music as though it consisted of a series of sounds strung together in time. However, psychologists have shown us that we perceive music not as a series of isolated events but rather in patterns, or *gestalts*. The practice of successful musicians confirms this, for they do not read note by note, but in terms of musical patterns. Therefore, we shall now turn to the patterns of durations that are possible with two-pulse groups and three-pulse groups. Since there are only five two-pulse patterns and thirteen three-pulse patterns (Ex. 3–6), it should be easy for you to learn to recognize, perform, and hear them. Remember to always focus on the whole pattern rather than reading sound by sound.

In Ex. 3–6, the numerical representation of each pattern designates the relative durations of sound and silence. The numerical 0 always equals 1 pulse of silence. The numeral 1 equals 1 pulse of sound; 2 equals 2 pulses of sound; 3 equals 3 pulses of sound. These "names" provide an easily remembered way of designating the various pulse patterns.

Ex. 3–6

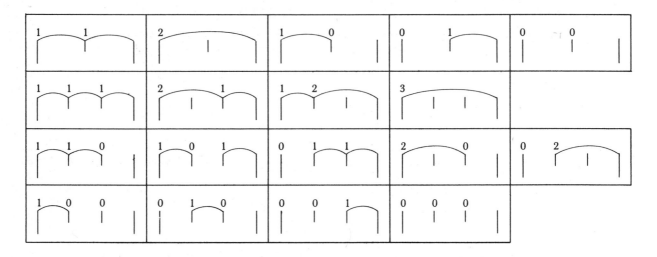

Practice these patterns by singing the durations while you clap the pulses.

GESTURES

The patterns in Ex. 3–6 are extremely short, and in actual compositions they may not be perceived as meaningful contextual units. Instead, a larger unit may be perceived as the basic contextual unit. We shall call these larger units *rhythm gestures*. When both pitch and rhythm are involved, they may be called *pitch-rhythm gestures*, or simply *gestures*. Sometimes the beginning and ending of a rhythm gesture coincide with the beginning and ending of a rhythm pattern. Sometimes the two do not coincide, as in Ex. 3–7 (based on "Hot Cross Buns" and "We Three Kings").

Ex. 3-7

a. gestures patterns

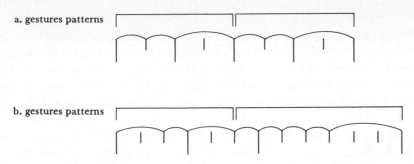

b. gestures patterns

If the perception and performance of music are to be truly meaningful, they must be based upon meaningful gestures rather than abstract patterns. However, this presents two serious pedagogical problems. The first is that although the number of rhythm patterns is limited (to the two- and three-pulse patterns in Ex. 3-6 plus some four-pulse and six-pulse patterns given in Chapter 12) the number of rhythm gestures is almost unlimited.

An even more vexing problem is deciding where a rhythm gesture begins and ends. To illustrate this point, let's return to Ex. 3-7b. In that example, the division into gestures was based primarily on the natural division of the text and somewhat on melodic considerations. However, in analyzing the end of a familiar German folk song, we find that even though its rhythm patterns are exactly the same as those of "We Three Kings," textual and melodic considerations could lead us to divide it into slightly different rhythm gestures (Ex. 3-8).

Ex. 3-8

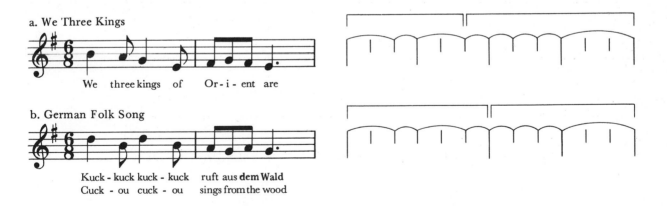

a. We Three Kings

We three kings of Or-i-ent are

b. German Folk Song

Kuck - kuck kuck - kuck   ruft aus dem Wald
Cuck - ou cuck - ou   sings from the wood

The delineation of musical gestures is not subject to rigid rules, and this is one reason why the interpretation of a musical composition varies slightly from one performer to another. In your advanced training in musical theory and applied music, you will learn some of the general principles, conventions, and traditions associated with the demarcation of musical gestures. For now, you should strive for absolute mastery in the performance and perception of the short patterns in Ex. 3-6. At the same time, you should creatively consider gestures with your teacher and fellow students whenever possible. (See p. 42 for a further discussion of musical gestures and phrasing.)

In performing music, it is always advisable to establish a clear temporal framework of regular pulses against which the durations of the music may be projected. This can be achieved, as we have done, by tapping or clapping, sounding the strong pulses louder and the weak pulses softer. Another effective technique is to conduct, using the patterns illustrated in Ex. 3-9.

Ex. 3-9

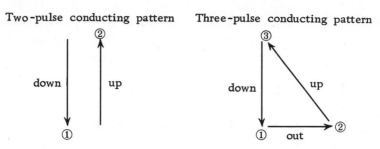

These patterns are performed with a rapid hand motion leading to the *ictus,* the point where the pulse occurs (indicated in Ex. 3-9 by the circled numbers). When the hand reaches this point, it pauses momentarily before moving to the next pulse.

In practice, conductors tend to make more supple, curving gestures (Ex. 3-10). Often, they will place the last pulse near the bottom of the pattern rather than at the top, as we have illustrated. A conductor, teacher, or advanced student can illustrate this for you in person far more effectively than we can in this book. You should learn these patterns so well that they become automatic.

Ex. 3-10

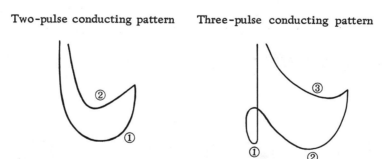

MUSIC-READING EXERCISES 3

The purpose of the five exercises is to develop your ability to maintain a steady pulse and to follow a given number of pulse groups. The top line will be sounded by the teacher, the bottom line by you. Use claps or taps. Be sure to accent the strong pulses by sounding them louder than the others. If you perform the exercises accurately, your last pulse should occur exactly with the pulse sounded by the teacher. Pay attention to the metronome markings.

1. Pulse = MM 60

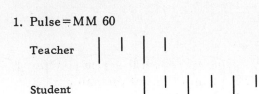

Teacher

Student

2. Pulse = MM 60

Teacher

Student

3. Pulse = MM 90

Teacher

Student

4. Pulse = MM 120

Teacher

Student

5. Pulse = MM 150

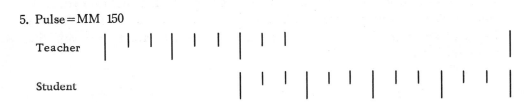

Teacher

Student

MUSIC-READING EXERCISES 3A

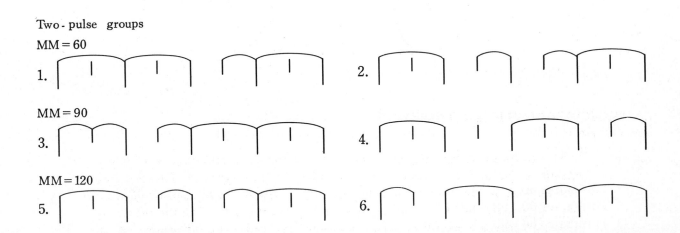

Two - pulse groups

MM = 60

1.   2.

MM = 90

3.   4.

MM = 120

5.   6.

Three-pulse groups

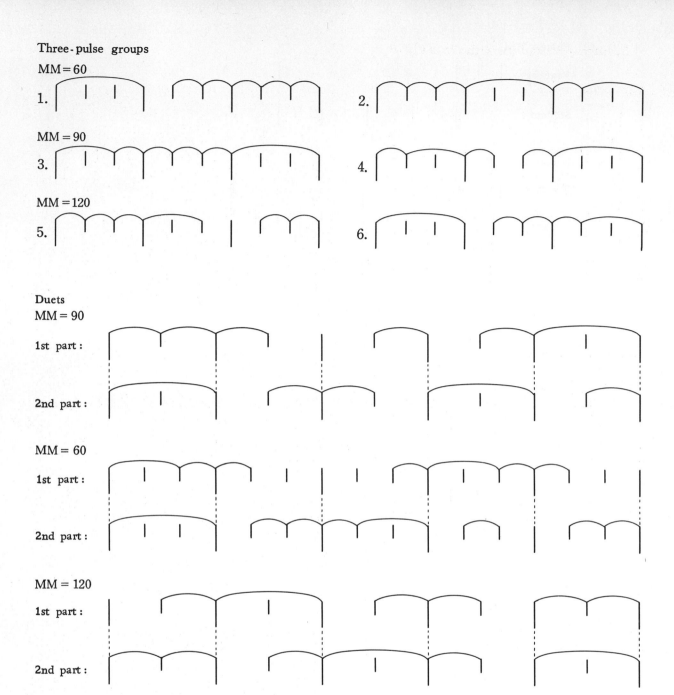

EAR-TRAINING EXERCISES 3

A. Listen to the musical examples and conduct them. When each excerpt is finished, underline the correct pulse rate and then check your answer.

1. Pulse rate: 60   90   120
2. Pulse rate: 60   90   120
3. Pulse rate: 60   90   120   150
4. Pulse rate: 60   90   120   150
5. Pulse rate: 60   90   120   150

1. 120
2. 60
3. 150
4. 120
5. 60

B. Indicate durations with arched lines.

Two - pulse groups

1.
2.
3.
4.
5.

Three - pulse groups

6.
7.
8.
9.
10.

Duets

1st part :
1.
2nd part :

1st part :
2.
2nd part :

EXAMPLES FROM LITERATURE

1. Beethoven: Symphony No. 7, third movement

2. Beethoven: Symphony No. 3, first movement

3. Borodin: *Polovetsion Dances* (adapted)

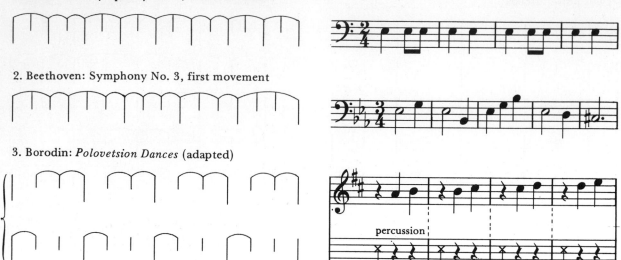

SUPPLEMENTARY EXERCISES 3

1. Write four examples in the style of, for instance, Ex. 3–2. Be able to sing them and use them as ear-training exercises for your partner.

2. Practice the conducting patterns in Ex. 3–9 while you listen to music.

3. Clap only the rhythm of familiar melodies and see if your partner can recognize them.

4. Create and perform examples, such as those shown below, that do not have clear pulse groups. Regard all pulses as being relatively equal. This exercise will help prepare you to understand the complexities of some very old and some very new music. It may also help you realize that clear pulse groups make performance and perception easier.

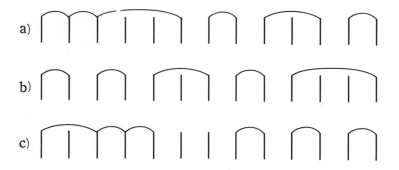

chapter 4

The system of notation used in the last chapter has given us some insight into the nature of the duration parameter in music, but it would be difficult to combine this system with pitch notation. Instead, we must now learn the more traditional system of notating duration, or rhythm.

NOTE VALUES

The durational symbols used in music are presented in Example 4–1.

Ex. 4–1

𝄺	Breve, or double whole note (rarely used)
𝅝	Whole note
𝅗𝅥	Half note
𝅘𝅥	Quarter note
𝅘𝅥𝅮	Eighth note
𝅘𝅥𝅯	Sixteenth note
𝅘𝅥𝅰	Thirty-second note
𝅘𝅥𝅱	Sixty-fourth note (rarely used)

Before you learn the meaning of these symbols, you should practice writing them. Follow the instructions carefully, writing the notes in the space provided. We shall utilize the usual five-line staff.

Whole notes. Be sure they are oval-shaped, not round.

Half notes. First draw the oval notehead, and then add the stem. Notes below the third line of a staff have stems up; notes above the third line have stems down. Notes on the third line may have stems in either direction.

Quarter notes. First draw an oval notehead, and then quickly black it in. Add stems according to the instructions above.

Eighth notes. First draw a quarter note according to the instructions above. Then add a flag. The flag always goes to the right, regardless of whether the stem goes up or down.

Smaller note values. Same as eighth notes, except add two flags for sixteenth notes, three flags for thirty-second notes.

In taking dictation, one should write black noteheads as a short diagonal line ( instead of ). The notehead should still be made first, and then the stem. Practice this in the following space.

♩ ♩   etc.

♪ ♪   etc.

♬ ♬   etc.

Now see if you can remember the durational symbols. Fill in the blanks, and then check your answers by referring to Ex. 4-1.

Sixty-fourth note   _____

Thirty-second note   _____

_____   ♪

_____   ♪

Quarter note   _____

_____   𝅗𝅥

Whole note   _____

_____   𝅝

The durational symbols indicate relative rather than absolute duration. An eighth note (♪), for example, may be very short in one piece and very long in another. What you must remember is that each note in Ex. 4-1 is twice as long as the note below it: the sixteenth note is twice as long as the thirty-second note; the half note is twice as long as the quarter note; and so forth. Elementary mathematics will show us the relationships between all of the notes. For example, the whole note is twice as long as the half note, four times as long as the quarter note, eight times as long as the eighth note, and so on.

RESTS

We use another set of symbols, called *rests,* to represent silence in music (Ex. 4-2). The rests stand in the same relationship to one another as do the corresponding notes. For example, a half rest is twice as long as a quarter rest.

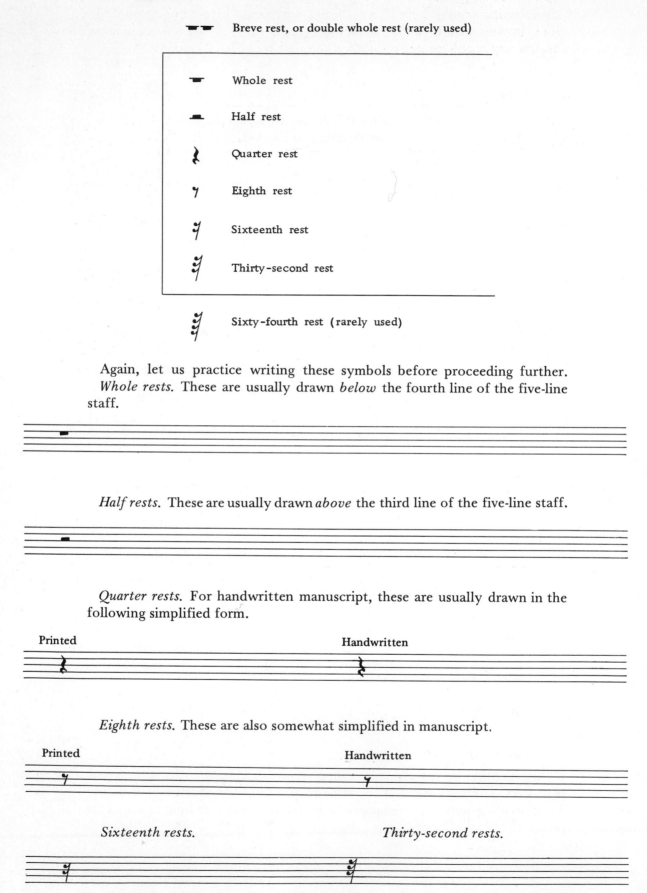

Ex. 4–2

Breve rest, or double whole rest (rarely used)

Whole rest

Half rest

Quarter rest

Eighth rest

Sixteenth rest

Thirty-second rest

Sixty-fourth rest (rarely used)

Again, let us practice writing these symbols before proceeding further.

Whole rests. These are usually drawn *below* the fourth line of the five-line staff.

Half rests. These are usually drawn *above* the third line of the five-line staff.

Quarter rests. For handwritten manuscript, these are usually drawn in the following simplified form.

Printed   Handwritten

Eighth rests. These are also somewhat simplified in manuscript.

Printed   Handwritten

Sixteenth rests.   *Thirty-second rests.*

The following exercise will help you review both notes and rests and the relationships among them. Cover the answer column before you begin. Write your answers in the blanks, and then check them with the answer column. Review any problems you encounter by referring to Ex. 4-1 and 4-2.

						Answers
1. One ♩ =	_____	♩ or	_____	♪		1. two, eight
2. One ♩ =	_____	♪ or	_____	♪		2. four, eight
3. One 𝄽 =	_____	𝄾 or	_____	𝄾		3. two, four
4. One 𝅝 =	_____	♩ or	_____	♩		4. four, eight
5. Four 𝄾 =	_____	𝄽 or	_____	𝄾		5. one, two
6. Two ♪ =	_____	♪ or	_____	♪		6. one, four
7. Four ♩ =	_____	♩ or	_____	𝄻		7. two, one
8. Eight 𝄾 =	_____	𝄽 or	_____	𝄻		8. four, one

Dotted notes or rests are used to represent durations three times as long as the next smaller note or rest. For example,

$$ \text{♩} = \text{♩} + \text{♩}, \qquad \text{♩.} = \text{♩} + \text{♩} + \text{♩} $$

Study Ex. 4-3, and this procedure should become clear.

Ex. 4-3

♪. = ♪ + ♪ + ♪   𝄾. = 𝄾 + 𝄾 + 𝄾

♪. = ♪ + ♪ + ♪   𝄾. = 𝄾 + 𝄾 + 𝄾

♩. = ♪ + ♪ + ♪   𝄽. = 𝄾 + 𝄾 + 𝄾

♩. = ♩ + ♩ + ♩   𝄻. = 𝄽 + 𝄽 + 𝄽

𝅝. = ♩ + ♩ + ♩   𝄻. = 𝄻 + 𝄻 + 𝄻

The traditional explanation of a dotted note or rest as being one and a half times as long as the note can lead to confusion, especially, as we shall see, in compound meters. Test your comprehension of the use of the dot by working the following exercises.

1. 𝄾 + 𝄾 + 𝄾 = _____ .

2. ♩ + ♩ + ♩ = _____ .

3. ♪ + ♪ + ♪ = _____ .

4. 𝄽· = _____ + _____ + _____ .

5. 𝅝· = _____ + _____ + _____ .

6. ♪· = _____ + _____ + _____ .

1. 𝄽·

2. 𝅗𝅥·

3. ♪·

4. 𝄾 + 𝄾 + 𝄾

5. ♩ + ♩ + ♩

6. ♪ + ♪ + ♪

We can now consider the relationship between traditional notation and the notation system used in the previous chapter. First, we choose one note value to represent one pulse span. Then we use the other notes and rests according to the principles we have discussed. Ex. 4–4 should make this clear.

Ex. 4–4

♪ = one pulse span

♩ = one pulse span

For ease in reading, we can substitute continuous lines, called *beams,* for flags. At this point, we will limit beams to notes within one pulse group. Later, we will learn to extend the use of beams. Ex. 4–5 shows how beams are used in two-pulse and three-pulse patterns. Study these patterns carefully, and practice singing and hearing them until you are thoroughly familiar with them. This is an essential foundation for your future work in the duration parameter.

Ex. 4–5

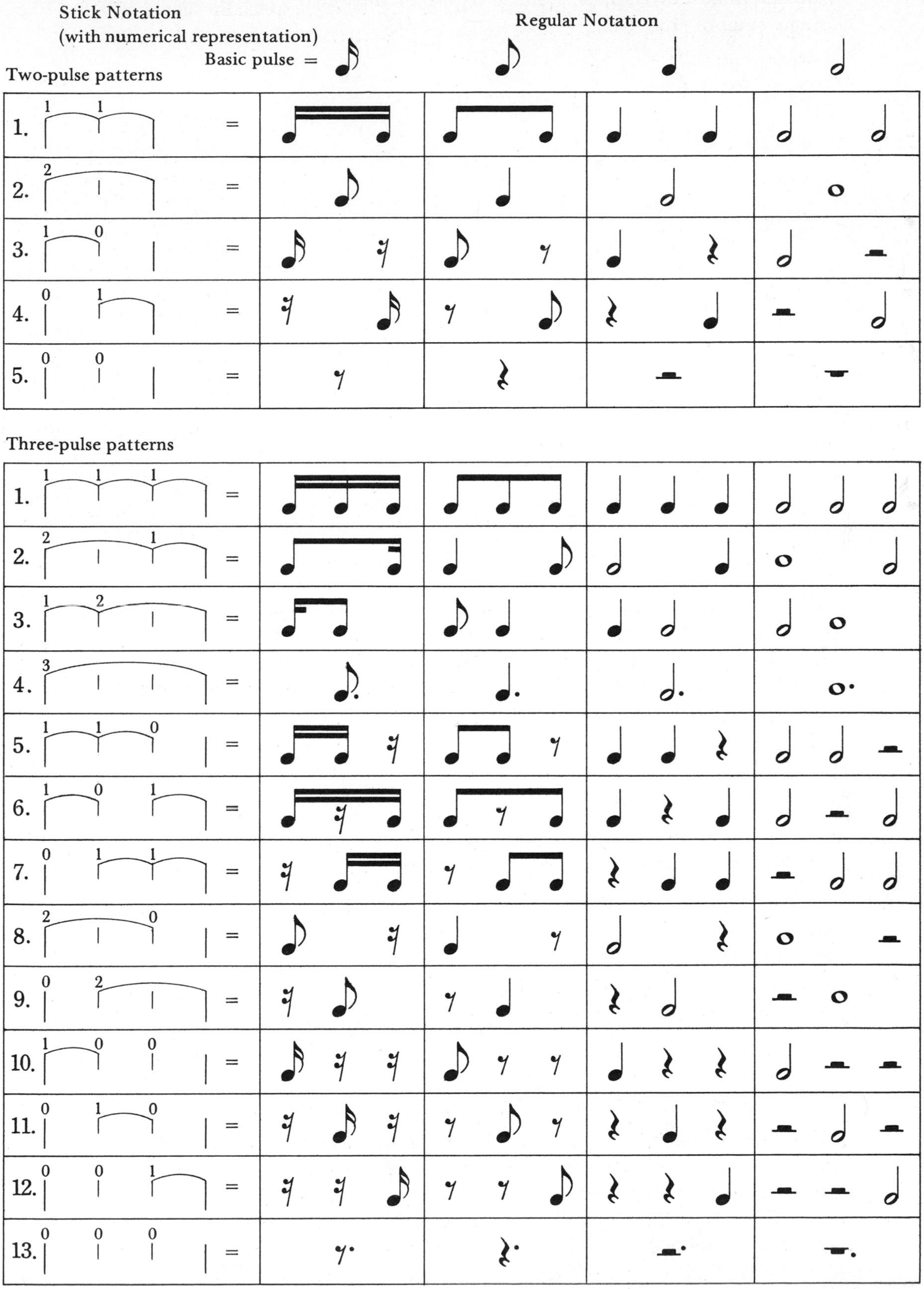
Stick Notation
(with numerical representation)
Basic pulse =
Regular Notation
Two-pulse patterns
1. 1 1 =
2. 2 =
3. 1 0 =
4. 0 1 =
5. 0 0 =
Three-pulse patterns
1. 1 1 1 =
2. 2 1 =
3. 1 2 =
4. 3 =
5. 1 1 0 =
6. 1 0 1 =
7. 0 1 1 =
8. 2 0 =
9. 0 2 =
10. 1 0 0 =
11. 0 1 0 =
12. 0 0 1 =
13. 0 0 0 =

One other principle should be borne in mind. Silence lasting for two pulse spans within a three-pulse group is represented by two rest symbols, not by a single symbol (Ex. 4–6).

Ex. 4–6

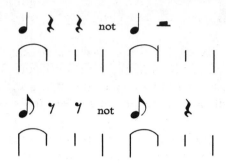

PULSE GROUP SIGNATURES

From this point on, in each example or exercise we shall use the format illustrated in Ex. 4–7 to indicate how many pulses are in each pulse group and what note value represents one pulse span.

Ex. 4–7

MEASURE LINES (BAR LINES)

To facilitate the organization of pulses into groups, we use vertical lines called *measure lines* or *bar lines*. The space (both visual and aural) between measure lines or bar lines is called a *measure* or a *bar*. Thus, 4–8 consists of five measures or bars, each of which contains three pulses.

Ex. 4–8

Notice that there is no bar line at the beginning of the first measure. Notice also that there is a small space between the bar line and the first note of the measure as it is written, but that there is no lapse of time between the bar line and the first note as it sounds. Ex. 4–9 might be a more accurate way of writing music with bar lines.

40

Here, the beginning of the measure and the beginning of the first note clearly coincide. This method, however, is not used because of possible difficulty in reading.

Notice also that in Ex. 4–8 and 4–9 the last measure ends with a double line, which is usually called a *double bar*. The double bar should always be used at the end of a composition or at the end of sections within a composition.

Finally, note that silence lasting an entire measure is always indicated by a whole rest.

Now see if you can translate stick notation into regular notation quickly and accurately. Indicate the proper durational values above the given stick notation.

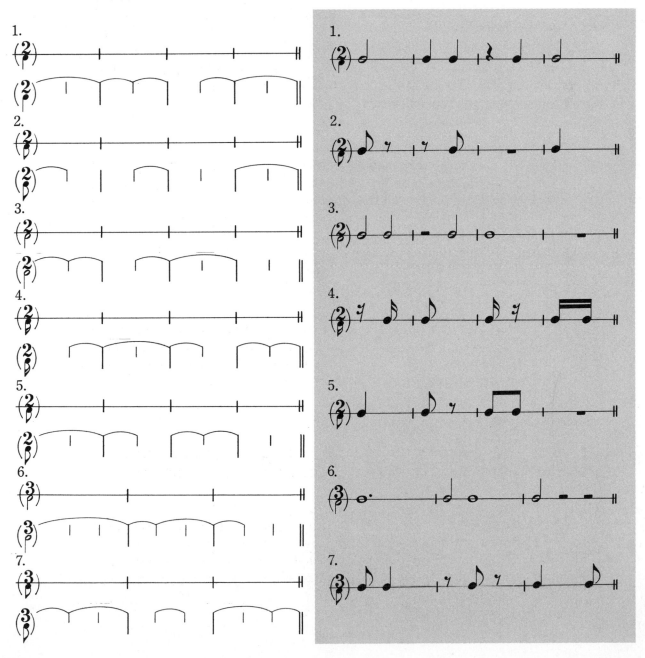

Referring to the number designation shown on p. 26, translate the following numerical representations into regular notation:

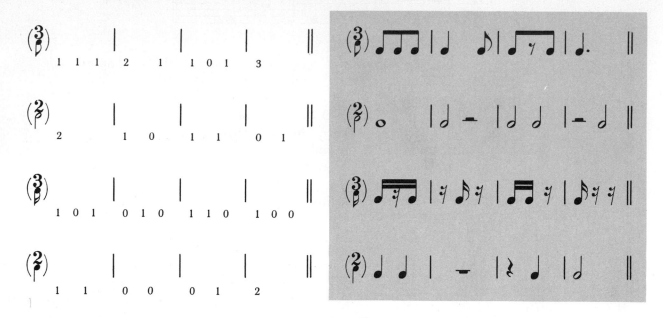

BAR LINES AND GESTURES

It is important to remember that bar lines divide music into pulse groups; they do not necessarily indicate musical gestures. In much music, it is customary to emphasize the first pulse of a measure. However, this should not be overdone, and above all this does not mean that the beginning of a measure always coincides with the beginning of a rhythmic gesture. Iannis Xenakis, the contemporary Greek composer, has said that bar lines in his music are like mile markers on a highway. That is, they indicate where one is in space or time, but they do not necessarily tell one how the music is organized. Keep this in mind as you work the following exercises. For additional exercises, you could perform the examples you write in the two preceding sets of exercises.

MUSIC-READING EXERCISES 4

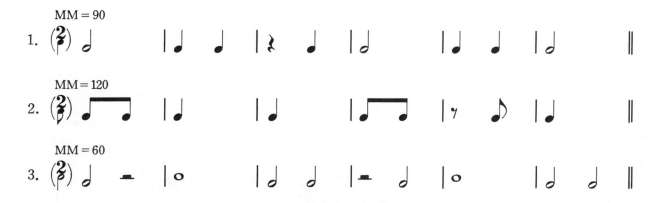

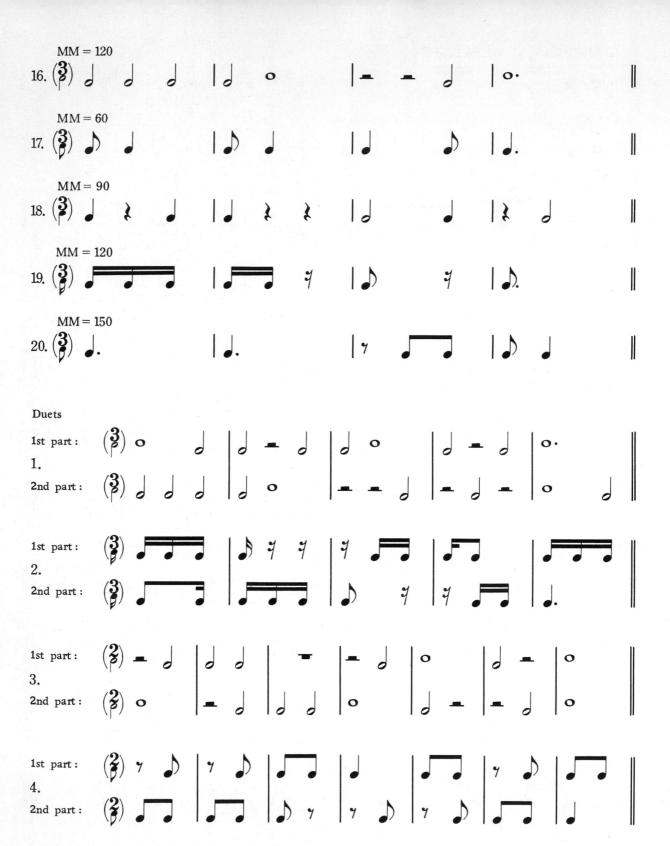

44

MM = 90

1.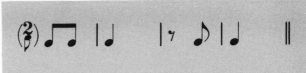

MM = 120

2.

MM = 60

3.

MM = 150

4.

MM = 90

5.

MM = 120

6.

MM = 60

7.

MM = 90

8.

MM = 120

9.

MM = 150

10.

Duets

1st part:

1.

2nd part:

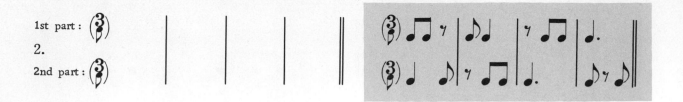

1st part:

2.

2nd part:

EXAMPLES FROM LITERATURE

These examples may be used for ear training and music reading. Even though we have not yet considered pitches, we include them in the examples so that you can begin to accustom yourself to them and so that the examples are complete. In performing the examples, you may (1) ignore pitch completely and sing on a single pitch, (2) try to approximate the general shape of the pitch pattern, or (3) learn the pitches by rote. In any event, you should focus upon the rhythmic aspect of these examples. You may sing on *la,* or on numbers representing the pulses in each note.

1. J. Strauss: "Blue Danube Waltz"

2. Brahms: Trio, Op. 40, second movement

3. Dvořák: Trio, Op. 90 "Dumky," first movement

4. Delibes: "Le Roi s'amuse"

5. J. S. Bach: Partita No. 2 in C Minor, Rondeau

1. Compose four examples in the same style as those in this chapter. Use them for ear-training exercises for your partner. Trade examples with your partner, and sight-sing each other's examples.

2. Practice conducting the two-pulse pattern as you listen to marches and similar pieces, and the three-pulse pattern as you listen to waltzes, minuets, and similar pieces.

3. (More challenging) Experiment with music that uses alternate or random arrangements of two- and three-pulse groups. Compose, perform, and use for ear training examples similar to the following:

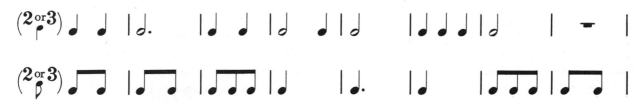

Keep a steady pulse throughout!

chapter 5

In the last chapter, we saw that the notation of duration is relative rather than absolute; that is, it shows the relationships between durations rather than showing precise length. In contrast, the notation of pitch used in most Western music is absolute, showing fairly precisely the location of a tone in terms of pitch. This was not always the case, however: earlier systems of pitch notation showed relationships between pitches rather than precise pitches. To understand some of the basic principles of the pitch parameters, let us return to a modified version of some of the earlier systems of relative pitch notation.

PITCH DIRECTION

Let us use a single horizontal line to represent a pitch. This pitch could be anywhere in the gamut of pitches. It is obvious that we can move from this first pitch in any one of three possible directions to a second pitch: we can ascend to a higher pitch, descend to a lower pitch, or repeat the same pitch (Ex. 5–1).

Ex. 5–1

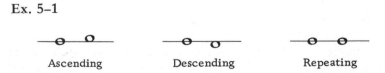

Ascending   Descending   Repeating

PITCH INTERVAL

In considering the movement from one pitch to another, it is important to describe not only the direction but also the distance, or *interval*, between pitches. In later sections of this text, we shall discuss pitch interval in more precise terms. At this point we are concerned only with developing a general awareness of gross differences in pitch interval, such as those illustrated in Ex. 5–2.

Ex. 5–2

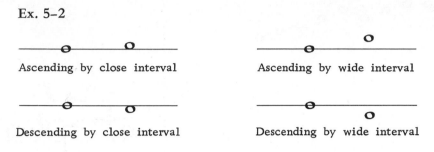

Ascending by close interval   Ascending by wide interval

Descending by close interval   Descending by wide interval

PITCH PATTERNS

If we add a third pitch, we find it possible to organize the three pitches into thirteen different patterns of pitch direction, disregarding the size of the pitch intervals employed. These patterns are illustrated in Ex. 5–3.

Ex. 5–3

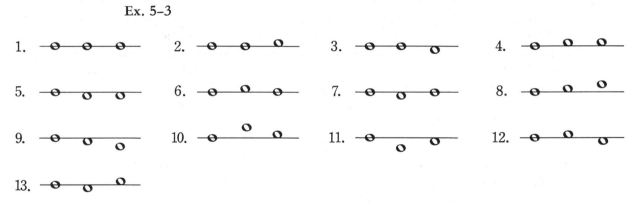

Try to sing or play pitches according to these patterns, and see if your partner can quickly recognize the patterns. We could list all of the patterns of four-pitch groups, five-pitch groups, and so on, but these would be so numerous that a list of them would be neither practical nor helpful. Instead, we shall consider larger pitch groups in terms of general contour types.

PITCH CONTOURS

Many pitch groups can be classified as one of the five pitch-contour types illustrated in Ex. 5–4. Not all of the pitches in a given contour follow the same direction. For example, in an ascending contour most of the pitches move upward, but there may be an occasional repeated or descending pitch or two. This does not change the essential type of contour.

Ex. 5–4

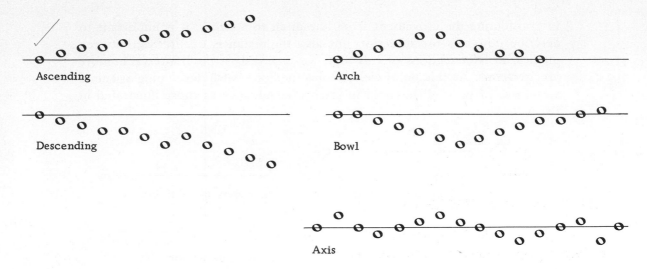

Ascending

Arch

Descending

Bowl

Axis

Many other pitch groups, such as the two in Ex. 5-5, may be heard as combinations or variants of these basic types.

Ex. 5–5

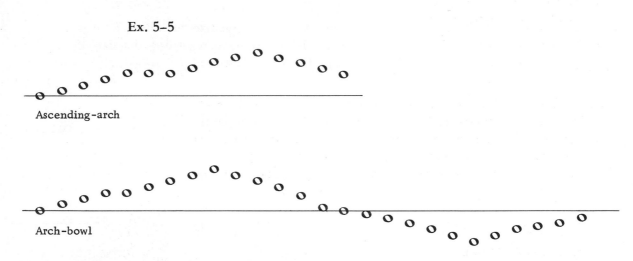

Ascending-arch

Arch-bowl

Other pitch groups have unique contours that are difficult to classify. Most extended melodies reveal such irregular contours. The important thing is not to find a correct label for the contour but rather to be aware of the general shape of the melody. You should be able to hear such significant aspects of the melody as the location of the highest pitch or climax, the location of the lowest pitch, and the relationship between the first pitch and the last pitch.

CONJUNCT AND DISJUNCT MOTION

Another general classification of pitch concerns the type of interval used predominantly. Pitch motion by narrow intervals, or *steps* (see Chap. 7), is called *conjunct* motion; pitch motion by wider intervals, or *leaps,* is called *disjunct* motion. These terms are useful even though most music moves by *mixed* motion—that is, by a combination of conjunct and disjunct motion. (See Ex. 5-6.)

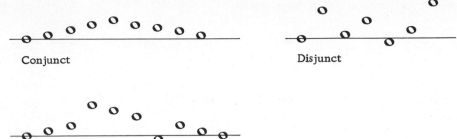

Conjunct   Disjunct

Mixed

EAR-TRAINING EXERCISES 5

A. Indicate by underlining whether the second pitch is the same as, higher than, or lower than the first pitch.

1. same higher lower	1. higher
2. same higher lower	2. same
3. same higher lower	3. higher
4. same higher lower	4. lower
5. same higher lower	5. same

The following pairs of pitches are separated by very close intervals, which are sometimes called *microtones*. The ability to make fine discriminations, such as are called for here, is essential for the development of good intonation. (Microtones may be found in the works of some modern composers, as well as in the music of some non-Western cultures.)

6. same higher lower	6. lower
7. same higher lower	7. higher
8. same higher lower	8. higher

B. Indicate by underlining whether the interval between the second pair of pitches is the same as, larger than, or smaller than the interval between the first pair of pitches.

1. same larger smaller	1. larger
2. same larger smaller	2. larger
3. same larger smaller	3. smaller
4. same larger smaller	4. same
5. same larger smaller	5. smaller
6. same larger smaller	6. smaller
7. same larger smaller	7. larger
8. same larger smaller	8. same

C. Each exercise has a pattern of three pitches. First listen, and then sing the pitches back in your own voice range. Then underline the correct representation of the pattern.

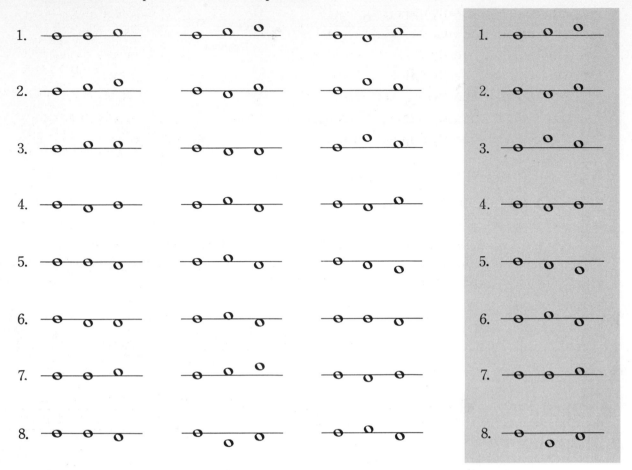

D. Listen to the melodic fragment, sing it back in your own voice range, and then underline the contour type.

1. ascending descending arch
   bowl axis other

2. ascending descending arch
   bowl axis other

3. ascending descending arch
   bowl axis other

4. ascending descending arch
   bowl axis other

5. ascending descending arch
   bowl axis other

6. ascending descending arch
   bowl axis other

7. ascending descending arch
   bowl axis other

8. ascending descending arch
   bowl axis other

1. bowl

2. ascending

3. descending

4. arch

5. axis

6. ascending

7. arch

8. bowl

E. Underline the correct description of the pitch motion.

1. mostly conjunct	mostly disjunct	mixed		1. mostly conjunct
2. mostly conjunct	mostly disjunct	mixed		2. mostly disjunct
3. mostly conjunct	mostly disjunct	mixed		3. mostly disjunct
4. mostly conjunct	mostly disjunct	mixed		4. mostly conjunct
5. mostly conjunct	mostly disjunct	mixed		5. mixed
6. mostly conjunct	mostly disjunct	mixed		6. mostly conjunct
7. mostly conjunct	mostly disjunct	mixed		7. mostly disjunct
8. mostly conjunct	mostly disjunct	mixed		8. mixed

EXAMPLES FROM LITERATURE

These examples may be analyzed for patterns and gestures and for their use of pitch direction, contour, and motion, even though some specific materials in them have not yet been discussed in the text.

1. Franck: Symphony in D Minor, first movement

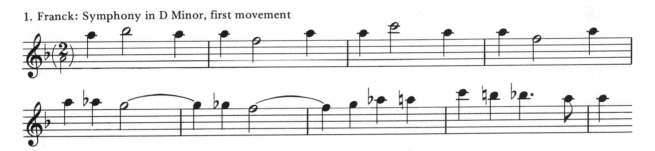

2. Beethoven: Symphony No. 5 in C Minor, second movement

3. Haydn: Quartet in B♭, Op. 64, No. 6, second movement

4. J. S. Bach: Concerto in D Minor for Two Violins and Orchestra, second movement

53

1. Sing or play a short section of a piece you know. Have your partner sing it back and then describe it in terms of direction, contour, and conjunct or disjunct motion.

2. Improvise short pitch patterns. Have your partner sing them back and then describe them.

3. Work on extending the length of pitch groups that you can sing or play back with accuracy.

4. Write a short piece, using the type of one-line notation that we have used in this chapter. Have various classmates sing it, and notice the variety of the versions they produce when reading this type of notation.

chapter 6

By now you have realized the necessity for a more precise type of pitch notation than the one we used in the last chapter. To understand the traditional system of pitch notation, which we are about to study, it is helpful if you read the next section of the text while seated at the piano or other keyboard instrument so that you may perform the suggested exercises.

PITCH DESIGNATION

The human ear can detect a wide range of pitches. For practical purposes, however, the eighty-eight notes of the piano provide most of the pitch material used in music. Familiarize yourself with the piano keyboard, noticing especially how the black keys are arranged in alternate groups of twos and threes. This arrangement facilitates the location of pitches on the keyboard. The pitch D, for example, is located between the group of two black keys. Study the piano keyboard in Ex. 6–1, and note the location of all the white keys in relation to the groups of black keys.

The white keys are designated by the first seven letters of the alphabet (A–G). To distinguish the various octave duplications of pitches, we employ small and capital letters with various subscript and superscript numbers. As you can see from Ex. 6–1, the type of designation changes at each C.

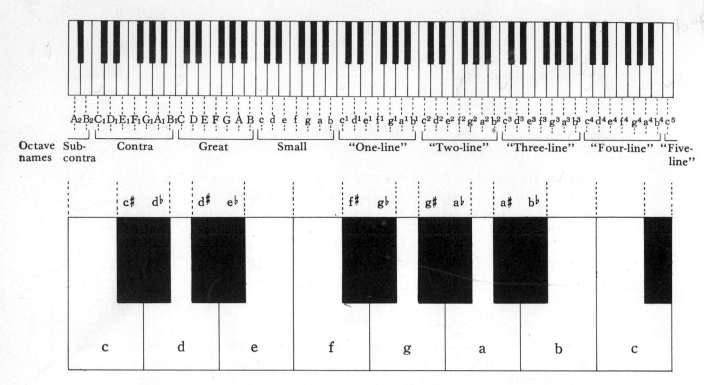

If you are not familiar with the piano keyboard, practice playing the following notes in the proper octave:

$$c^1 \ E \ a^3 \ G_1 \ d^2 \ f \ b^4$$

Now try to play these same notes without looking at the keyboard. You can locate the notes by feeling for the black notes and relating the other notes to them. You can extend this exercise by having your drill partner call out notes for you to play. Continue practicing until you have a very clear mental and aural picture of the arrangement of notes on the keyboard.

The black keys are named according to their relationship with the white keys. The black key between C and D, for example, is called either *C-sharp*, indicating that it is right above C, or *D-flat,* indicating that it is right below D. Other black keys are named similarly as you can see from Ex. 6-1.

We use the following customary abbreviations:

♯ sharp

♭ flat

♮ natural (used to indicate a return to a white key after a sharp or flat has been used)

These signs are called *accidentals*.

Now locate and play the following notes on the piano. A note with no accidental following it is assumed to be natural.

$$f\sharp^1 \ A\flat \ c\sharp^3 \ d\flat^2 \ A\sharp_1 \ b \ d\sharp^1 \ G\sharp \ e\flat^2 \ B\natural$$

Play the same notes without looking at the keyboard. Continue the exercise by having your partner call out notes for you to play. Do not continue in this chapter until you can easily and quickly locate any of the notes on the piano.

In music, pitches are usually represented on a group of five parallel lines called a *staff*. The lines and spaces are numbered from the bottom.

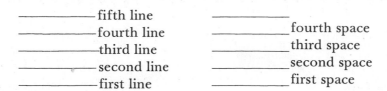

A *clef sign* is placed on the staff to indicate the location of a specific pitch. The *treble clef*, or *G clef*, indicates the location of the pitch g^1 on the second line. Practice drawing this as shown below, making sure that the loop encircles the second line.

A staff with the treble clef at the beginning is called a *treble staff*. To write the pitch g^1 on this staff, place the notehead of the rhythmic symbol on the second line. Other pitches are located in relation to this pitch, as shown in Ex. 6-2.

Ex. 6-2

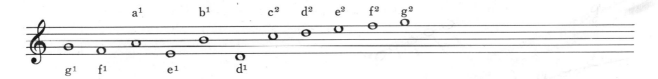

Identify the following pitches, check your answers in the answer column, and then play the pitches on the piano, using whatever fingering is convenient.

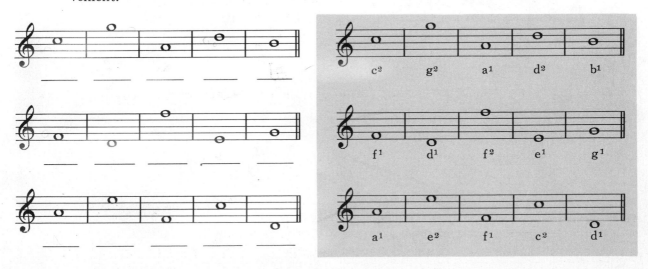

The *bass clef,* or *F clef,* indicates the location of the pitch f on the fourth line. Practice drawing this clef sign as shown below, making sure that one dot is above the fourth line and the other dot is below it.

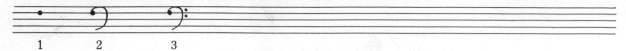

1   2   3

Ex. 6–3 shows the location of notes on the bass staff.

Ex. 6–3

f   e   g   d   a   c   b   B   A   G   F

Identify the following notes on the bass staff, check your answers in the answer column, and then play the notes on the piano in the proper octave.

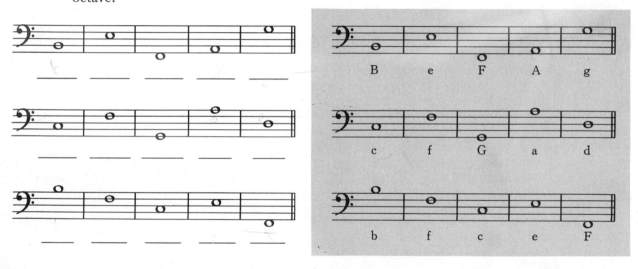

Write the indicated notes.

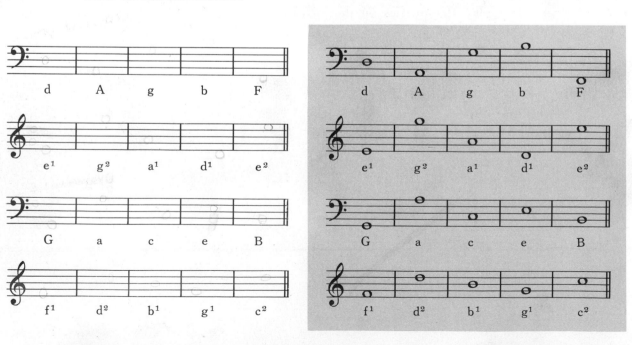

Other clefs will be introduced in later chapters.

LEDGER LINES

The range of any staff may be extended by the use of short lines, called *ledger lines,* above or below the staff (Ex. 6-4). Notice that these lines are the same distance apart as the staff lines, and that they are always drawn with spaces between them, not as continuous lines.

Ex. 6-4

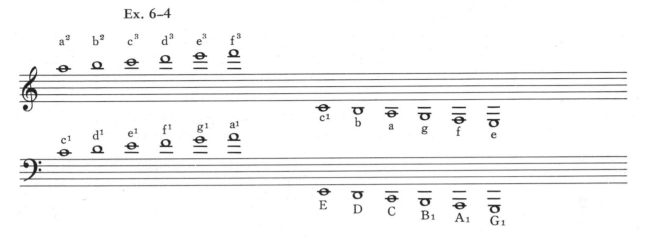

Identify the following notes, and then play them on the piano.

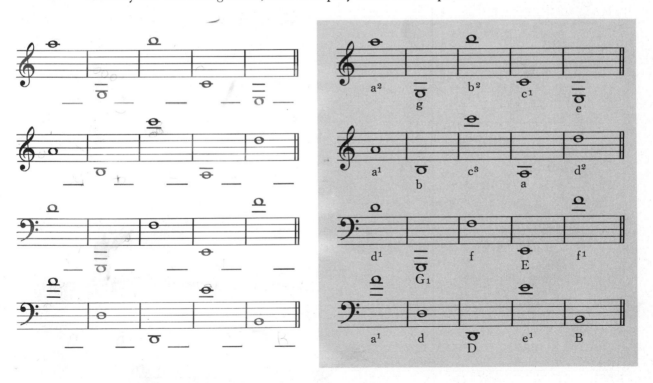

Another way of extending the range of any staff is through the use of *octave signs* (Ex. 6-5). An octave is the distance between a note and the next higher or lower note with the same letter name. By using octave signs, one can avoid excessive use of ledger lines. The sign *8ve* means one octave higher; *8ve basso* means one octave lower.

Ex. 6–5

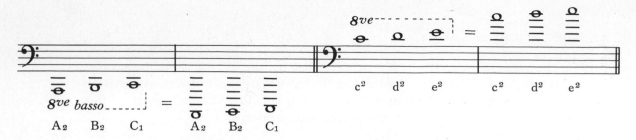

Identify the following notes, and play them on the piano.

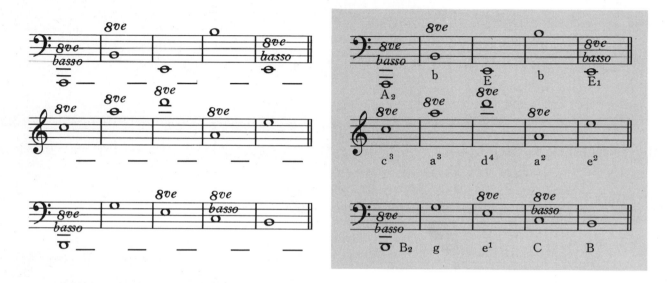

Accidentals (♯ ♭ ♮) are always placed *before* the notehead in staff notation (Ex. 6–6).

Ex. 6–6

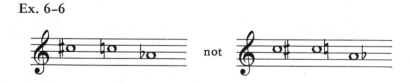

The combination of a treble staff and a bass staff, used often in piano and choral music, is called a *great staff* (Ex. 6–7).

Ex. 6–7

Identify the following pitches.

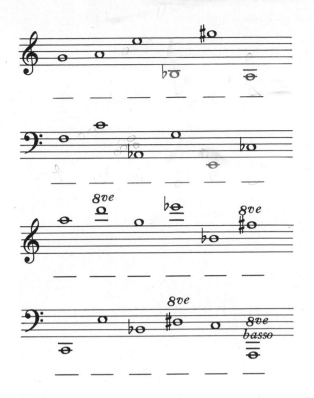

Write the following pitches.

f#¹   b²   e¹   db²   g#¹   f²

G   eb   F   a   c   A#

c³   f⁴   d²   ab³   g#²

B²   Eb   G¹   F#   d

The use of sharps and flats can be extended. We have located A#, C#, D#, F#, and G#, but not B# or E#. A glance at the keyboard shows us that there is no black key above B or E. Therefore, B# is the same as C and E#

is the same as F, at least in the tempered intonation used for the piano. Similarly, C♭ is the same as B and F♭ is the same as E. Any two pitches that have the same sound but are designated with different letter names are called *enharmonic pitches*.

In the preceding chapter, we used a simplified notation to illustrate some basic characteristics of the pitch parameter. It should be easy for you to recognize these same characteristics in staff notation.

Under each pitch pair, write whether the pitch motion is ascending, descending, or repeated.

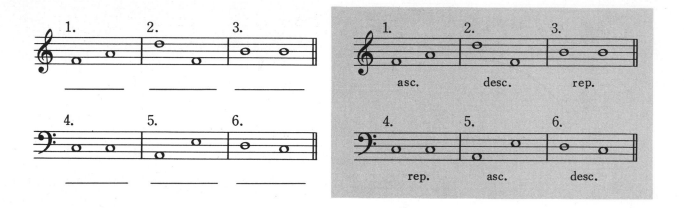

Look at the following groups of intervals, and circle the widest pair in each group.

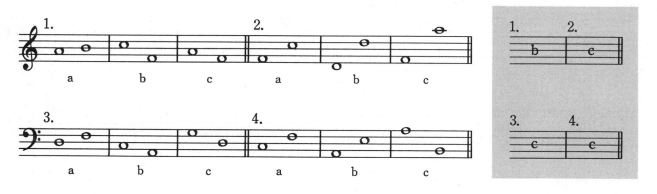

Indicate which basic contour type is illustrated (ascending, descending, arch, bowl, axis, or other).

3.
Arch

4.
Descending

5.
Bowl-descending

MUSIC-READING EXERCISES 6

Play the following examples on the piano at the indicated rate. Use any fingering that is convenient.

EAR-TRAINING EXERCISES 6

Multiple choice.

64

EXAMPLES FROM LITERATURE

You may use these examples for additional music-reading and ear-training exercises, and you may analyze them in terms of their patterns and gestures and their use of pitch direction, contour, and motion.

1. Verdi: *Aïda,* "Celeste Aïda"

2. Dvořák: Symphony in F Minor,"New World," first movement

3. Ashanti Air

4. Handel: *Messiah,* "The Trumpet Shall Sound"

5. Rimsky-Korsakov: *Scheherezade*, Op. 35, first movement

SUPPLEMENTARY EXERCISES 6

1. One of the best ways to gain proficiency in writing music (and, incidentally, familiarity with the conventions of good notation) is simply to copy music. This is the training that composers such as Bach and Mozart had. Start a notebook, and each day copy in it some music you like. Later, as you develop skill in ear training, you can write down music just from hearing it.

2. Write four melodies, using simple rhythmic patterns and any pitches you like.

3. Continue the type of ear-training exercises given in this chapter in the following manner. Show your partner a page of music, and then play one measure or so. See if he or she can tell which measure you played.

chapter 7

Now that you know the basic symbols of pitch notation, you can begin to develop the ability to hear and perform pitches. There are at least three main methods of achieving this: absolute pitch, or pitch memory; relative pitch, or interval recognition; and functional pitch, or a recognition of relationships implied in tonally organized music.

True absolute pitch—the ability to recognize or produce a pitch without reference to any previously heard pitch—is a relatively rare ability, even among musicians. Most musicians and psychologists have concluded that it is not possible to develop this ability unless it is established at a very early age. It is, however, definitely possible and advisable for musicians to develop short-term pitch memory—that is, the ability to recall pitches that have recently been sounded. For example, if you were to sing the following passage, you could sing the second d merely by recalling what the first d sounded like and returning to this pitch.

Whenever possible, you should work to develop and extend your sense of pitch memory. No specific exercises will be given in this text for doing this, but you can employ pitch memory with any passage that involves a return to previously heard pitches. In the remainder of this chapter, we will begin the study of interval recognition. In the following chapter, we shall introduce the concept of pitch function, or pitch focus. Ultimately, success in working with the pitch parameter of music involves a combination of these three aspects—pitch memory, pitch distance, or interval, and pitch function.

We have already learned that an interval is the musical distance between two pitches. The smallest interval commonly used in Western music is the *half step.* On the piano, we can find half steps between any two adjacent keys (Ex. 7–1).

Ex. 7–1

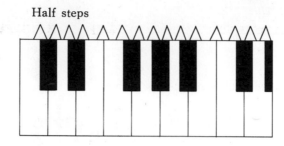

Half steps

A half step that spans two pitches with the same letter name (C–C♯, G–G♭, and so forth) is called a *chromatic half step;* a half step that spans two pitches with consecutive letter names (C–D♭, G–F♯, and so forth) is called a *diatonic half step.*

A *whole step* spans two half steps. Most whole steps span two pitches with consecutive letter names and are therefore diatonic whole steps (C–D, F♯–G♯, E♭–F, and so on). Chromatic whole steps spanning two pitches with the same letter name (for example, C♭–C♯) are possible, but are rarely encountered.

Identify the intervals (DHS = diatonic half step, CHS = chromatic half step, DWS = diatonic whole step, CWS = chromatic whole step).

Write the given interval above the given note.

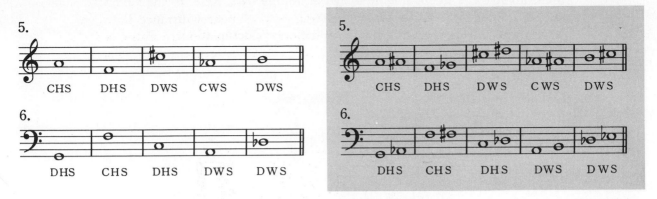

Write the given interval below the given note.

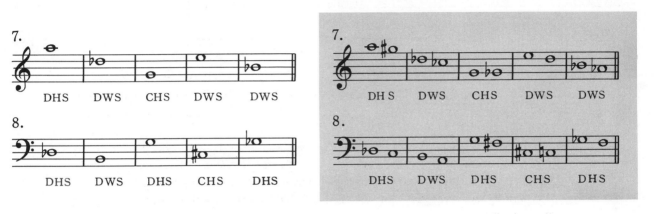

DOUBLE SHARPS AND DOUBLE FLATS

If we use only natural notes, sharps, and flats, we find it impossible to write certain intervals, such as a chromatic half step below a♭ or a diatonic whole step above b♯. To handle situations like this we must use double sharps (𝄪) or double flats (♭♭). We use sharps and flats to raise or lower a pitch by one chromatic half step, double sharps and double flats to raise or lower a pitch by two chromatic half steps (Ex. 7–2).

Ex. 7–2

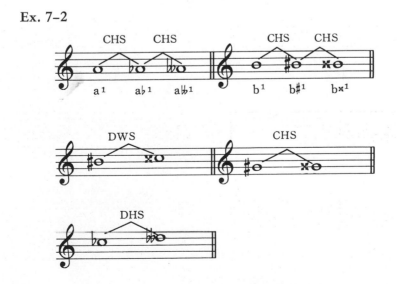

The following exercises are similar to the preceding exercises, but most of them involve the use of double sharps or double flats. Refer to the keyboard in determining the relationships.

Identify the following notes; include the octave designation.

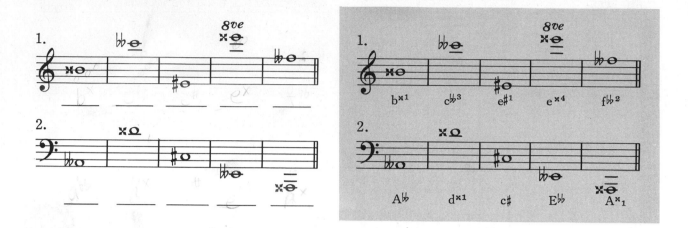

Write the indicated notes.

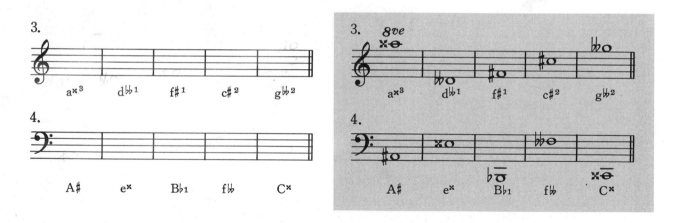

Identify the following intervals.

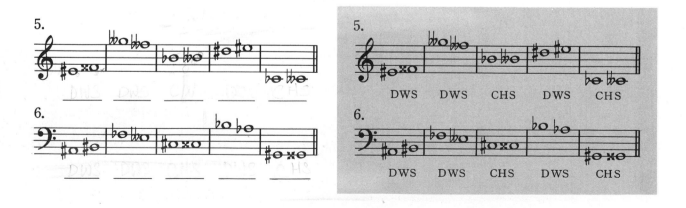

Write the given interval *above* the given note.

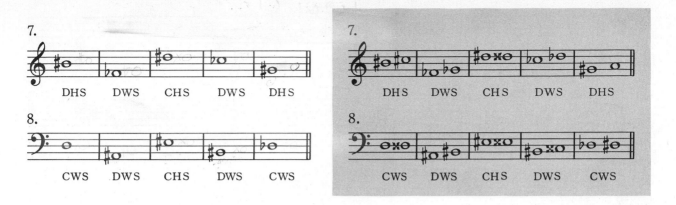

Write the given interval *below* the given note.

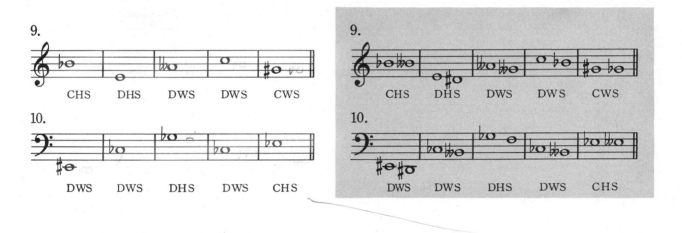

TWO-PITCH SETS

On p. 8, we discussed the concept of a pitch set, defining it simply as a collection of a certain number of pitches. A pitch set is the raw material from which a composition can be realized. To begin, we shall use two-pitch sets in two forms, as indicated in Ex. 7–3.

Ex. 7–3.

In the music-reading exercises that follow, we shall learn to distinguish between these two types of pitch sets and to use them in melodies. At first, you may play both notes of a set and then sing them. But you should soon develop the ability to play just the first note and then sing the other one.

EAR-TRAINING EXERCISES 7

Use only diatonic intervals.

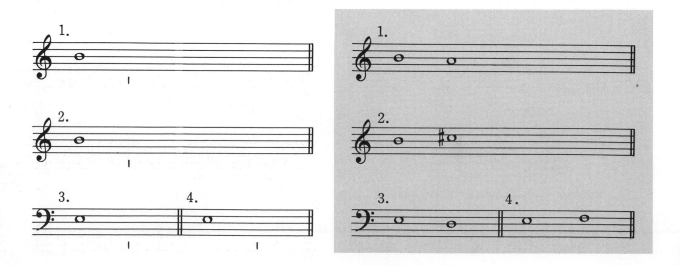

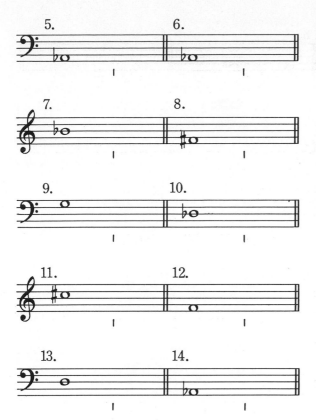

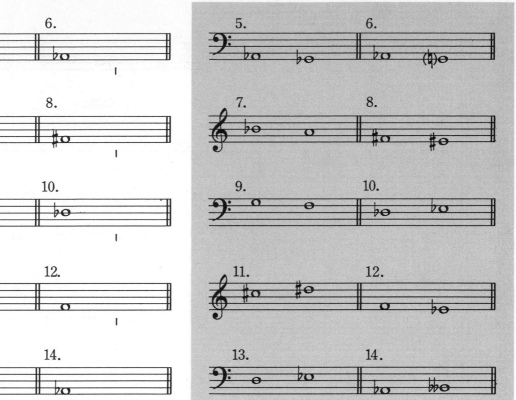

MUSIC-READING EXERCISES 7A

Use only diatonic intervals.

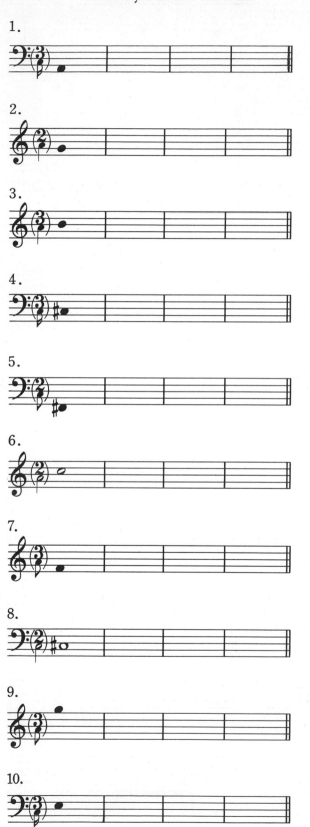

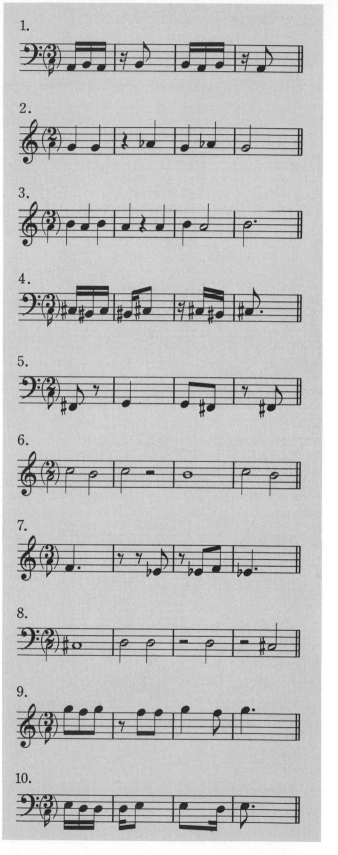

EXAMPLES FROM LITERATURE

1. Beethoven: Symphony No. 3, third movement

2. Beethoven: Symphony No. 3, third movement

3. Botocudos Folk Melody

4. Fuegian Folk Melody

5. Rimsky-Korsakov: "La Grande Pâque Russe"

SUPPLEMENTARY EXERCISES 7

1. Study your own music and see how many examples you can find of chromatic half steps, diatonic half steps, and whole steps. Sing them, play them, and listen carefully to them.

2. Play examples of half and whole steps on the piano for your partner. Tell your partner the starting pitch and then have him or her sing back the notes, using letter names.

3. Write four examples in the same style as those in this chapter. Sing and play them, and use them for ear training with your partner.

Integer Notation

Integer notation is a recently developed analytical and pedagogical tool that involves the use of integers (whole numbers) to represent pitches or pitch sets. We shall use zero (0) to represent the *lowest* pitch in a set, and we shall designate other pitches in the set by their distance in half steps from this pitch. Accordingly, the pitch set (0,1)* consists of two pitches, one of which is *one* half step above the other; the (0,2) pitch set comprises two pitches, one of which is *two* half steps above the other.

In integer notation, the enharmonic spelling of the pitches is not significant: e-f♯, e-g♭, and d✗-g♭, would all be considered the same (0,2) ("oh-two") pitch set.

Test your comprehension of these principles by answering the following questions.

1. A collection of pitches may be called a

_____ .

1. pitch set

2. Zero (0) is used to designate the (highest, lowest, first, last) _____ pitch of a set. The remaining pitches are designated by a number or integer indicating the number of (half steps, whole steps)

_____ above the lowest pitch.

2. lowest; half steps

3. Give the integer notation of the following pitch sets.

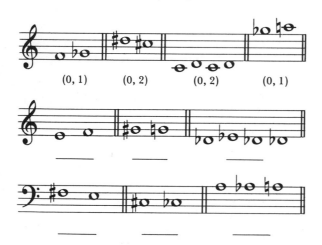

(0, 1)   (0, 1)   (0, 2)

(0, 2)   (0, 2)   (0, 1)

In integer notation, a half step or a whole step in traditional notation may be labeled "interval 1," and "interval 2," respectively, or, in abbreviated form, "I 1," and "I 2." When a pitch is repeated, we designate it "I 0."

*Usually spoken "oh-one."

Designate the following intervals. Remember that enharmonic spelling is not significant.

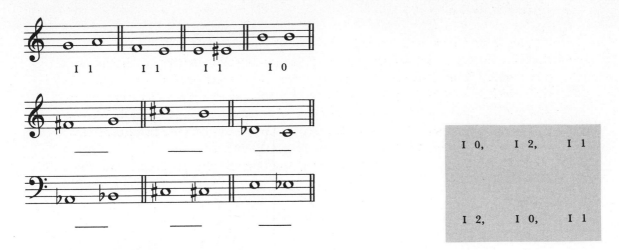

If direction is to be specified, this can be done by means of an arrow following the interval (for instance, "I 2 ↑" or "I 2 ↓").

You may wonder at this time why it is necessary to learn two ways of designating pitches. One answer is that we are in a period of transition from traditional pitch designation to the modern system of integer notation. Integer notation has the advantage of being applicable to a wide variety of music literature. It not only has been adopted by leading music-theory journals, but is also establishing itself in the undergraduate curriculum of many leading music schools. The second answer is that even if you never use integer notation after finishing this book, it should still help you to understand the traditional system. This should become clearer as we progress through the chapters on pitch.

chapter 8

In this chapter, we shall expand our discussion of pitch activity to cover three-pitch sets, and we shall begin our study of traditional interval designations. Since our study of pitch activity at this point is still limited to such a narrow range, we recommend that teachers and students occasionally return to some of the more general notions of pitch activity discussed in Chapter 5, in order to provide some interest and variety in study and practice.

NUMERICAL NAMES OF INTERVALS

In traditional terminology, each interval has a two-part name—a *descriptive* name and a *numerical* name. The numerical name is determined by counting the letter names spanned by the interval (accidentals are disregarded). Thus, g–d is a fifth (g a b c d).
                    (1 2 3 4 5)

The six intervals in Ex. 8–1 are all fifths.

Ex. 8–1

The numerical names of other intervals are determined similarly (Ex. 8–2).

Ex. 8–2

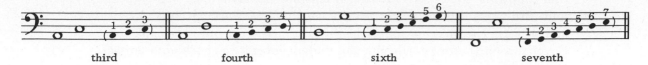

third   fourth   sixth   seventh

The numerical name for intervals spanning two pitches with exactly the same letter designation is a *prime,* or *unison.* The numerical name for two pitches that have the same letter name but are located eight notes apart is an *octave.*

In staff notation, it is easy to determine the numerical name of an interval if you remember the chart in Ex. 8–3.

Ex. 8–3

Primes or unisons:
same line or same space

Seconds:
line to space or
space to line

Thirds:
line to line or
space to space

Fourths:
line to two spaces above or below or
space to two lines above or below

Fifths:
line to two lines above or below or
space to two spaces above or below

Sixths:
line to three spaces above or below or
space to three lines above or below

Sevenths:
line to three lines above or below or
space to three spaces above or below

Octaves:
line to four spaces above or below or
space to four lines above or below

Give the numerical names of the intervals between consecutive notes in the following melodies. Use the following abbreviations: 1 me (prime), 2nd, 3rd, 4th, 5th, 6th, 7th, 8ve (octave). Work as accurately and quickly as you can. The answers appear in the line directly below the blank spaces. Cover this line before you begin, and then uncover it to check your answer.

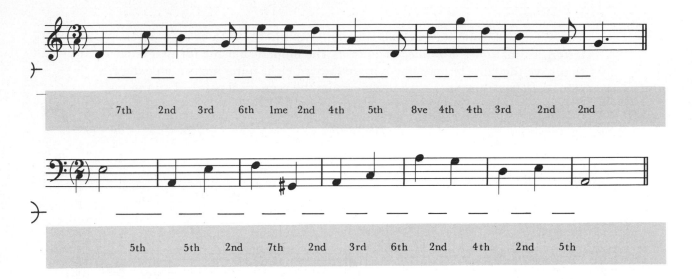

7th   2nd   3rd   6th   1me   2nd   4th   5th   8ve   4th   4th   3rd   2nd   2nd

5th   5th   2nd   7th   2nd   3rd   6th   2nd   4th   2nd   5th

DESCRIPTIVE NAMES OF INTERVALS

The descriptive names of intervals are somewhat more complicated to determine. In this chapter we shall concern ourselves only with the perfect prime and with major and minor seconds and thirds, reserving a discussion of other intervals until later chapters. Probably the simplest way to learn the descriptive names of these first intervals is to consider them in terms of half steps and whole steps. Study the following table carefully.

Descriptive Name	Numerical Name	Abbreviation	Half Steps and Whole Steps	Examples
perfect	prime	P1	0 (repeated tone)	C–C
minor	second	m2	one diatonic half step	C–D♭
major	second	M2	one whole step (or two half steps)	C–D
minor	third	m3	one whole step plus one diatonic half step (or three half steps)	C–E♭
major	third	M3	two whole steps (or four half steps)	C–E

Identify the following intervals, using abbreviations.

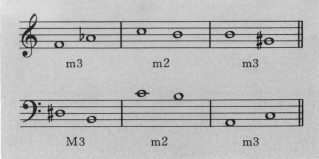

m3   m2   m3

M3   m2   m3

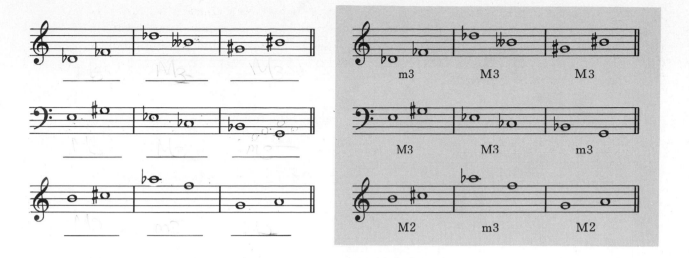

Write the indicated interval above (↗) or below (↘) the given note.

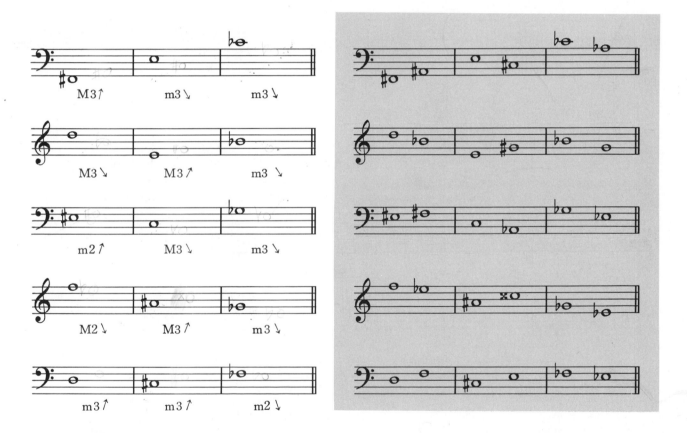

THREE-PITCH SETS

We can now expand our pitch material and work with three-pitch sets in the arrangements shown in Ex. 8-4. Other arrangements are possible, but for the present we shall limit ourselves to these three commonly used sets. Study the interval structure of each. Play and sing them, and notice the difference in the sounds of each.

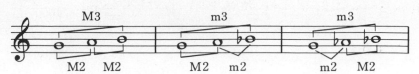

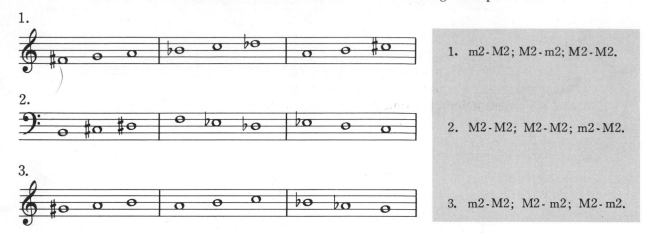

Indicate the intervallic structure of each of the following three-pitch sets.

1.

1. m2-M2; M2-m2; M2-M2.

2.

2. M2-M2; M2-M2; m2-M2.

3.

3. m2-M2; M2-m2; M2-m2.

Fill in the missing notes according to the intervals indicated, so as to create ascending three-pitch sets.

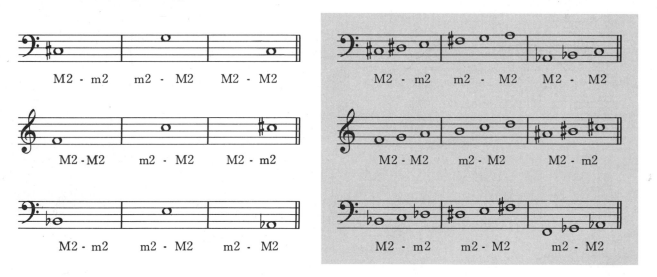

M2 - m2   m2 - M2   M2 - M2

M2 - M2   m2 - M2   M2 - m2

M2 - m2   m2 - M2   m2 - M2

M2 - m2   m2 - M2   M2 - M2

M2 - M2   m2 - M2   M2 - m2

M2 - m2   m2 - M2   m2 - M2

PITCH FOCUS

If we move from a theoretical consideration of pitch to an actual musical situation where pitches are animated by the interaction of duration, loudness, and timbre, we often find that one pitch in a melody tends to be more prominent than the others. The other pitches seem to focus upon or be dependent upon this central pitch. This phenomenon of pitch focus can be created by many factors, and in this chapter we shall examine some of them, including position, duration, and frequency.

Sometimes, all three of these factors combine to establish very clearly one pitch as the focal pitch of a group. Play Ex. 8–5 on the piano.

Ex. 8–5

The pitch g♭¹ is established very convincingly as the focal pitch because it is the first and last pitch, because it is sounded the most frequently, and because it is sounded for the longest total duration.

In other melodies, some factors may emphasize one pitch while others emphasize other pitches. Play Ex. 8–6, and try to determine its focal pitch.

Ex. 8–6

Here, the pitch b♭¹ would tend to be perceived as the focal pitch, because it is the first accented pitch and the last pitch, even though the pitch a¹ is heard more frequently and for a longer total duration. Other factors, such as pitch configuration and harmony, may also influence the perception of pitch focus, as we shall see in later chapters. Ultimately, the judgment of pitch focus must be made by the sensitive ear rather than on the basis of rules or visual analysis.

Study the following melodies and then indicate which pitch you hear as the focal pitch. Sing or play the melodies through before making your final judgment. Circle the factors that tend to establish pitch focus.

1. The focal pitch is ____ .
   The factors that tend to establish pitch focus are
   (a) position, (b) duration, (c) frequency.

1. e¹
   (a), (b), (c)

2. The focal pitch is ____ .
   The factors that tend to establish pitch focus are
   (a) position, (b) duration, (c) frequency.

2. A♭
   (a), (c)

3. The focal pitch is ___.
   The factors that tend to establish pitch focus are
   (a) position, (b) duration, (c) frequency.

Knowing the pitch focus of a melody can help you to hear and perform it more accurately and more musically. In a three-pitch set, for example, you can clearly establish the focal pitch and then relate the other pitches to it, as shown in Ex. 8–7. In this example, the focal pitch is indicated by a white note and the other two pitches by black notes.

Ex. 8–7

As you hear and perform the exercises that follow, try to think of pitch focus or pitch function as well as of interval and pitch memory. Try also to read always by patterns rather than by single notes.

MUSIC-READING EXERCISES 8

Sound the starting pitch and sing the examples at a moderate tempo in your own voice range.

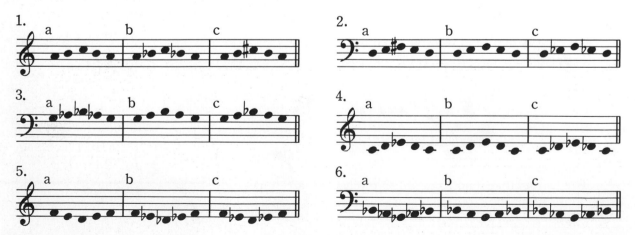

EAR-TRAINING EXERCISES 8

Fill in the blanks with the missing notes.

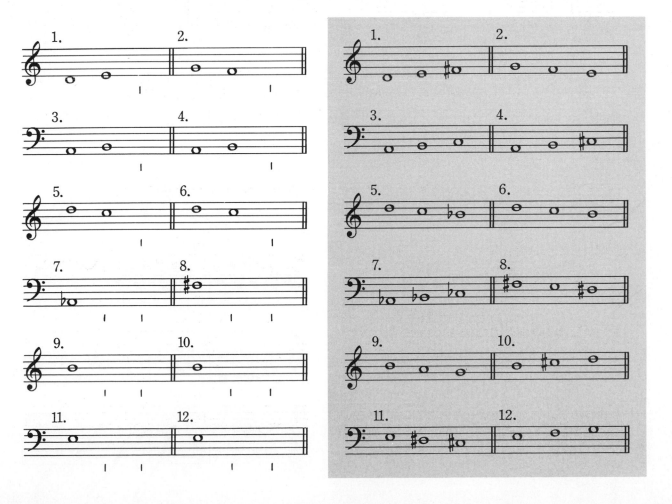

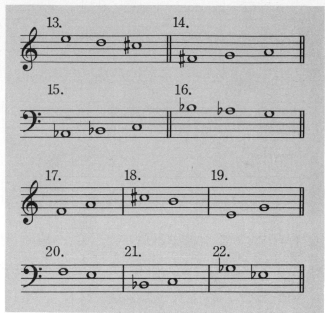

MUSIC-READING EXERCISES 8A

EXAMPLES FROM LITERATURE

To be used for music reading and ear training.

1. Brahms: Quartet in A Minor, Op. 51, No. 2, second movement

2. Mahler: Symphony No. 1, third movement

3. Brahms: Serenade in A, Op. 16, fifth movement

4. Mendelssohn: "Capriccio Brilliant," Op.22

5. Slave Beat Song,"Sold off to Georgy"

SUPPLEMENTARY EXERCISES 8

1. Listen to the following pieces for their use of thirds:

   Gershwin: "I loves you, Porgy," from *Porgy and Bess*
   Brahms: Symphony No. 4, first movement, first theme
   Brubeck: "Rondo à la Turk"

2. Devise and practice exercises for the piano that emphasize both major and minor thirds.

3. Compose short melodies, using the following rhythm and pitch material. For example, in the first melody use rhythmic patterns based upon two-pulse groups with the half note as the pulse, and use the pitches f, g, and ab. Establish ab as the focal pitch through such means as position, duration, and frequency.

etc.

4. Sing and play your own melodies and those written by your partner. Dictate your melodies to your partner.

OPTIONAL MATERIAL

Integer Notation for Larger Intervals

Now that you have learned the basic principles of integer notation with I0, I1, and I2, it should be relatively easy to expand the concept to larger intervals. Counting the lower note always as 0, you simply count up to the highest note. It is helpful to have a keyboard in front of you as a "musical ruler" to facilitate counting. Direct your attention to the back of the keyboard, where the alternation of black and white keys is clear. Count each key (black or white) as 1. With practice, you should be able to visualize the piano keyboard. Remember that you can designate a two-note interval in two ways, as shown in Ex. 8–8. Remember also that spelling is not critical; the sound, or the distance between the notes on the keyboard, is.

Ex. 8–8

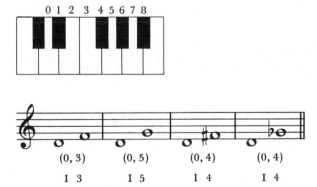

Identify the following intervals, as shown in Ex. 8–8.

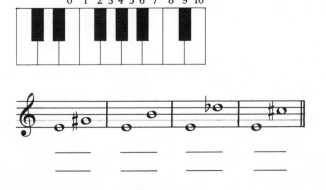

(0, 4)	(0, 7)	(0, 9)	(0, 9)
I 4	I 7	I 9	I 9

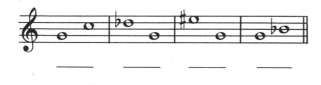

(0, 5)　(0, 6)　(0, 6)　(0, 11)
I 5　　I 6　　I 6　　I 11

(0, 5)　(0, 6)　(0, 10)　(0, 3)
I 5　　I 6　　I 10　　I 3

(0, 6)　(0, 9)　(0, 10)　(0, 8)
I 6　　I 9　　I 10　　I 8

Write the indicated intervals in the direction shown by the arrow.

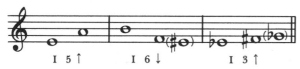

I 5 ↑　　　I 6 ↓　　　I 3 ↑

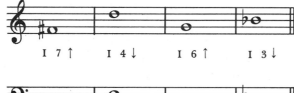

I 7 ↑　　I 4 ↓　　I 6 ↑　　I 3 ↓

I 11 ↑　　I 4 ↓　　I 5 ↑　　I 6 ↓

Three-pitch sets may be designated in integer notation as shown in Ex. 8–9.

Ex. 8–9.

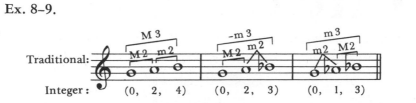

Traditional:

Integer :　　(0, 2, 4)　　(0, 2, 3)　　(0, 1, 3)

Indicate in integer notation the intervallic structure of each of the following three-pitch sets.

1. (0,1,3) (0,2,3) (0,2,4)

2. (0,2,4) (0,2,4) (0,2,3)

Fill in the missing notes according to the intervals indicated, so as to create ascending three-pitch sets.

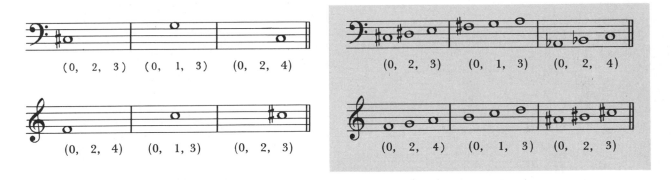

(0, 2, 3) (0, 1, 3) (0, 2, 4)

(0, 2, 4) (0, 1, 3) (0, 2, 3)

(0, 2, 3) (0, 1, 3) (0, 2, 4)

(0, 2, 4) (0, 1, 3) (0, 2, 3)

Focal Pitches in Integer Notation

In integer notation, we designate the focal pitch as "0." When the focal pitch of a set is the lowest pitch, we can easily use the approach discussed on p. 82. For example, the first item in Ex. 8-7 is based on the (0,2,3) set.

When the focal pitch is not the lowest pitch, as in the case of the last two items in Ex. 8-7, we are presented with some problems. In these situations, it is helpful to look at a larger context. Imagine a composition that used the pitches from B♭ to b♭², as in Ex. 8-10, and clearly established b♭ (in all of its octave occurrences) as the focal pitch. We could represent the pitch spectrum of this composition as in Ex. 8-10.

Ex. 8–10

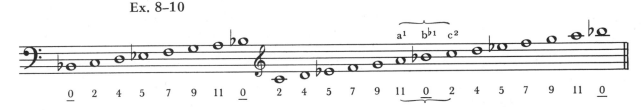

Notice that the numbering of the pitches begins with B♭ as 0 and progresses consecutively to the pitch a as 11. After this we return to the pitch b♭, and, therefore, it is logical to return to the designation "0."

Now imagine that a section of this composition used only the pitches a¹, bb¹, and c². We would designate this pitch set (11,0,2). Returning to the second item of Ex. 8–7, we see that an identical situation exists, namely an (11,0,2) pitch set, with the pitch d as the focal pitch. Using an analogous procedure, we see that the set used in the third item is (9,10,0), with f¹ as the focal pitch.

Here is a step-by-step procedure for numbering pitch sets to pitch sets with a focal pitch:

1. Write the given pitches of the set in ascending order. Write the focal pitch as a whole note and the other pitches as stemless quarter notes. Designate the focal pitch as 0.

2. Determine the integer number of each pitch *above* 0 by counting the number of half steps between the pitch and 0.

3. Determine the integer number of each pitch *below* 0 by counting the number of half steps between the pitch and 0 and then subtracting this number from 12.

These three steps are illustrated in Ex. 8–11 for each of the pitch sets in Ex. 8–7.

Ex. 8–11

In later chapters, the usefulness of these concepts will become clearer to you. To test your comprehension, complete the following exercises.

Example (focal pitches are whole notes)

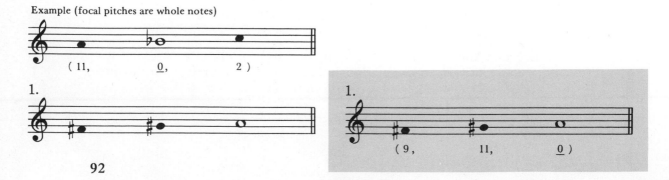

92

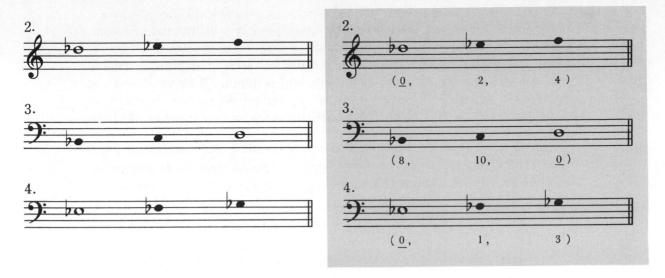

Remember that in some situations focal pitches are clearly established and you can use the techniques described above. When the focal pitch is ambiguous, simply assign "0" (not underlined) to the lowest pitch. In Music Reading Exercises 8, where no rhythm is assigned to the pitches, it is virtually impossible to establish a clear focal pitch. Therefore, these pitches should be sung with "0" as the lowest pitch.

Pitch Class

If we were concerned with pitch focus in a melody with a large range, we would recognize that not just a single pitch but all of the octave duplications of that pitch could serve as the pitch focus. We would also recognize that, at least on an equal-tempered instrument, it would not make any difference which of the several possible enharmonic spellings we chose for this pitch. A pitch, its octave duplications, and its enharmonic spellings are all said to belong to a given *pitch class* (abbreviated "p.c."). Thus, F, e♯[1] and g♭♭[3] all belong to the same pitch class.

In addition to using 0 to represent the lowest pitch of a set of pitches, or the focal pitch of a set of pitches (0), we can use it to refer always to pitch class c (b♯ and d♭♭). Pitch class 1 would be c♯, pitch class 2 would be d, and so on, as shown in the following table.

Pitch class in integer notation	*Pitch class in letter notation*
0	c, b♯, d♭♭
1	c♯, d♭
2	d, cx, e♭♭
3	d♯, e♭
4	e, dx, f♭
5	f, e♯, g♭♭
6	f♯, g♭
7	g, fx, a♭♭
8	g♯, a♭
9	a, gx, b♭♭
10	a♯, b♭
11	b, ax, c♭

From now on in this text, most of the pitch sets we will use will have a pitch focus. When you are working with melodies in which there is no clear pitch focus, however, you can use the three-step procedure described above. Many recent books and articles on the use of pitch in twentieth-century music have adopted this practice. See, for example, "Sets and Ordering Procedures in Twentieth-Century Music" by Gary Wittlich (pp. 388–476) in *Aspects of Twentieth-Century Music,* Wittlich, Gary, ed. (Englewood Cliffs, N.J.: Prentice-Hall, 1975).

You may now wish to return to the music-reading and ear-training exercises in this and earlier chapters and apply some aspects of integer notation to your performance and perception.

chapter 9

Rhythmic activity in music can occur on several different levels. Until now, we have been concerned only with rhythmic activity on one level. In this chapter we shall investigate rhythmic activity on two levels, and in subsequent chapters, three or more levels.

To understand the concept of rhythmic activity on two levels, sing the familiar songs in Ex. 9–1. Notice that on one level of rhythmic activity, both songs are organized in three-pulse groups. We shall represent each song with the eighth note as one pulse. Tap these pulses with your left hand as you sing.

Ex. 9–1

Now sing each song again, and this time focus on rhythmic activity on a slower level—the dotted quarter note. Tap eighth-note pulses with your left hand and conduct dotted-quarter-note pulses with your right hand as you sing each song. Notice that the slower pulses (𝅗𝅥.) are organized into groups of twos in the first song and into groups of threes in the second song (Ex. 9–2).

Ex. 9–2

"Drink to Me Only with Thine Eyes"

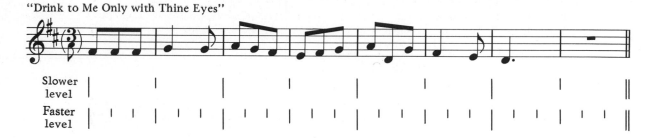

"Beautiful Dreamer"

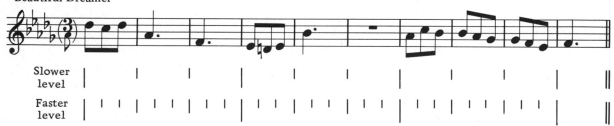

Using two-pulse groups and three-pulse groups on two levels, we can form the four regular combinations illustrated in Ex. 9–3. Practice sounding these combinations by tapping one level with one hand and the other level with the other hand, or by singing one level and clapping the other. These combinations could be represented by various note values, as we shall see in subsequent sections of this chapter.

Ex. 9–3

A.		B.	
Slower level Two-pulse groups	| | |	Slower level Three-pulse groups	| | | |
	etc.		etc.
Faster level Two-pulse groups	| | | | |	Faster level Two-pulse groups	| | | | |
C.		D.	
Slower level Two-pulse groups	| | |	Slower level Three-pulse groups	| | | |
	etc.		etc.
Faster level Three-pulse groups	| | | | | |	Faster level Three-pulse groups	| | | | | | |

BEAT

To this point, we have used the term *pulse* rather than the term *beat*, even though you may be more familiar with the latter term. Like the pulse, the beat may be defined as one of a series of regularly recurring stimuli. The difference between pulse and beat is that for any given section of music, pulses may be heard on various levels at various rates of speed, ranging from very fast to very slow; beats, however, are heard only on one level and at a rate of speed that is appropriate or "natural" for the particular piece of music. Sing a march or a college "fight song" and clap as you sing. You will probably find that you are clapping at the rate of about 120 to 140 claps per minute. You are clapping the beat. At the same time, you can be aware of pulses at other levels, both faster and slower.

Try singing "Drink to Me Only With Thine Eyes" at various speeds, and you will notice that you will tend to hear the beat on the eighth-note level (groups of threes) when you sing very slowly and on the dotted-quarter-note level (groups of twos) when you sing very fast. At a moderate speed, you could hear the beat at either level.

No hard and fast rules can be made regarding beats. Indeed, the selection of the appropriate level for the beat is one of the most difficult problems facing a conductor. In general, we tend to hear beats in a range of approximately 70 to 140 per minute, but musical characteristics and individual preferences are sometimes just as decisive as the mere speed involved.

To simplify matters at this point, we shall arbitrarily say that what we have called the slower level will be the *beat level*. What we have called the faster level will be the *division level*; that is, pulses at this level will be heard as divisions of the beat. In later chapters, we will modify this distinction somewhat.

METER

Meter refers to the basic temporal organization of a composition or a section thereof. It is customary to designate meters with two terms. The first refers to the division level and indicates if the grouping is by twos (*simple* meters) or by threes (*compound* meters). The second term refers to the beat level and indicates if the grouping here is by two (*duple* meters) or by three (*triple* meters). In other words, duple or triple indicates whether there are two or three beats in each measure; simple or compound indicates whether there are two or three divisions of each beat. Ex. 9–4 illustrates four basic meters. Study and memorize this chart. Practice tapping the division (or faster) level with the left hand and conducting the beat (or slower) level with the right hand.

Ex. 9–4

Simple duple meter:

	1.	2.	1.
Beat level in groups of two						

etc.

Division level in groups of two						
	1.	2.	1.	2.	1.

Simple triple meter:

	1.	2.	3.	1.
Beat level in groups of three							

etc.

Division level in groups of two								
	1.	2.	1.	2.	1.	2.	1.

Compound duple meter:

	1.	2.	1.
Beat level in groups of two							etc.

Division level in groups of three
| | | | | | |
1. 2. 3. 1. 2. 3. 1.

Compound triple meter:

	1.	2.	3.	1.
Beat level in groups of three								etc.

Division level in groups of three
| | | | | | | | | |
1. 2. 3. 1. 2. 3. 1. 2. 3. 1.

Meter Signatures

Meter signatures are double numbers placed at the beginning of a section of music to indicate the metric organization. They are similar to the pulse-group designations that we have been using until now, except that a number is used in place of a note value (Ex. 9-5).

Ex. 9-5

$$\left(\frac{3}{\text{♩}}\right) = \frac{3}{4} \qquad \left(\frac{2}{♪}\right) = \frac{2}{8} \qquad \text{etc.}$$

In simple meters, the bottom figure indicates the note value representing one beat and the top figure indicates the number of beats in a measure. Ex. 9-6 illustrates simple meters with meter signatures and shows the beat level (top) and the division level (bottom). Notice that measure lines are now used only on the beat level. In some meters, beams aid the eye in perceiving beat groupings or divisions of the beat. However, in meters involving quarter notes or half notes on the division level, the musician must grasp the grouping without the aid of beams.

Ex. 9-6

Simple duple

Simple triple

* The meter signature for $\frac{2}{2}$ is sometimes indicated by ¢ .

Simple meters that call for sixteenth notes or whole notes on the beat level are rarely used.

The problem of representing compound meters is somewhat complicated if the beat is a dotted note, for such notes cannot be translated directly into whole numbers.

Ex. 9-7

Because of this, it is necessary to represent the division level in the meter signature of a compound meter. Thus, the metric organization in Ex. 9-8

Ex. 9-8

would be represented by the meter signature of $\frac{6}{8}$, which indicates that there are six eighth notes in a measure. Example 9-9 shows compound meters with meter signatures and indicates the beat level (top) and the division level (bottom).

Ex. 9-9

Compound duple

Compound triple

Compound meters that call for thirty-second notes or half notes on the division level are rarely used.

Now let us review your comprehension of meters and meter signatures. Before answering the questions below, review carefully Ex. 9-6 and 9-9. Remember that meter signatures whose upper number is 2 or 3 indicate simple meters. In this case, the upper figure indicates the number of beats per measure and the lower figure indicates the note value representing one beat. The division level will consist of note values that are half the value of the beat. These notes will be grouped in twos.

Meter signatures whose upper figure is 6 or 9 indicate compound meters. In this case, the upper figure indicates the number of divisions in a measure and the lower figure indicates the note value representing one division. On the division level, the notes will be grouped in threes. The beat level will consist of dotted notes that are three times as long as the note value of the division level. If the upper figure of the meter signature is 6, there will be two beats per measure; if the upper figure of the meter signature is 9, there will be three beats per measure.

Write the beat level and the division level of the following meters.

1. **3/4** Beat level:
Division level:

2. **9/16** Beat level:
Division level:

3. **2/8** Beat level:
Division level:

4. **3/16** Beat level:
Division level:

5. **6/4** Beat level:
Division level:

6. **¢** Beat level:
Division level:

7. **9/8** Beat level:
Division level:

8. **6/2** Beat level:
Division level:

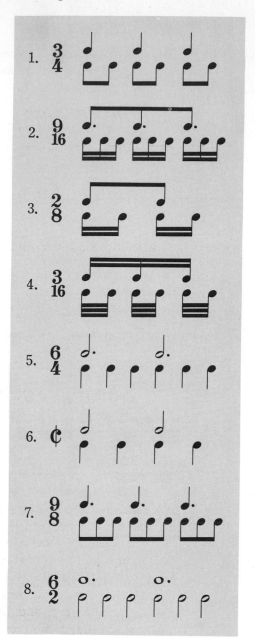

Supply the proper meter signature for the following examples.

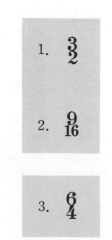

Supply the proper meter signature for the following examples. Only the beat level is given.

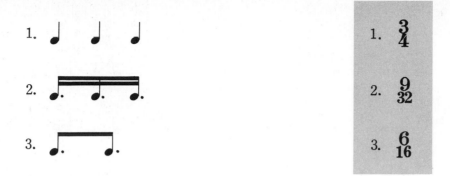

1. ♩   ♩   ♩   1. $\frac{3}{4}$

2. ♩. ♩. ♩.   2. $\frac{9}{32}$

3. ♩.　　♩.   3. $\frac{6}{16}$

Supply the proper meter signature for the following examples. Only the division level is given.

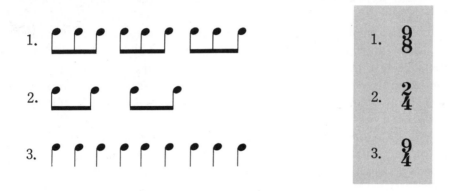

1.   1. $\frac{9}{8}$

2.   2. $\frac{2}{4}$

3.   3. $\frac{9}{4}$

Rhythmic Patterns in Simple and Compound Meters

When you are thoroughly familiar with the basic concepts of the simple and compound meters studied in the last section, you are ready to learn to hear and perform the basic rhythmic patterns in Ex. 4–5 within the context of these meters. You should learn to perform and hear these patterns on both the beat level and the division level. We shall begin by learning these patterns on the division level.

First, establish the basic metric pattern by tapping divisions with the left hand and conducting with the right hand. While doing this, sing the various patterns in the selected meter. For example, if the selected meter is $\frac{2}{4}$, you would first establish the meter as shown in Ex. 9–10.

Ex. 9–10

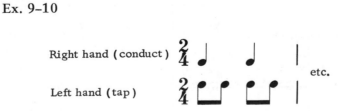

Since the eighth note represents one pulse on the division level, you would refer to the eighth-note column and then sing the two-pulse patterns as shown in Ex. 9–11.

Ex. 9–11

Sing (on "tah")

Right hand (conduct)   etc.

Left hand (tap)

Next, sing the patterns in random order and use them for ear training with your partner. Repeat the procedure with other meters. After you have sung many examples, try to do the same exercise but merely conduct on the beat level. In the back of your mind, however, imagine the pulses on the division level so that your performance is accurate. Eventually, you should also be able to eliminate conducting, or reduce it to an imperceptible gesture, and imagine the pulses on both levels as you sing. This skill of imagining steady pulses without actually sounding them is of utmost importance. Obviously, you could not perform in public and conduct and tap as you play or sing. But with a firm background of steady pulses on both levels, your performance can be accurate and vital. Later in your musical development, you can take the subtle liberties with rhythmic patterns that are required for the expressive performance of music, but these liberties must always be taken against a clearly established metric background.

Finally, practice the same patterns on the beat level. For compound meters, it is necessary to learn these patterns written with dotted notes (Ex. 9–12). Notice that a note value lasting three beats in a compound meter must be written as a two-beat note tied to a one-beat note.

Ex. 9–12

Basic pulse =	♪.		♩.		♩.	
1 1	♩.	♩.	♩.	♩.	♩.	♩.
2	♩.		♩.		o·	
1 0	♪	ɣ·	♩.	ɤ·	♩.	▬·
0 1	ɣ·	♪	ɤ·	♩.	▬·	♩.
0 0	ɣ·		▬·		▬·	

Two-pulse groups

Basic pulse =   ♪.   ♩.   𝅝.

Three-pulse groups	(♪.)	(♩.)	(𝅝.)
1 1 1	♪. ♪. ♪.	♩. ♩. ♩.	𝅝. 𝅝. 𝅝.
2 1	♩. ♪.	𝅗𝅥. ♩.	o. 𝅝.
1 2	♪. ♩.	♩. 𝅗𝅥.	𝅝. o.
3	♩.⌣♪.	𝅗𝅥.⌣♩.	o.⌣𝅝.
1 1 0	♪. ♪. 𝄾.	♩. ♩. 𝄽	𝅝. 𝅝. ⬓.
1 0 1	♪. 𝄾. ♪.	♩. 𝄽 ♩.	𝅝. ⬓. 𝅝.
0 1 1	𝄾. ♪. ♪.	𝄽 ♩. ♩.	⬓. 𝅝. 𝅝.
2 0	♩. 𝄾.	𝅗𝅥. 𝄽	o. ⬓.
0 2	𝄾. ♩.	𝄽 𝅗𝅥.	⬓. o.
1 0 0	♪. 𝄾. 𝄾.	♩. 𝄽 𝄽	𝅝. ⬓. ⬓.
0 1 0	𝄾. ♪. 𝄾.	𝄽 ♩. 𝄽	⬓. 𝅝. ⬓.
0 0 1	𝄾. 𝄾. ♪.	𝄽 𝄽 ♩.	⬓. ⬓. 𝅝.
0 0 0	𝄼. 𝄾.	⬓. 𝄽	𝄻. ⬓.

TEMPO

Tempo may be defined simply as the speed of the beat in music. In our discussion of beat, we saw that it was possible to hear the beat at different levels, depending upon the piece, the performer, or the listener. Since tempo is dependent on beat, it is possible to have the same variety of perception of tempo.

The only precise method of designating the tempo of a section of music is to indicate the metronome marking for a specific note value:

(♩ = 120,   ♪ = 144, etc.)

We often use words as tempo indicators, but these are not as exact as metronome indications and may be interpreted differently from piece to piece or from performer to performer. Still, it is important for a musician to be acquainted with these terms in at least the four languages represented in the following tables. It is especially important to know the Italian terms, for they are the most frequently used. Notice that many of the terms really refer to the character of a piece rather than directly to the speed of the piece.

English	Italian	German	French
SLOW TEMPOS			
broad	largo	breit	large
slow	lento	langsam	lent
	adagio (literally, "at ease")	getragen	lent
heavy	grave	schwer	lourd
MODERATE TEMPOS			
moderate	andante (literally, "walking")	gehend	allant
	moderato	mässig	moderé
FAST TEMPOS			
fast	allegro (literally, "cheerful")	schnell	vite
lively	vivace	lebhaft	vif
very fast	presto	eilig	rapide

Slight adaptations or modifications of these tempos can be indicated thus:

English	Italian	German	French
very	molto	sehr	très
somewhat	poco or un poco	ein wenig or etwas	un peu
more	più	-er	plus
even more	-issimo	noch -er	encore plus
not too	non troppo	nicht zu	pas trop
less	meno, -ino, or -etto	weniger	moins

Tempo in music does not always remain the same. Sudden or gradual changes in tempo can be indicated by the following terms:

English	Italian	German	French
accelerate	accelerando	schneller werden	accélérer
becoming faster	stringendo (literally, "tightening")	drängend	en pressant
faster	piu mosso	bewegter	plus animé
retard (gradually)	ritardando	langsamer werden	ralentissant
	rallentando	zurückhalten	ralentir
held back (immediately)	ritenuto	zurückgehalten	retenu
broaden	allargando	verbreitern	élargissant
less fast	meno mosso	weniger bewegt	moins vite
freely	rubato (literally, "robbed")	frei	liberé
gradually	poco a poco	allmählich	peu à peu
suddenly	subito	plötzlich	tout à coup
decrease in tempo and loudness	calando	nachlassen	en diminuant

decrease in tempo and loudness, dying away	smorzando	verlöschen	en s'effaçant
decrease in tempo and loudness, dying down	morendo	ersterben	en mourant
return to original tempo	a tempo or tempo primo	erstes Zeitmass	premier tempo

Give the proper Italian term for each of the following:

1. broad (slow) _____

2. very fast _____

3. moderate (walking) _____

4. less fast _____

5. accelerate _____

6. gradually (little by little) _____

7. suddenly _____

8. decrease in tempo and loudness

   (dying down) _____

9. return to original tempo _____

10. broaden _____

1. largo

2. molto allegro, or presto

3. andante

4. meno allegro, or meno mosso

5. accelerando

6. poco a poco

7. subito

8. calando,

   smorzando, or morendo

9. a tempo, or tempo primo

10. allargando

"RHYTHM SHORTHAND" FOR EAR-TRAINING EXERCISES

Ultimately, the most effective way to take rhythm dictation is to listen directly for the patterns involved and to write these down in regular notation. For some students, however, an intermediate step of writing the rhythms in a simple form of "shorthand" may prove helpful in the beginning stages of ear training.

First, write out numbers for each beat of the example. Then, using these as reference points, write long lines for long notes and short lines or dots for short notes. When you have completed these two steps, you can translate the results into regular notation. Ex 9–13 illustrates this technique for Ear-Training Exercises 9, numbers 1–4.

Ex. 9–13

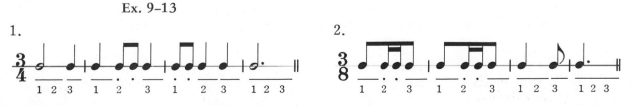

105

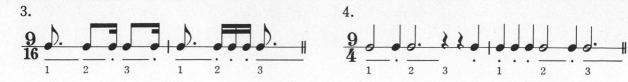

A shorthand system such as this has but limited value, and we suggest that you learn to think in patterns of regular notation as soon as possible.

One other suggestion may be helpful for ear-training exercises involving pitches. We suggest that you first sketch dots for noteheads and then fill in the rest of the notehead and the necessary stems, flags, dots, and accidentals later. (See Ex. 9–14.)

Ex. 9–14

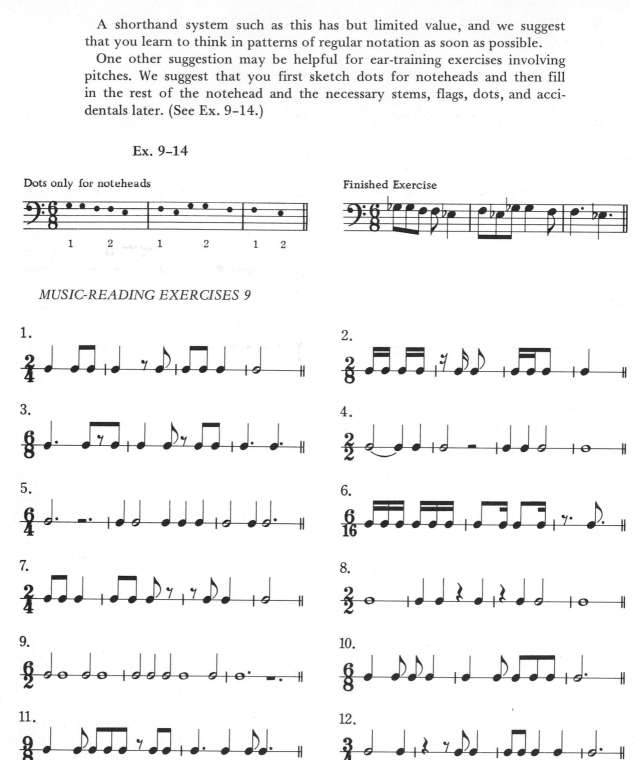

MUSIC-READING EXERCISES 9

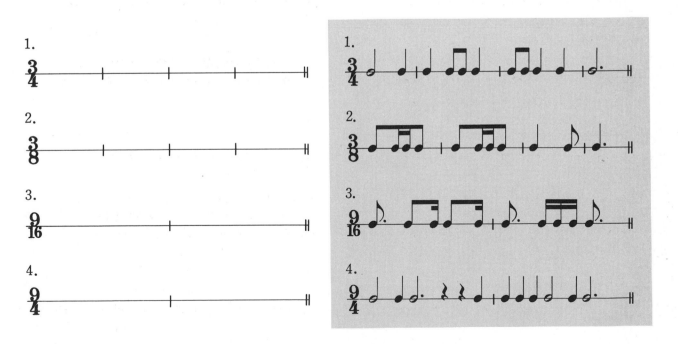

EAR-TRAINING EXERCISES 9

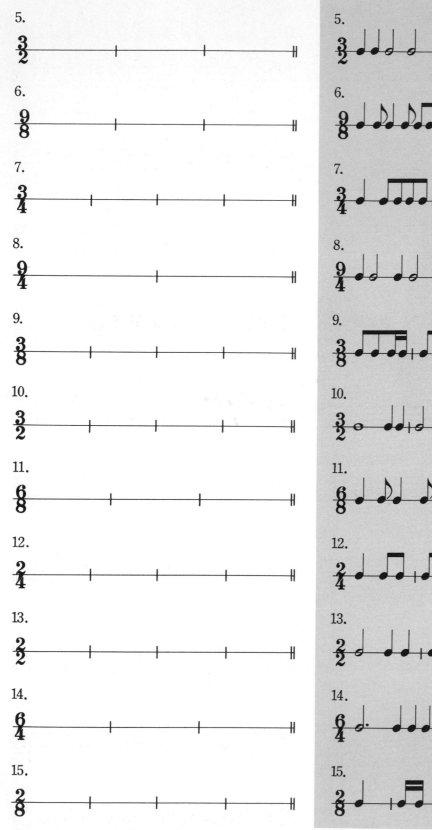
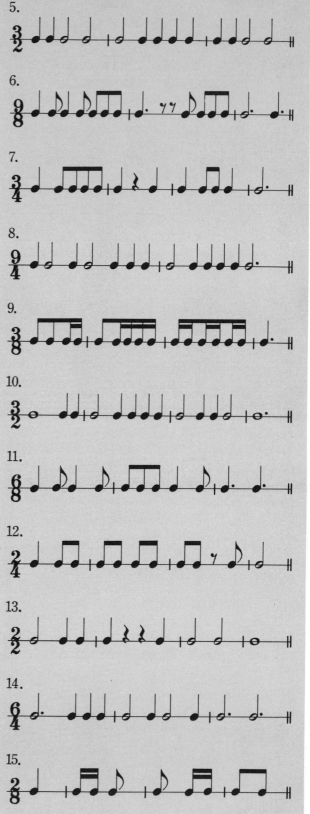

108

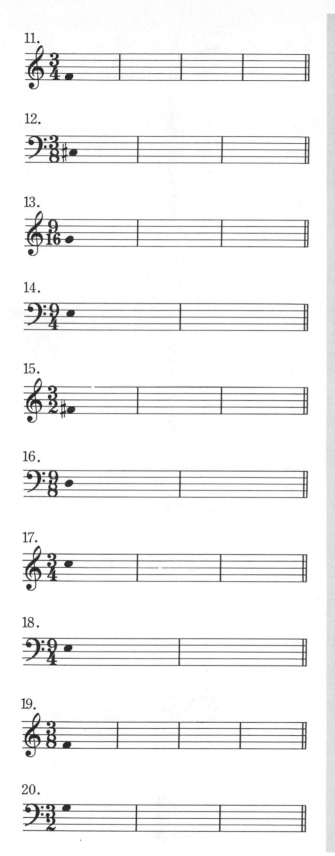

Meter recognition. After listening to each of the following excerpts, underline the meter that best fits the passage.

1. simple duple   simple triple
   compound duple   compound triple
2. simple duple   simple triple
   compound duple   compound triple
3. simple duple   simple triple
   compound duple   compound triple
4. simple duple   simple triple
   compound duple   compound triple
5. simple duple   simple triple
   compound duple   compound triple
6. simple duple   simple triple
   compound duple   compound triple
7. simple duple   simple triple
   compound duple   compound triple

1. simple duple

2. compound duple

3. simple triple

4. simple duple

5. compound triple

6. compound duple

7. simple duple

EXAMPLES FROM LITERATURE

1. New Guinea Tribal Song

2. Landino: "Benche ora piova"

3. Offenbach: *Tales of Hoffman,* Barcarolle

4. Mozart: Symphony No. 38, first movement

5. Brahms: Symphony No.2, third movement

1. Compose four examples similar to the ear-training exercises in this chapter. Work with your partner, using each other's melodies for sight singing and ear training.

To make your melodies more interesting and coherent, repeat rhythmic patterns or motives in consecutive measures, in every second measure, or in some other fashion.

2. Sing or play familiar tunes for your drill partner and see if he or she can identify the tune and write down the rhythm.

chapter 10

In the preceding chapter, we studied rhythmic activity that occurred either on the beat level or on the division level and that involved patterns of two pulses or three pulses that were complete within a beat or within a measure. In this chapter, we shall study more complex patterns that involve durations extending from one beat to the next or from one measure to the next. Before we learn to hear and perform these patterns, we must learn the notational principles involved.

There are two guiding principles for all rhythmic notation:

1. The notation should show as clearly as necessary the underlying metric organization.
2. The notation should be as concise as possible.

Sometimes these two principles will conflict with each other. It is the musician's task to find an acceptable solution to problems of rhythmic notation, based upon common sense and a knowledge of the notational conventions employed by composers through the years.

It is not always possible to say that a given rhythmic notation is right or wrong. Instead, we could use the familiar letter grades (A, B, D, F) to evaluate a given example:

A = correct, clear, concise; probably the way this passage would be written by careful, knowledgeable writers; shows the metric organization (that is, the beat and its divisions) of the composition clearly, but does not have unnecessary symbols.

B = possible, but not in accordance with established practices; errs slightly either in not showing the beat and its divisions or in having too many symbols.

D = understandable with great difficulty; completely different from established practices; obscures the metric structure completely, or has far too many rhythmic symbols.

F = incomprehensible; impossible to interpret in accordance with standard notational procedures; for example, uses incorrect or nonexistent symbols, or has too few or too many symbols.

We might illustrate this rating system as follows:

1. Rating: A
   This example shows the beat clearly, but has no unnecessary symbols. Rests are handled with more care than notes.

2. Rating: B
   This example goes too far in the direction of showing the beat and its divisions: it uses too many unnecessary symbols.

3. Rating: B–
   This example goes too far in the direction of using as few symbols as possible; it does not show the beat and its divisions. Notice that this version is rated B–, indicating that it is worse to err in the direction of confusion than in the direction of being too careful.

4. Rating: D
   This is about as confusing as notation can be and still convey a message to the performer. It does not show the beat and its divisions, yet it uses more symbols than are necessary.

5. Rating: F
   This is musical nonsense: it conveys no clear meaning to anyone. It uses some strange or incorrect versions of standard symbols, and combines them in a meaningless way. It may be visually pleasing, but try to perform it.

A tie is a curved line connecting two or more adjacent notes of the same pitch and indicating that the sound is to be continued from one note to the next without any intervening pause or articulation. The following rules apply to the use of ties.

1. Ties are always used for durations that extend from one measure to the next measure(s) (Ex. 10-1).

Ex. 10-1

When the tie between measures connects notes with accidentals, it is not necessary to repeat the accidental after its first occurrence.

2. Ties are always used for sound durations that could not be represented by a single note value (Ex. 10-2).

Ex. 10-2

3. Ties should not be used for durations that begin on one beat and extend through the next complete beat. These should be represented by a single note value whenever possible (Ex. 10-3).

Ex. 10-3

4. Ties may or may not be used for durations that extend from one beat to the next beat(s) and involve one or two incomplete beats or durations. Here, we encounter the problem of finding an acceptable compromise between clarity and conciseness, and it is difficult to lay down hard and fast rules.

In general, musicians tend to use a single note value where possible in simple meters and to use ties more often in compound meters (Ex. 10-4).

Ex. 10-4

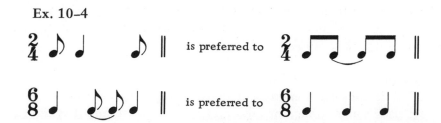

One exception to this general rule is illustrated in Ex. 10-5.

116

Ex. 10–5

BEAMS

In the meters and rhythms studied to this point, it is proper to beam notes within one beat or within one measure. Any other usage of beams should be avoided. (See Ex. 10–6.)

Ex. 10–6

RESTS

1. A silence lasting for a whole measure is represented with a whole rest, regardless of the meter (Ex. 10–7).

Ex. 10–7

2. Silence lasting for two beats in simple triple meters or for two divisions of the beat in any compound meter are usually written as two rests rather than as a single rest (Ex. 10–8).

Ex. 10–8

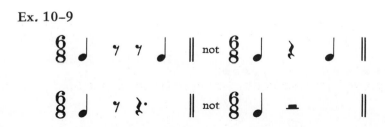

3. Silence that extends from one beat to the next beat(s) and involves one or two incomplete beats is usually written as two or more rests rather than as one united rest (Ex. 10–9).

Ex. 10–9

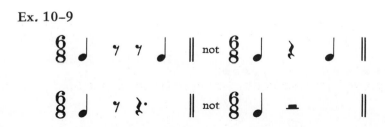

4. Do not use dotted rests in simple meters (Ex. 10–10).

Ex. 10–10

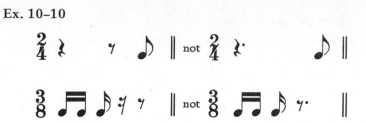

To develop and test your competence in dealing with these notational principles, complete the following exercises. Use the model exercise as a guide.

SYNCOPATION

Often, the rhythmic patterns used in a composition tend to confirm or reinforce the natural accentuation of the meter in which they are written. Sometimes, however, the rhythmic patterns tend to contradict the natural accentuation of the meter, producing a special effect called *syncopation*. Ex. 10–11 illustrates syncopation achieved by means of ties or rests.

Ex. 10–11

Not all ties and rests produce syncopation. Some, as in Ex. 10–12, do not disturb the normal metric accentuation and therefore do not result in syncopation.

Ex. 10–12

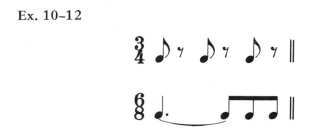

Another method of achieving syncopation is to place an accent or stress on a normally unaccented or weak beat or division of the beat (Ex. 10–13).

Ex. 10–13

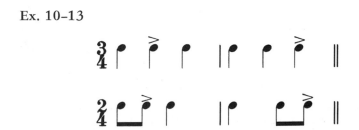

TRIPLETS, DUPLETS, AND OTHER IRREGULAR DIVISIONS

Composers sometimes wish to have fewer or more notes sounded in the allotted time. They indicate this as shown in Ex. 10–14.

Ex. 10–14

a)   b)   c)

In Ex. 10–14a, the triplet sign (⌐—*3*—¬) indicates that on the division level three even notes are to be sounded in the time normally occupied by two even notes. In Ex. 10–14b, the duplet sign (⌐—*2*—¬) indicates that on the division level two even notes are to be sounded in the time normally occupied by three even notes. In Ex. 10–14c, the quintolet sign (⌐—*5*—¬) indicates that on the subdivision level five even notes are to be sounded in the time normally occupied by four even notes.

When triplets or duplets occur on the beat level, it is helpful to hear them in terms of the division level shown in Ex. 10–15.

Ex. 10–15

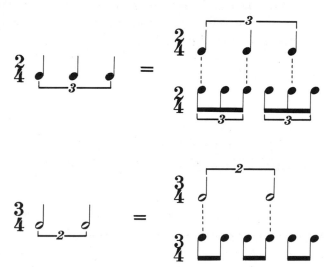

AGOGIC ACCENT AND PITCH ACCENT

The accents in Ex. 10–13 were *dynamic accents;* they were achieved by sounding some notes louder than others. It is also possible to achieve accents by sounding some notes longer than others. This type of accent is called *agogic accent* (Ex. 10–16).

Ex. 10–16

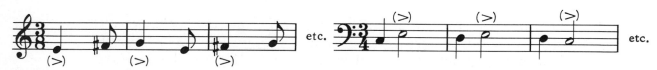

Pitch accent is usually achieved by sounding some notes higher than others (Ex. 10–17).

Ex. 10–17

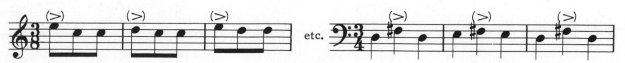

Agogic accent and pitch accent are generally less obvious than dynamic accent, but they can play a significant role in musical organization.

ARTICULATION

Articulation in music refers to the manner in which notes are performed. We shall consider three basic types of articulation—*legato, nonlegato* or *portato,* and *staccato.*

In legato articulation, the notes are connected as smoothly as possible; no pause or accent occurs between notes. Legato articulation is usually indicated with a *slur,* a curved line connecting tones of different pitch (compare the definition of "tie," p. 116). In singing, legato articulation may best be achieved by remaining on the same vowel, with no intervening consonants, as in Ex. 10–18.

Ex. 10–18

dah _____

In nonlegato or portato articulation, there is no intervening pause between notes, but there is a slight accent or articulation on each note. Portato articulation may be indicated by short lines, as in Ex. 10–19. In singing, nonlegato or portato articulation may best be achieved by placing a consonant on each note.

Ex. 10–19

dah   dah   dah   dah   dah   dah   dah   dah

In staccato articulation, there is both a short pause between notes and a slight articulation or accent on each note. Staccato articulation is usually indicated with a dot above or below the notehead (Ex. 10–20a). In effect, this dot usually cuts the value of the note in half and replaces the other half with a rest, as indicated in Ex. 10–20b.

Ex. 10–20

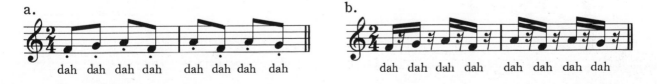

a.

dah dah dah dah   dah dah dah dah

b.

dah dah dah dah   dah dah dah dah

121

When no articulation signs are present, the performer can choose the type of articulation that best fits the music. In this text, we have limited the use of articulation signs largely to duets and longer melodies. We suggest that you experiment with various articulations on the other exercises. In general, however, the exercises on rhythm alone are best performed with a nonlegato or staccato articulation, for the sake of clarity.

PHRASING

The term *phrasing* is applied most properly to the division of a long melody into shorter units called *phrases* (see p. 8). In practice, it may also be used to refer to the division of a melody into melodic gestures or even shorter units; in this sense, it is nearly synonymous with articulation.

The same sign—namely, a curved line—may be used for phrasing as well as for slurs and ties. In Ex. 10-21a and 10-21b, it is obvious that the curved line does not represent a tie or slur, for if it did, the repeated notes in these examples would coalesce into a single duration. Rather, the sign represents the phrasing intended by the composer—that is, the division of the melody into its constituent gestures. Notice that in Ex. 10-21b and 10-21c, the gestures are indicated across the bar line, something that is fairly typical in music. A common occurrence in an amateur performance is to allow the bar line to assume the role of indicating the end of musical gestures. The alert performer should be sensitive to this, even when the composer does not supply phrasing, as has been done in Ex. 10-21. It is not the case, as some nineteenth-century theorists postulated, that *every* musical gesture must cross the bar line. Certainly, however, many gestures in common musical practice tend to do this.

Ex. 10-21

a. Chopin: Etude, 25, No. 11

b. Chopin: Ballade, Op. 23

c. Chopin: Mazurka, Op. 7, No. 1

CHARACTER

In addition to signs and terms indicating tempo, dynamics, and articulation, other terms may be used in music to indicate the general character, mood, or spirit of the music. Some of the most common terms are listed below. Again, we recommend that you concentrate on the Italian terms, which are used more frequently. These terms may be used alone or in combination with tempo terms. *Allegro con moto,* for example, signifies "fast (cheerful), with motion."

English	Italian	German	French
affectionate	*affettuoso*	*innig*	*affectueux*
agitated	*agitato*	*lebhaft bewegt*	*agité*
amiable	*amabile*	*lieblich*	*aimable*
animated	*animato*	*belebt*	*animé*
caressingly	*lusingando*	*schmeichelnd*	*caressant*
expressive	*espressivo*	*ausdrucksvoll*	*expressiv*
with fire	*con fuoco*	*feurig*	*ardent*
gracefully	*grazioso*	*zierlich*	*gracieux*
grieving	*dolente*	*klagend*	*triste*
held	*tenuto*	*gehalten*	*tenu*
impassioned	*appassionato*	*leidenschaftlich*	*passionné*
joyously	*gioioso*	*freudig*	*joyeux*
lightly	*leggiero*	*leicht*	*léger*
majestically	*maestoso*	*feierlich*	*majestueux*
martially	*marziale*	*kriegerisch*	*martiale*
mournfully	*mesto*	*traurig*	*triste*
mysteriously	*misterioso*	*geheimnisvoll*	*mystérieux*
with movement	*con moto*	*bewegt*	*mouvementé*
playfully, joking	*giocoso, scherzando*	*scherzhaft, scherzend*	*en badinant*
resolutely	*risoluto*	*entschlossen*	*résolu*
simple	*semplice*	*einfach*	*simple*
singing	*cantabile*	*gesangvoll*	*chantant*
smoothly	*piacévole*	*gefällig*	*plaisant*
with spirit	*con anima*	*munter*	*avec verve*
sustained	*sostenuto*	*getragen*	*soutenu*
sweet	*dolce*	*zart*	*doucement, doux*
tenderly	*teneramente*	*zärtlich*	*tendre*
with vigor	*con brio*	*schwungvoll*	*avec force*

MUSIC-READING EXERCISES 10

EAR-TRAINING EXERCISES 10

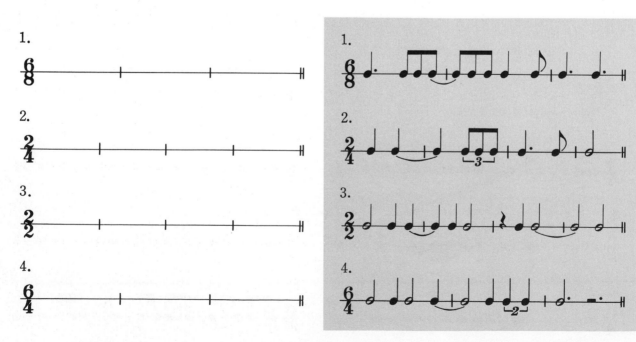

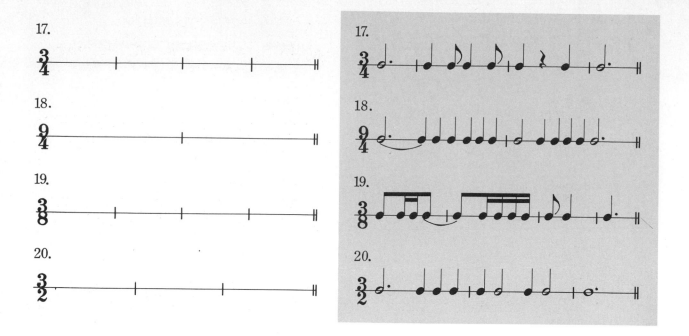

MUSIC-READING EXERCISES 10A

We have added indications of tempo and character to the brief examples below primarily as means of reviewing these terms. You can, however, attempt to perform the examples according to the performance indications. We suggest that in future music-reading exercises you add indications of tempo and character to at least some of the exercises before you perform them.

1. Getragen, klagend

2. Breit, traurig

3. Un peu lent

4. Adagio non troppo

5. Allegro, gioioso

6. Andante, grazioso

7. Lebhaft

8. Prestissimo, agitato

9. Moderé

10. Largo

EAR-TRAINING EXERCISES 10A

128

EXAMPLES FROM LITERATURE

1. Stravinsky: *Firebird Suite,* "Dance of Kastchei"

2. Slave Song, "Jesus on de Water-Side

3. Lalo: *Symphonie Espagnole,* first movement

4. Schumann: Quartet, Op. 41, No. 3, second movement

5. Schubert: String Quartet in D Minor, "Death and the Maiden"

6. Beethoven: Symphony No. 7, second movement

SUPPLEMENTARY EXERCISES 10

1. Use phrase marks to analyze musical gestures in selected exercises and examples from the literature.

2. Compose four examples similar to the ear-training exercises in this chapter, and work with your drill partner on them.

3. One way to make your compositions more musical and more unified is to repeat a pitch pattern or gesture. You can repeat the pattern immediately with the same rhythm; you can repeat the pattern immediately with a change of rhythm; or you can return to the pattern after writing a contrasting pattern. The following example illustrates the application of these techniques. Study it, and then use these techniques to compose examples of your own.

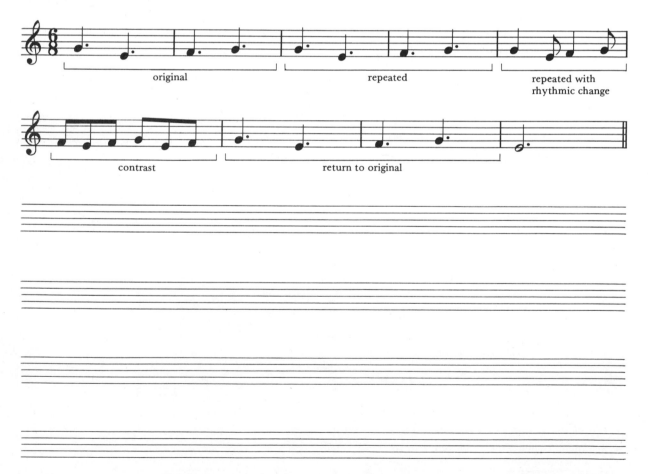

4. Another way to make your original compositions interesting and more unified is to apply techniques of rhythmic variation. Three of these techniques are augmentation, diminution, and change of meter.

For augmentation, you start with a rhythmic pattern or gesture and then double each durational value. It is also possible to triple or quadruple each note.

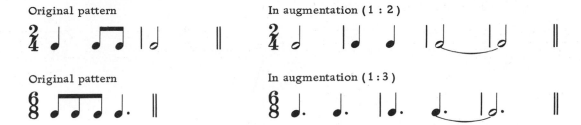

For diminution, you start with a rhythmic pattern or gesture and then halve each durational value. It is also possible to reduce each note to one third or one fourth of its original value.

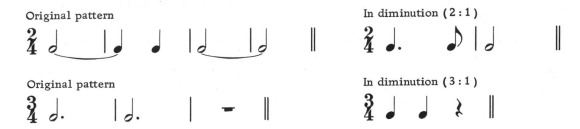

You can also vary a motive by rewriting it in another meter but preserving the basic long-short relationships of the original.

Compose examples that incorporate these techniques.

chapter 11

In this chapter, we shall widen the range of our pitch sets to five pitches. This will allow us to use more melodies drawn from music literature. First, however, we must learn some additional principles of interval designation.

FOURTHS AND FIFTHS

We have already learned that intervals are designated with a descriptive name and a numerical name. The numerical name of an interval is determined simply by counting letter names from the bottom note of the interval to the top note inclusive. The descriptive name is determined by the number of half steps and whole steps in the interval. Let us review the intervals we have studied thus far, plus two new intervals—the perfect fourth and perfect fifth.

Interval Name	Abbreviation	Half Steps	Whole Steps	Examples
Perfect prime	P1	0	0	A–A; e–e
Minor second	m2	1	$\frac{1}{2}$	b–c; d♯–e
Major second	M2	2	1	F–G; A♭–B♭
Minor third	m3	3	$1\frac{1}{2}$	b–d; C–E♭
Major third	M3	4	2	c♯–e♯; F–A
Perfect fourth	P4	5	$2\frac{1}{2}$	D–G; B♭–e♭
Perfect fifth	P5	7	$3\frac{1}{2}$	B–f♯; C–G

Notice that primes or unisons, fourths, and fifths are designated with the descriptive name of *perfect*, seconds and thirds with the descriptive names of *major* and *minor*. Later, we shall examine the reasons for this terminology. For now, it is important that you remember which descriptive names are to be used with specific numeric names.

Rather than counting half steps and whole steps, there is a simple way to identify perfect fourths and perfect fifths. All fourths or fifths that have the same accidental sign for both members are perfect, except for the fourth from F to B and the fifth from B to F. Thus, all of the fourths and fifths in Ex. 11-1 are perfect.

Ex. 11-1

To create perfect fifths or fourths involving F and B, the B must be one accidental "lower" than the F. Thus, each of the intervals in Ex. 11-2 is a perfect fifth or fourth. Notice that if the F is natural, the B must be flat; if the F is sharped (♯), the B must be natural.

Ex. 11-2

Identify each of the following intervals, using P, M, and m for perfect, major, and minor and using numbers for the numerical descriptions (P5, M3, m2, etc.).

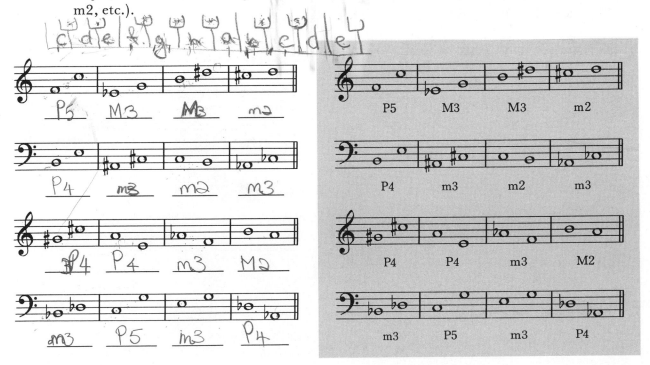

Write the indicated intervals above the given notes.

Write the indicated intervals below the given notes.

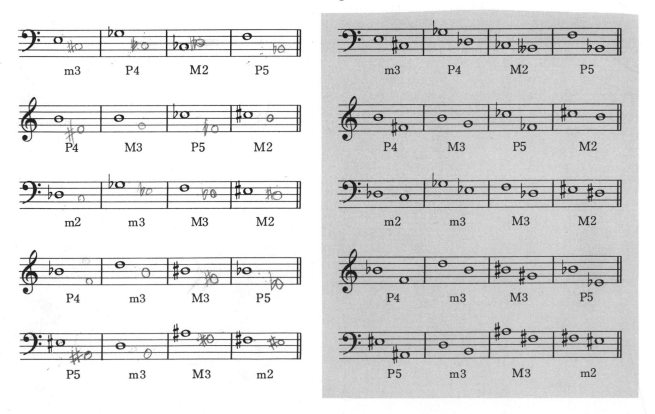

134

AUGMENTED AND DIMINISHED INTERVALS

We can expand an interval by raising the top note a chromatic half step or by lowering the bottom note a chromatic half step (Ex. 11–3).

Ex. 11–3

f¹ —— a¹   expanded to   f¹ —— a♯¹   or   f♭¹ —— a¹

We can contract an interval by lowering the top note a chromatic half step or by raising the bottom note a chromatic half step (Ex. 11–4).

Ex. 11–4

f¹ —— a¹   contracted to   f¹ —— a♭¹   f♯¹ —— a¹

If we expand a major or perfect interval, we produce an *augmented interval* (Ex. 11–5).

Ex. 11–5

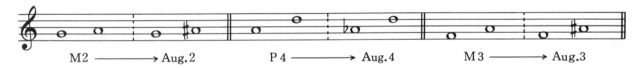

M2 ⟶ Aug.2   P4 ⟶ Aug.4   M3 ⟶ Aug.3

If we contract a minor or perfect interval, we produce a *diminished interval* (Ex. 11–6).

Ex. 11–6

m2 ⟶ dim.2   P4 ⟶ dim.4   m3 ⟶ dim.3

The one exception to these principles is the perfect prime or perfect unison. We can produce an augmented prime or unison by expanding the interval—that is, by lowering or raising one note of the interval a chromatic half step. However, it is impossible to have a diminished prime or unison. It is impossible to contract a perfect prime or unison; it is impossible to have any smaller distance between two notes than 0 half steps.

Expand the following intervals by raising the top note one chromatic half step. Then identify the new interval, using + for augmented and ° for diminished in addition to the terms given before.

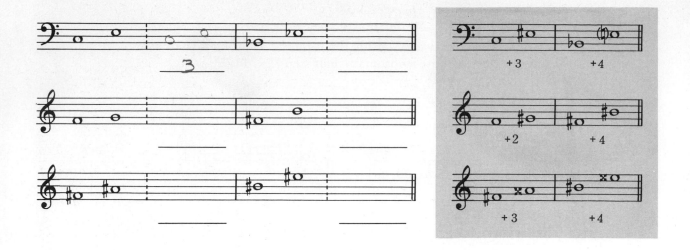

Expand the following intervals by lowering the bottom note one chromatic half step, and then identify the new interval.

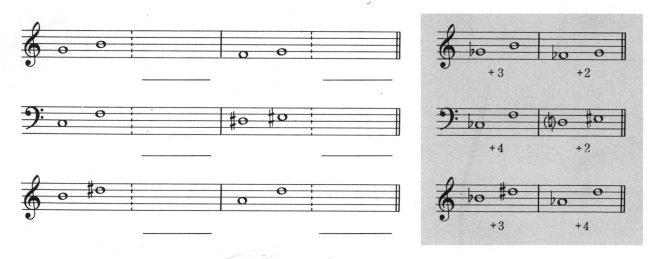

Contract the following intervals by lowering the top note one chromatic half step, and then identify the new interval.

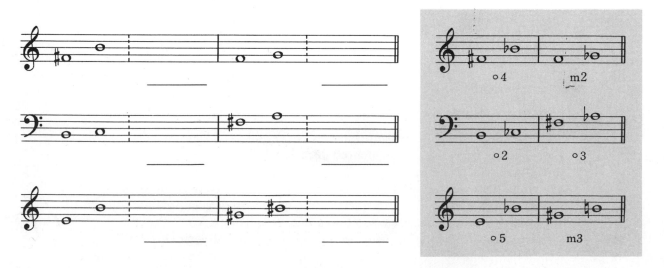

Contract the following intervals by raising the bottom note one chromatic half step, and then identify the new interval.

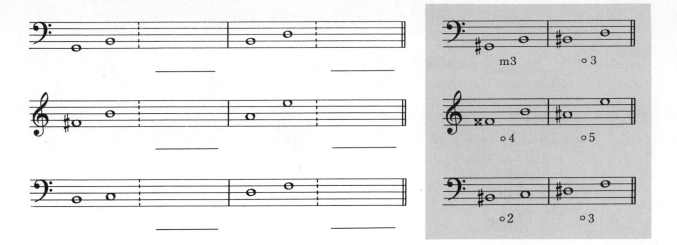

ENHARMONIC TONES AND INTERVALS

Two notes that sound the same (in equal temperament, at least) and yet are written with two different letter names are called *enharmonic notes* or *enharmonic equivalents* (Ex. 11-7).

Ex. 11-7

Two intervals that sound the same but are written differently may be called *enharmonic intervals* (Ex. 11-8).

Ex. 11-8

The term *tritone* is applied to the interval of the augmented fourth or diminished fifth. The name reflects the fact that the interval spans three whole tones (Ex. 11-9). "Tritone" may be abbreviated "TT."

Ex. 11-9

INTERVALS TO THE FIFTH

The following table lists all intervals, including diminished and augmented intervals, up to the fifth.

Interval Name (descriptive)	Abbreviation (numerical)	Half Steps	Whole Steps	Examples
Perfect prime (perfect unison)	P1	0	0	c–c; E♭–E♭
Augmented prime (augmented unison)	+1	1	$\frac{1}{2}$	d–d♯; a–a♯
Diminished second	°2	0	0	b–c♭; c♯–d
Minor second	m2	1	$\frac{1}{2}$	f–g♭; A–B♭
Major second	M2	2	1	G–A; e–f♯
Augmented second	+2	3	$1\frac{1}{2}$	f–g♯; D–E♯
Diminished third	°3	2	1	c♯–e♭; F♯–A♭
Minor third	m3	3	$1\frac{1}{2}$	d–f; c–e♭
Major third	M3	4	2	B–d♯; a–c♯
Augmented third	+3	5	$2\frac{1}{2}$	C–E♯; f♯–a✕
Diminished fourth	°4	4	2	f♯–b♭; g–c♭
Perfect fourth	P4	5	$2\frac{1}{2}$	A–d; c–f
Augmented fourth (tritone)	+4 or TT	6	3	c–f♯; e♭–a
Diminished fifth (tritone)	°5 or TT	6	3	c♯–g; d–a♭
Perfect fifth	P5	7	$3\frac{1}{2}$	D–A; A♭–e♭
Augmented fifth	+5	8	4	f–c♯[1]; c–g♯

Identify the following intervals with both their descriptive and their numerical names. Use abbreviations.

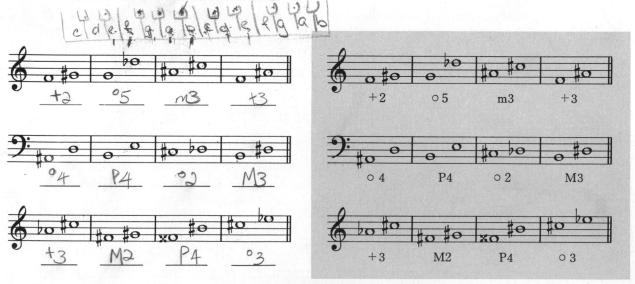

138

Write the indicated intervals above the given notes.

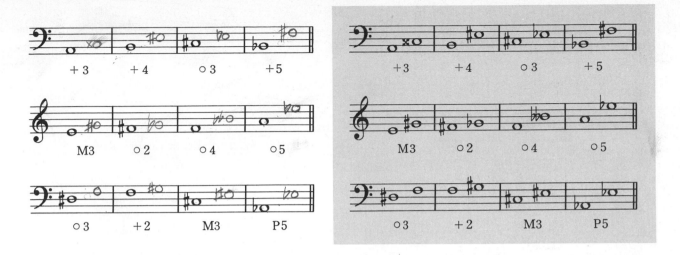

Write the indicated intervals below the given notes.

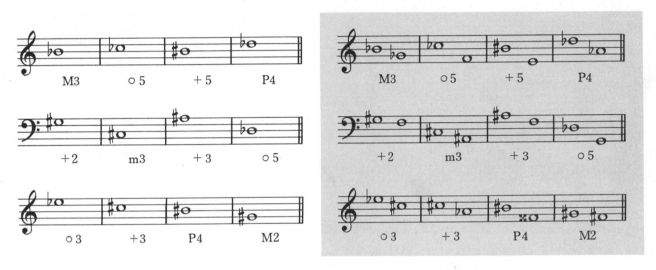

FIVE-PITCH SETS

We shall base our study of pitch in this chapter upon four specific five-pitch sets. These sets, with their names and intervallic structures, are given in Ex. 11-10.

Ex. 11-10

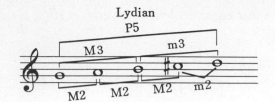 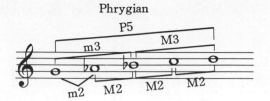

Study the intervallic structure of these four pitch sets, and relate them to the piano keyboard. Notice the placement of half steps and the disposition of major and minor thirds.

Identify each of the following five-pitch sets.

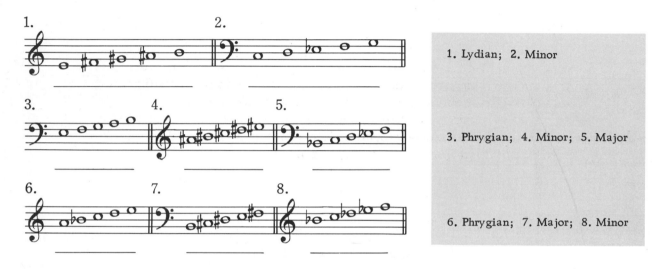

1. Lydian; 2. Minor

3. Phrygian; 4. Minor; 5. Major

6. Phrygian; 7. Major; 8. Minor

Write the indicated five-pitch sets in ascending order above the given note.

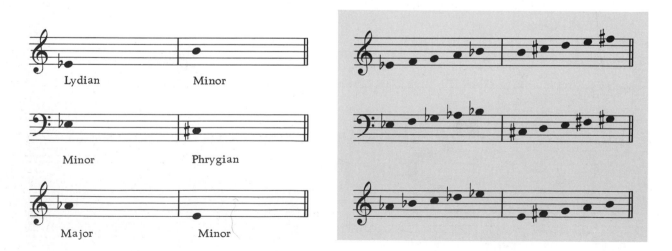

140

Write the indicated five-pitch sets in descending order below the given note.

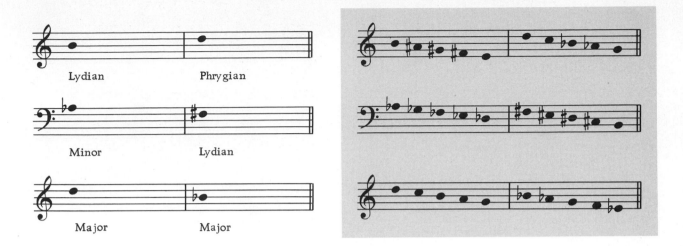

THE TRIAD

Sing through the notes of the major five-pitch set in ascending order. Now sing the first, third, and fifth notes of this pitch set. This pitch configuration, one of the most common in Western music, is called the *major triad*. If you sing the first, third, and fifth pitches of the minor pitch set, you produce another common pitch configuration, the *minor triad*. Study the interval structure of the major and minor triads in Ex. 11-11.

Ex. 11-11

Identify the following triads as major (M) or minor (m).

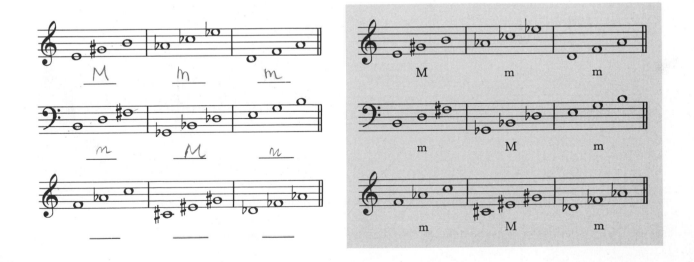

Write major triads in ascending order above the given notes.

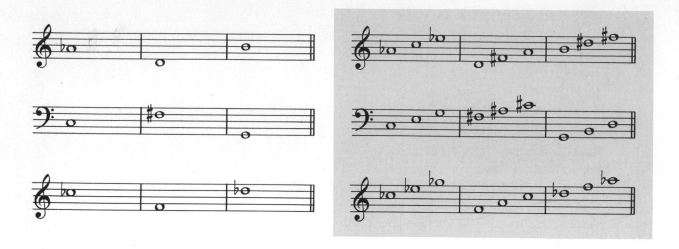

Write minor triads above the given notes.

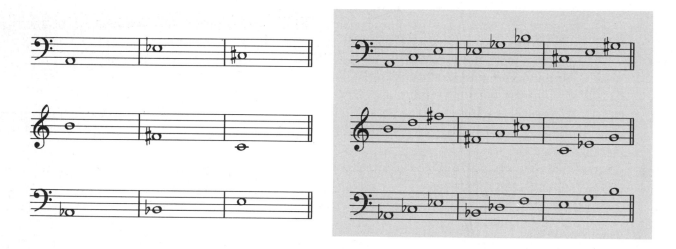

You should now learn to recognize, perform, and hear the triad patterns in Ex. 11–12, which use both major and minor triads.

Ex. 11–12

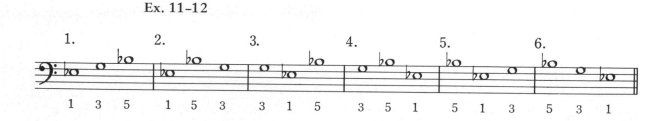

In practicing these patterns, you can use a single starting pitch. Or you can use various starting pitches, as shown in Ex. 11–13, by using one of the notes of the previous pattern as the beginning note of the next pattern.

142

Ex. 11–13

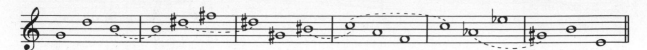

PITCH PATTERNS

In our study of rhythm, we have emphasized the importance of seeing and hearing patterns rather than isolated notes. The same holds true for pitch. By now you should be able to recognize, hear, and perform many different pitch patterns—two-pitch sets, three-pitch sets, five-pitch sets, major triads, minor triads, and intervals up to the perfect fifth.

Ex. 11–14 can help you consolidate your knowledge of all of these patterns. Practice it in the following ways as preparation for the music-reading and ear-training exercises that follow in this chapter.

1. Play each pattern on the piano, and sing the pattern immediately afterward. Sing on pitch names or neutral syllables.
2. Sound the first pitch only. Then sing each pattern, and play it immediately afterward on the piano in order to check your accuracy.
3. Sound the first pitch only, and then sing the patterns in random order. Play the patterns in order to check your accuracy.
4. Teacher or drill partner sings the pattern on a neutral syllable. You sing it back on pitch names.
5. Teacher or drill partner plays a pattern on the piano while you turn your head away. Then you play the pattern back on the piano.
6. Teacher or drill partner plays a pattern on an instrument. You write down the notes played.
7. Repeat Ex. 11–14 but start the patterns on a different pitch and use a different pitch set.

Several half-hour drill periods spent on Ex. 11–14 will help enormously in developing your ability to work with these patterns. Then, as you sing the music reading exercises in this and other chapters, try to apply what you have learned from this drill.

Ex. 11–14

PITCH CONFIGURATION AND PITCH FOCUS

In Chapter 8, we saw how the factors of duration, frequency, and position can create a focus upon a particular pitch. Now we shall begin to explore ways in which pitch focus can be accomplished by factors in the pitch parameter itself.

In the music of most cultures, the bottom note of the interval of a perfect fifth will usually be heard as the most important or focal pitch. To test this, improvise a passage using only the notes d^1 and a^1 and see which note makes the most convincing concluding note for the passage. For most people, d^1 will be the most satisfying ending. We shall not go into the psychological or acoustical explanations of this phenomenon.

PITCH FUNCTION

When you perform and listen to melodies involving five-pitch sets, such as those in the music-reading and ear-training exercises that follow in this chapter, you should make use of all of the techniques we have discussed. You can easily make use of pitch memory, since you have only five pitches to remember. You can also use your sense of pitch distance or interval, for in any given exercise there will be only a limited number of intervals possible. And now that we are dealing mostly with melodies having a clear pitch focus, you can use a third approach—the sense of pitch function. This means that you consider each pitch in terms of its hierarchical relationship to the other pitches, as shown in Ex. 11–15. The note values indicate the relative importance of the pitches.

Ex. 11–15

In terms of performance and perception, this notation implies that you clearly establish the triad pitches and then relate the remaining pitches to them.

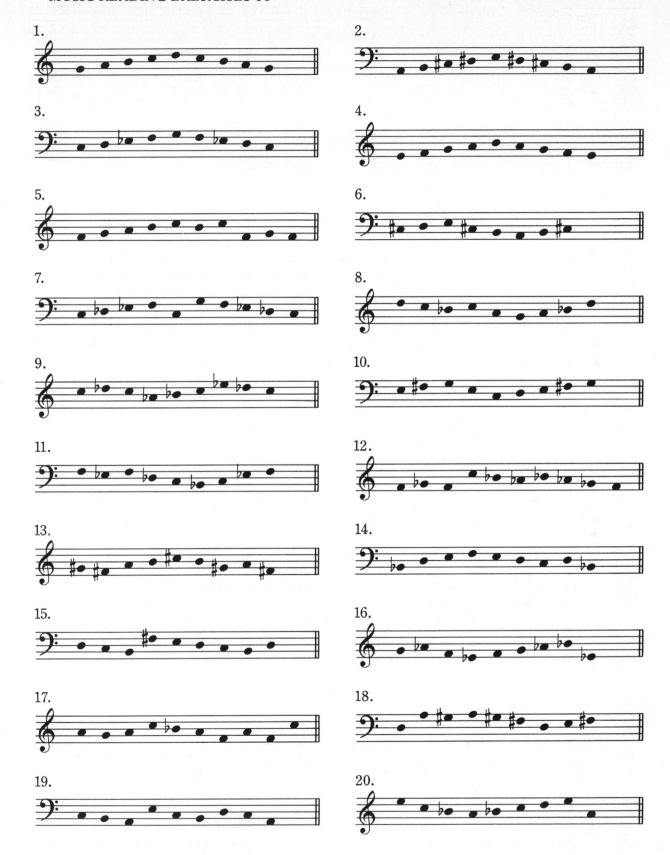

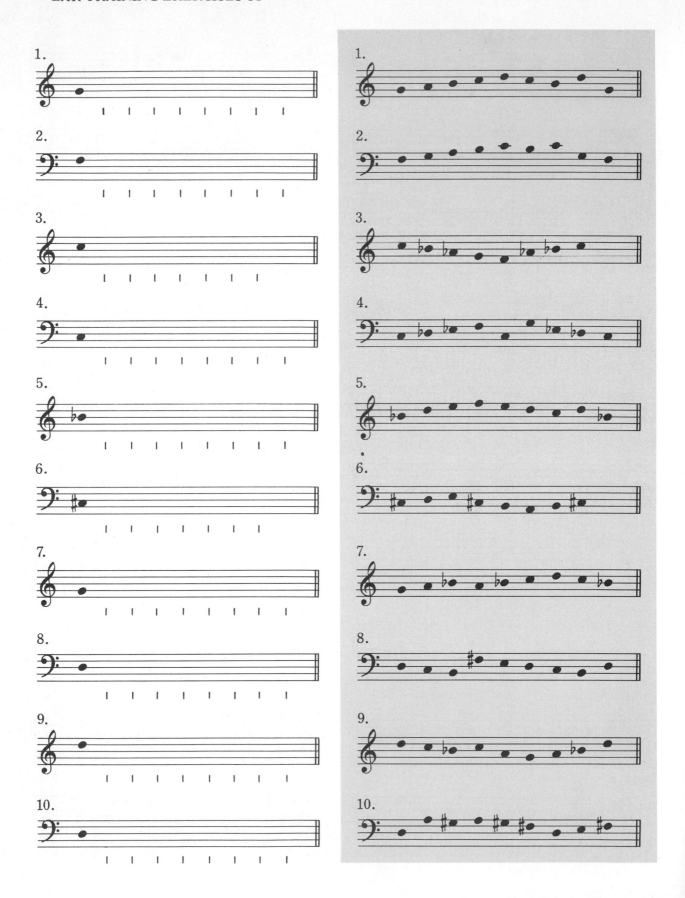

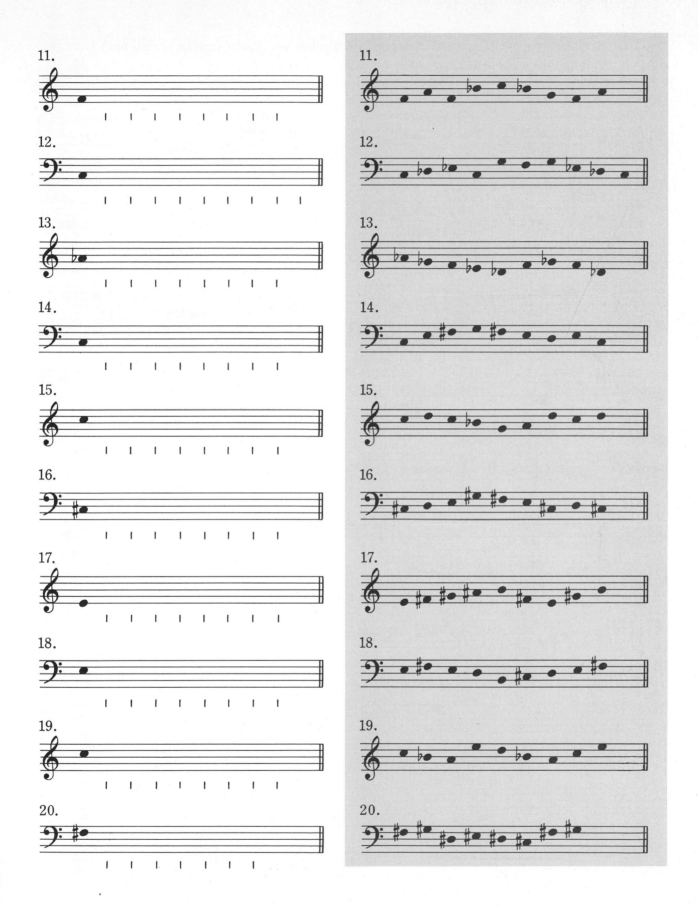

As you perform these exercises, remember to supply various tempo and dynamic markings.

Duets

1. ♪=100

2. Allegro molto

11.

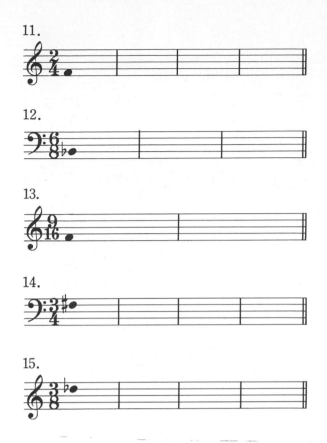

12.

13.

14.

15.

Duets
1.

2.

EXAMPLES FROM LITERATURE

1. Brahms: Symphony No. 1, third movement

2. Barber: Symphony No. 1, Op. 9

3. Haydn: String Quartet, Op. 3, No. 3, third movement

4. Vaughn Williams: A London Symphony, first movement

5. Vaughn Williams: Fantasia on a Theme by Tallis

6. Mozart: *Musical Joke*, K. 522, first movement

7. Mozart: *Musical Joke*, K. 522, second movement

8. Mozart: *Musical Joke*, K. 522, third movement

9. Beethoven: Symphony No. 9, second movement

10. Beethoven: Symphony No. 5, fourth movement

1. Many folk songs are based on the major and minor five-pitch sets. See how many you can write and sing. Start them on various pitches.

2. Compose examples similar to the music-reading exercises in this chapter and work on them with your drill partner.

3. Just as we learned to vary rhythmic motives and patterns by using such techniques as augmentation, diminution, and change of meter, so we can vary pitch motives by such techniques as sequence, interval expansion or contraction, added notes, and deleted notes. A sequence involves the repetition of a pitch pattern on a different pitch level. The following example illustrates this and the other techniques mentioned. Study these techniques, then compose examples that incorporate them. Also, see if you can find examples from the literature that incorporate these techniques.

OPTIONAL MATERIAL

Integer Notation

The integer notation of our four five-pitch sets and its relationship to traditional interval designation are shown in Ex. 11–16.

Ex 11–16

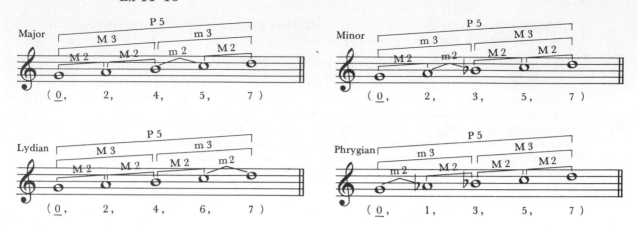

Identify each of the following five-pitch sets in integer notation, as shown in Ex. 11–16.

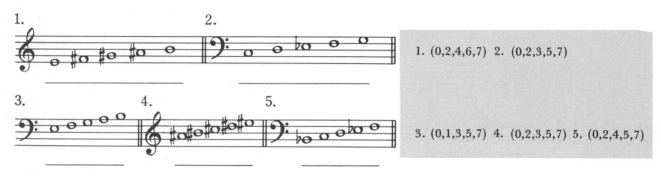

1. (0,2,4,6,7)   2. (0,2,3,5,7)

3. (0,1,3,5,7)   4. (0,2,3,5,7)   5. (0,2,4,5,7)

Write the indicated five-pitch sets in *ascending* order.

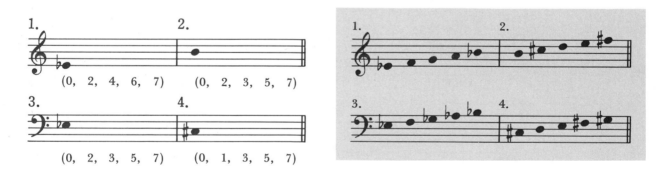

1. (0, 2, 4, 6, 7)   2. (0, 2, 3, 5, 7)

3. (0, 2, 3, 5, 7)   4. (0, 1, 3, 5, 7)

The Triad in Integer Notation

The integer notation of the major and minor triads is shown in Ex. 11–17.

Ex. 11–17

Identify the following triads in integer notation.

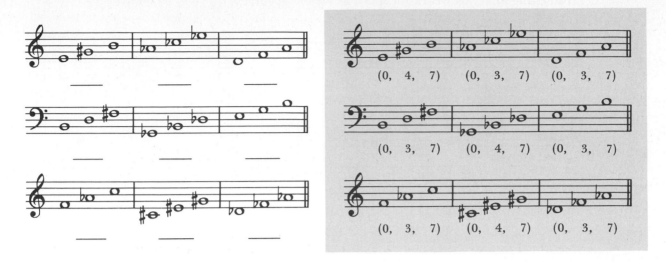

(0, 4, 7)   (0, 3, 7)   (0, 3, 7)

(0, 3, 7)   (0, 4, 7)   (0, 3, 7)

(0, 3, 7)   (0, 4, 7)   (0, 3, 7)

Write major triads (0,4,7) above the indicated notes in ascending order.

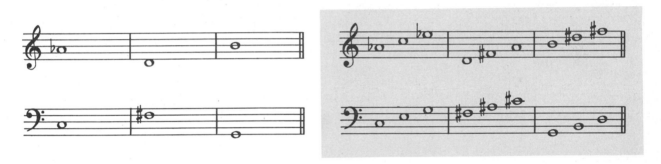

The triad can also be useful in determining the integer notation of larger intervals. If you know that d–f♯–a is a major triad (0,4,7), then you can determine the size of an interval such as d–b not by laboriously counting, but by adding the intervals d–a (I 7) and a–b (I 2), which results in I 9, the interval from d to b. Ex. 11–18 shows some further instances of this procedure.

Ex. 11–18

(0,   4,   7)

I 7 + I 2   =   I 9

I 7 − I 1   =   I 6

(0,   4,   7,   0)
                 (12)

I 12 − I 1   =   I 11

I 12 − I 2   =   I 10

Using the procedure illustrated in Ex. 11-18, determine the size of the following intervals. Work for speed as well as accuracy.

I 10,   I 11,   I 10

I 6,   I 11,   I 10

chapter 12

In this chapter and the next one, we shall continue our exposition of the rudiments of the duration parameter in music. In this chapter, we discuss rhythmic activity on three levels, four-pulse and six-pulse patterns, and incomplete measures.

RHYTHMIC ACTIVITY ON THREE LEVELS

We have worked with rhythmic activity on the beat level and the division level, and we have seen that it is possible to organize pulses on either level into groups of twos or threes. On the third or subdivision level, pulses are regularly organized only into groups of twos. (See Ex. 12–1.)

Ex. 12–1

In simple meters, there are regularly four pulses per beat on the subdivision level (two groups of two pulses each); in compound meters, there are regularly six pulses per beat on the subdivision level (three groups of two pulses each). Example 12–2 shows all three levels for the most frequently used simple and compound meters. An effective way to practice these patterns is to conduct the beats with the right hand, tap the division with the

157

left hand, and sing the subdivisions on some neutral syllable or pair of syllables, such as "tah-kah."

Ex. 12-2

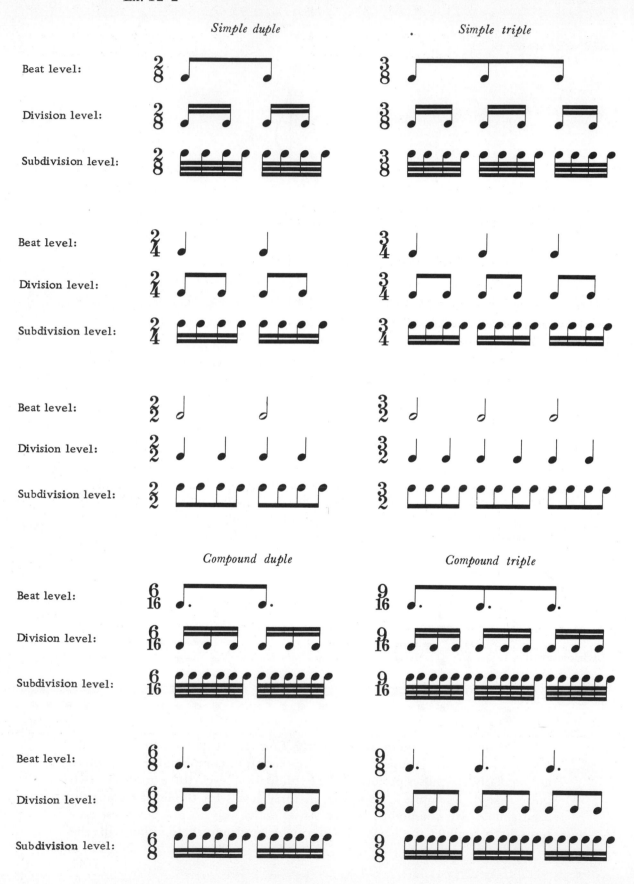

FOUR-PULSE PATTERNS

Ex. 12-3 lists the eight possible combinations of notes in a group of four pulses. These patterns would be used on the subdivision level of a simple meter. Learn to hear, perform, and write them as a pattern or gestalt, rather than as a collection of separate notes.

These patterns may be practiced as follows:

1. Tap or clap the subdivisons as you sing the patterns.
2. Tap subdivisons with one hand, conduct a beat pattern (duple or triple) with the other hand, and sing the pattern.
3. Tap beat *divisions* with the left hand, conduct with the right hand, and sing the pattern.
4. Conduct the beat with the right hand, mentally hear the divisions or subdivisions, and sing the pattern.

Ex. 12-3

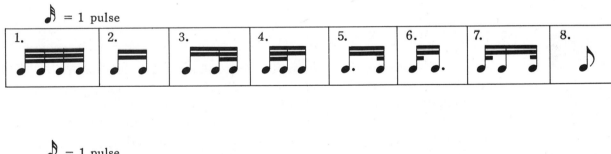

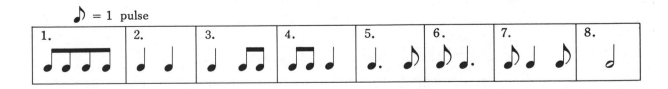

SIX-PULSE PATTERNS

Ex. 12-4 lists some of the possible patterns that could be formed with six-pulse groups and that would be used on the subdivision level of a compound meter. To learn all the possible patterns in a six-pulse group would be impractical; Ex. 12-4 merely illustrates some of the most commonly used ones.

Ex. 12-4

= 1 pulse

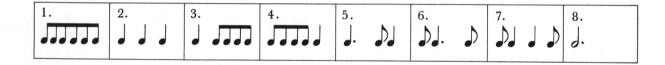

UPBEATS AND INCOMPLETE MEASURES

Often, a piece of music begins with one or more upbeat notes that lead to a downbeat in the following measure. Traditionally, in a composition or section of a composition that begins with an incomplete measure, the last measure is also an incomplete measure, written such that the first and last measures together make up a whole measure.* Ex. 12-5 should make this clear.

Ex. 12-5

Beats: 3   1   2   3   1   2   3   1   2

          2   1   2   1   2   1   2

*This convention is not necessarily observed in all periods of music literature.

160

Write a note in the last measure, according to the convention that the first and last measures together make up a whole measure.

Add rests to the last measure so that it conforms to the convention that the first and last measures should add up to a complete measure.

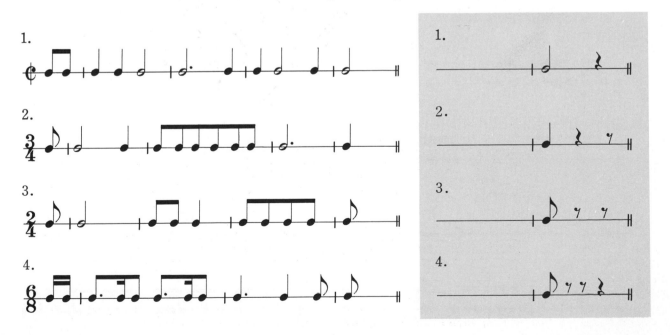

To save labor in writing out literal repetitions in music, we may employ the various signs illustrated in Ex. 12–6.

Ex. 12–6

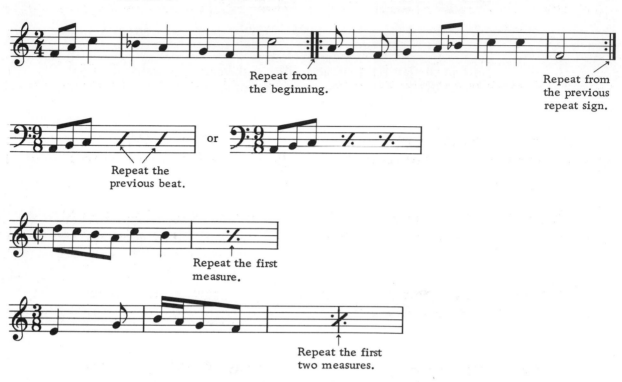

Da capo or *D.C.* signifies "repeat from the beginning." *D.C. al segno* signifies "repeat from the beginning to the sign."

MUSIC-READING EXERCISES 12

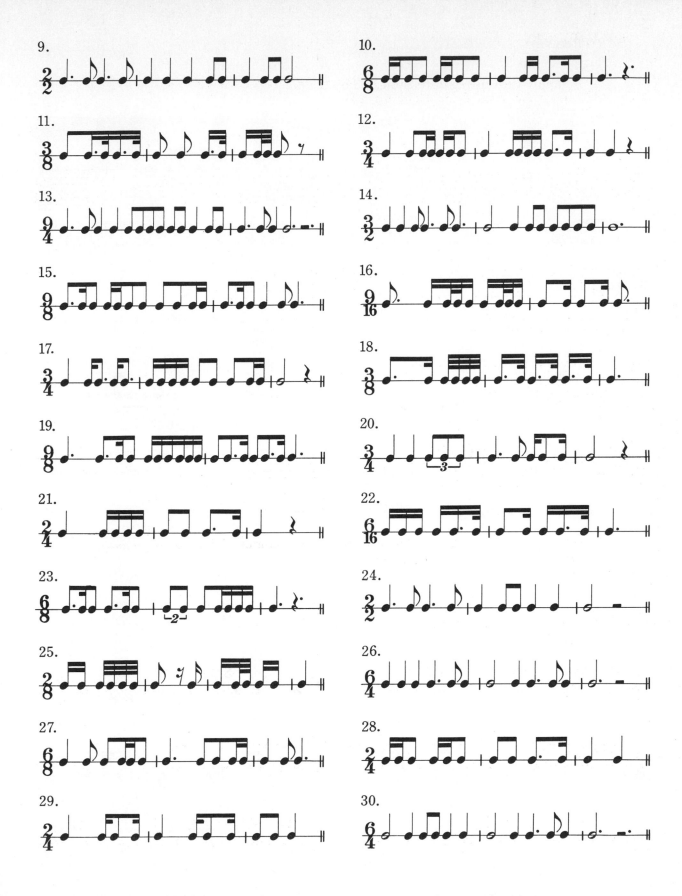

Supply the missing notes indicated by the brackets.

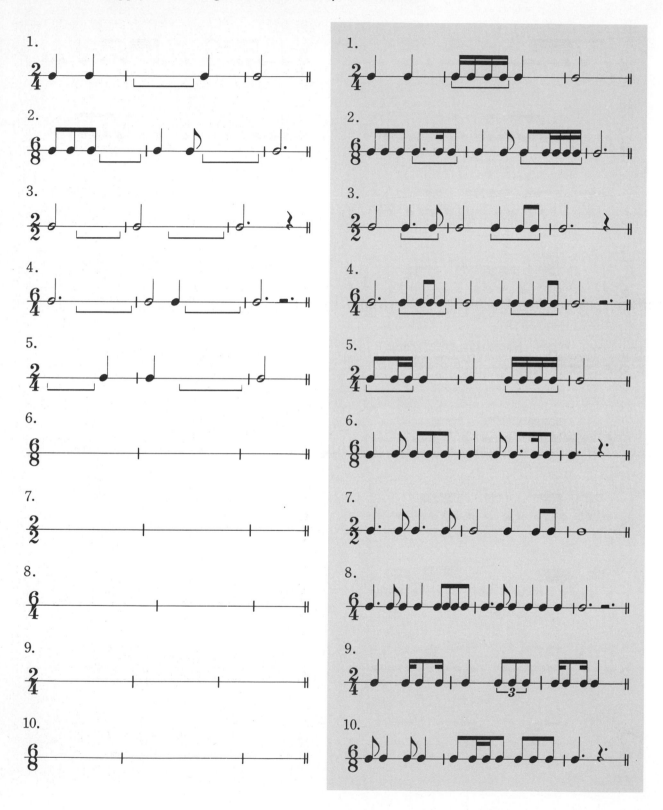

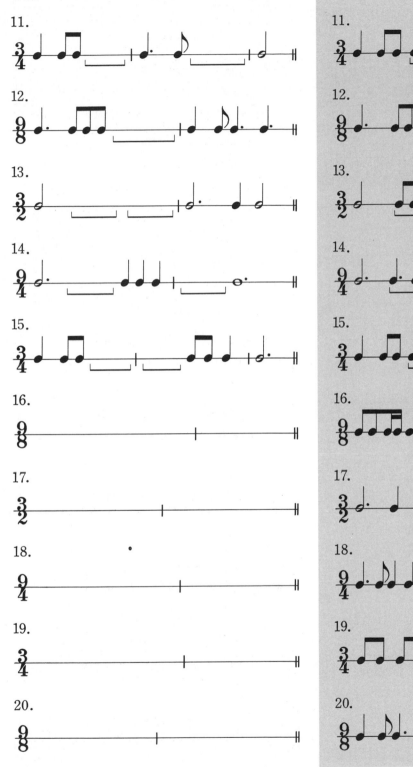

Duets

1. Allegro

2. Andante

11.

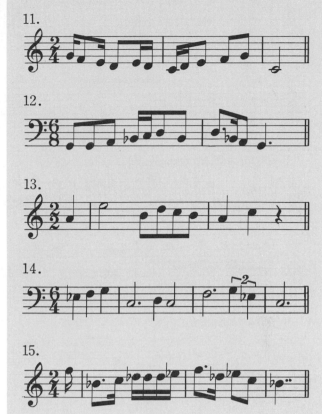

12.

13.

14.

15.

Duets

EXAMPLES FROM LITERATURE

1. Rimsky-Korsakov: *Capriccio Espagnol*, Variations

2. Respighi: Ancient Dances and Airs for Lute

3. Beethoven: Andante in F

4. Bartók: *Rumanian Folk Dances.* I

5. Haydn: String Quartet, Op. 64, No. 5, second movement

6. Mozart: Sonata, K. 331

7. Dufay: *In lumen, tu splendor patris*

8. Anonymous, "L'Homme armé"

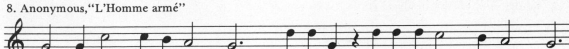

9. Gregorien Chant

10. Traditional, "Roll, Jordan, Roll"

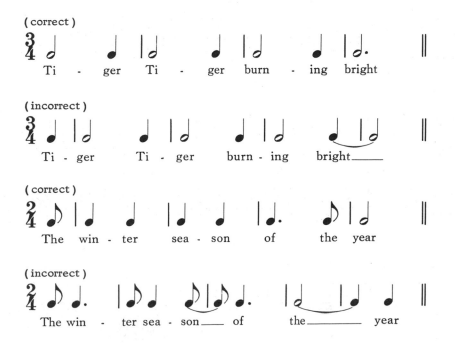

SUPPLEMENTARY EXERCISES 12

1. Compose examples similar to the music reading exercises in this chapter and work on them with your partner.

2. Compose rhythmic settings (no pitches) of poetry. Be sure that the rhythm gestures and the accentuation of the music match that of the words.

(correct)

Ti - ger Ti - ger burn - ing bright

(incorrect)

Ti - ger Ti - ger burn - ing bright___

(correct)

The win - ter sea - son of the year

(incorrect)

The win - ter sea - son___ of the___ year

A more creative version would be:

$\frac{2}{4}$ Ti - ger Ti - ger burn-ing bright

chapter 13

In this chapter, we conclude our discussion of rhythm by introducing quadruple meter, shift of beat level, unusual meters, multimeter, and polymeter.

QUADRUPLE METER

As we have frequently indicated, we tend to perceive rhythmic activity in groups of twos and threes. In the last chapter, however, we saw that it was possible, on the subdivision level of a simple meter, to work with a group of four pulses (two groups of two pulses each). It is also possible to have four pulses on the beat level, or, in other words, *quadruple meter.* In terms of strong and weak beats, quadruple meters could be represented as follows:

1	2	3	4
strong	weak	moderately strong	weak

The standard conducting pattern for quadruple meter is shown in Ex. 13–1.

Ex. 13–1

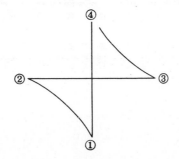

Ex. 13-2 shows the commonly used quadruple meters, both simple and compound. Pulses on the beat level, division level, and subdivision level are shown for each meter.

Ex. 13-2

Simple Quadruple

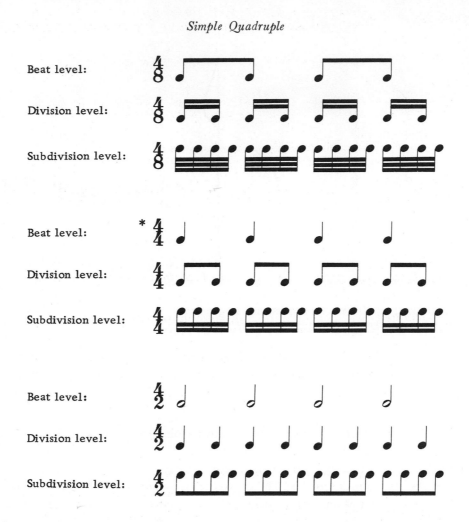

* The meter signature for 4/4 is sometimes indicated by 𝄴 .

Compound Quadruple

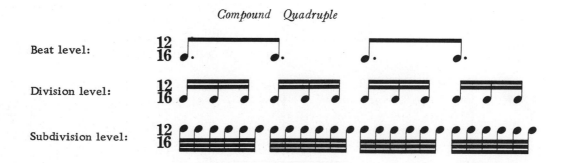

SHIFT OF BEAT LEVEL

Until this point, we have arbitrarily said that meter signatures for simple meters show the beat level of the meter and that meter signatures for compound meters show the division level of the meter. We shall continue to do this in most of the exercises that follow, but it is important for the student to be aware of certain musical situations in which the beat level should be shifted from that indicated by the meter signature. Let us illustrate this with some examples.

Ex. 13–3

Adagio

We have said that meter signatures in compound meter regularly show the division level of the meter. Therefore, in Ex. 13–3 the beat would be the dotted quarter. In this particular passage, however, the tempo is so slow and there is such frequent usage of thirty-second notes that it is more helpful to consider the eighth note as the beat, sixteenth notes as the division level, and thirty-second notes as the subdivision level.

Now look at Ex. 13–4, which reverses the situation.

Ex. 13–4

Presto

In this example, the indicated meter signature would suggest that the quarter note should be the beat. But in this particular case, the tempo is so fast that it is more efficient to hear the half note as the beat—in other words, to regard the piece as being in $\frac{2}{2}$.

In waltzes and other pieces in simple triple meter, the tempo is very often so fast that it is impractical to hear or conduct beats on the level indicated in the meter signature. Instead, each measure in effect becomes a beat. Conductors usually refer to this phenomenon as "one in a bar," and they conduct such music with a circular motion for each measure. Your teacher can demonstrate this for you.

If each measure is regarded as a beat, then it is not possible from the rhythmic notation alone to determine how these "measure beats" are organized. The musician must examine other musical factors to determine this. Generally, it will be found that the "measure beats" are organized into sets of two as in Ex. 13–5 and 13–6. Occasionally, as in Ex. 13–7, the composer will specify or the music will indicate that the "measure beats" are organized into sets of three. This organization of measures into strong and weak measures is sometimes referred to as *macrorhythm* (large rhythm).

Ex. 13–5

Ex. 13–6

Ex. 13–7

Macrorhythm can be considered even in cases in which the measure is not regarded as the beat.

176

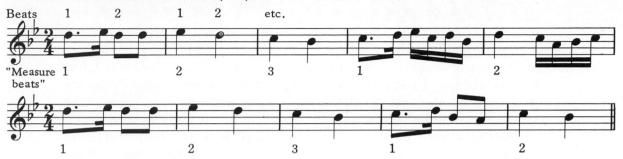

Ex. 13-8

Brahms: Variations on a Theme by Haydn

ADDITIONAL NOTATIONAL PRINCIPLES
FOR QUADRUPLE METER

If you bear in mind that quadruple meter is in effect two groups of two beats each, then you will understand the reasons behind the following principles.

1. Whenever possible, the third beat in quadruple meter should be made obvious in the notation (Ex. 13-9).

Ex. 13-9

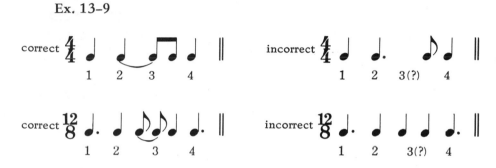

2. Beaming in quadruple meters may be done by beat, by half measure, or by measure. Careful beaming can clearly indicate the individual beats even if several beats are beamed together. Notice in Ex. 13-10 that the top beam runs through several beats but that the lower beams group by beats.

Ex. 13-10

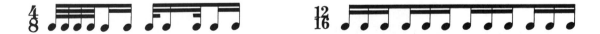

ADDITIONAL NOTATIONAL PRINCIPLES
FOR SUBDIVISIONS

Notation of durations must be handled with more care on the subdivision level than on the division level. Most writers use ties for durations that extend from one beat to the next beat(s) and involve incomplete beats (Ex. 13-11).

177

Ex. 13–11

preferable 2/4 [musical notation] ‖   less clear 2/4 [musical notation] ‖

DOUBLY AND TRIPLY DOTTED NOTES

We have already learned that a note having a duration of three pulses is represented by a dotted note. In simple meters, notes having a duration of seven pulses may be represented by a doubly dotted note; notes having a duration of fifteen pulses may be represented by a triply dotted note. (See. Ex. 13–12.) Notice that a dotted note is one level slower than the three pulses, a doubly dotted note is two levels slower than the seven pulses, and the triply dotted note is three levels slower than the fifteen pulses. Doubly dotted notes are occasionally used and should be learned. Triply dotted notes are hardly ever encountered, and are included here for reference only.

Ex. 13–12

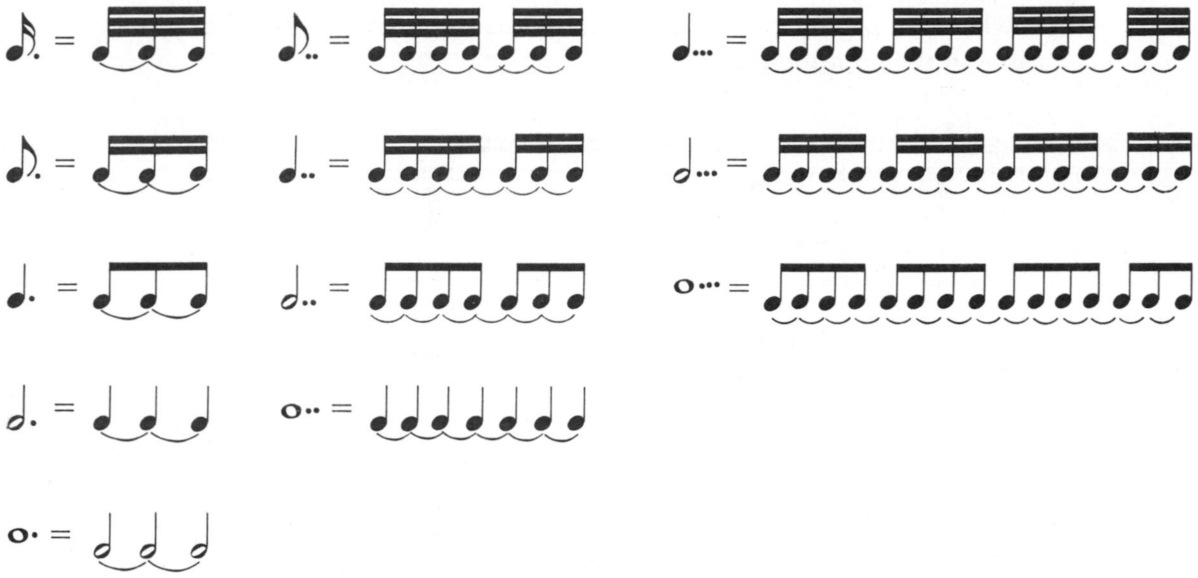

[Musical notation examples showing equivalences of singly, doubly, and triply dotted notes in terms of beamed notes.]

Another way of viewing the dotted notes is that each dot adds half the value of the preceding note or dot (Ex. 13–13).

Ex. 13–13

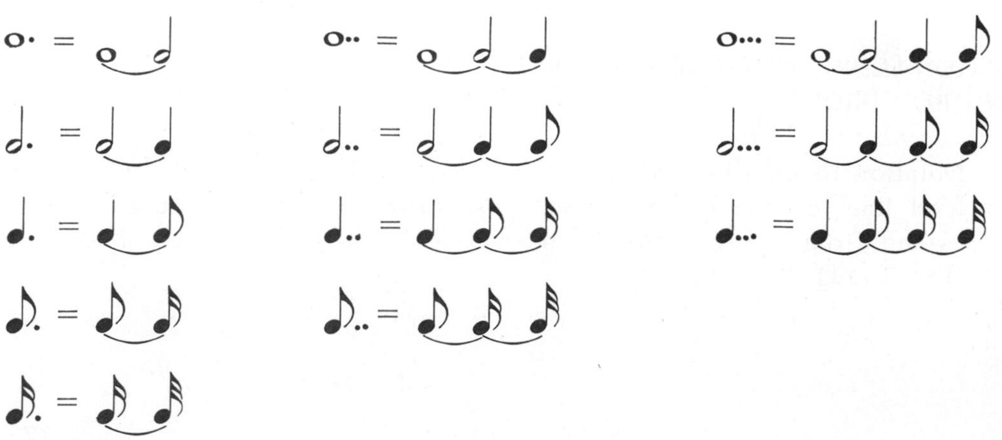

[Musical notation examples showing dotted notes as sums of tied notes.]

In order to avoid confusion, one should use doubly and triply dotted notes with great care. They are not used in compound meters. Doubly and triply dotted rests are not used at all.

RESTS IN FOUR-PULSE AND SIX-PULSE GROUPS

We have illustrated the patterns of four-pulse and six-pulse groups with notes only. It is possible to substitute rests for any of the notes in these patterns, thereby creating varied patterns which should also be practiced. In all exercises involving rests, it is important to make the rests active rather than merely dead silence. It is also important to consider whether rests are used to signal the end of a gesture or whether they are an integral part of the gesture. An effective way to practice patterns involving rests is as follows:

1. Given pattern:

2. First, practice with notes substituted for rests:

3. Then, practice saying the word "rest" whenever rests are indicated:

4. Finally, perform the pattern as indicated, but be sure to think actively of the durations involved in each rest:

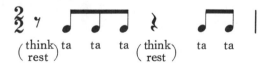

To test your comprehension of the notational principles we have discussed, rewrite the following examples, using fewer notes whenever possible. Be careful, however, to show the metric organization (that is, the beat or division) in complicated passages. Remember to be stricter with rests than with notes, and stricter with compound meters than with simple meters. In some of the examples, more than one solution is acceptable. Discuss such examples with your teacher.

OTHER METERS

All of the meters we have studied to this point can be regarded as being built of repeated groups of two pulses or three pulses. On any one level of rhythmic activity, only one type of pulse group was used.

It is also possible to construct meters out of various combinations of two-

180

and three-pulse groups. In Ex. 13–14, we present these meters on two levels. The beat could be heard on either level, depending on the tempo and character of the music.

Ex. 13–14

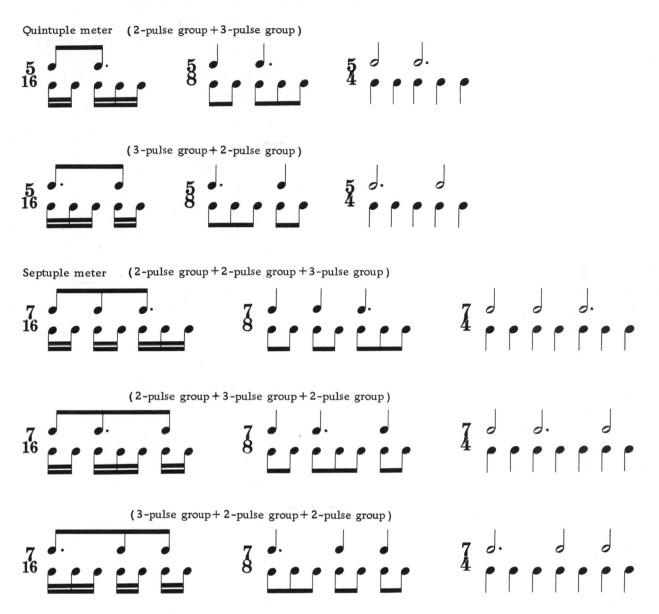

Perform these examples by tapping the faster (lower) level and conducting the slower (upper) level. Be sure to perform the faster level at a regular, even rate. The slower level will result in duple or triple patterns with one beat longer than the others.

Many other unusual meters are possible, some of which are shown in Ex. 13–15. If you understand the basic principles of meter, then it should not be too difficult for you to interpret these meters and others you may encounter. Notice how the signature may indicate the organization.

Ex. 13–15

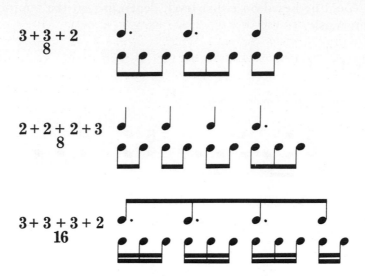

Normally, the next faster level (subdivision) would be in groups of two, unless specifically indicated to be otherwise (Ex. 13–16).

Ex. 13–16

Sometimes, the subdivision level is specifically indicated in groups of three (Ex. 13–17).

Ex. 13–17

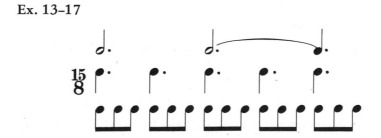

Note that these meters are unusual only in Western music prior to the twentieth century. They are encountered more frequently in twentieth-century music and in non-Western music. These meters are sometimes called *asymmetrical* or *complex.**

---

*For a full discussion of these meters, see Allen Winold, "Rhythm in Twentieth-Century Music," in *Aspects of Twentieth-Century Music*, ed. Gary Wittlich (Englewood Cliffs, N.J.: Prentice-Hall, 1975), pp. 208–69.

Composers sometimes use one or more changes of meter within a composition. When these changes occur frequently, the technique is referred to as *multimeter* or *changing meter*. In hearing or performing these changes, it is important that you understand which note value of the old meter is equivalent to which note value of the new meter. This is usually specified, but if not, assume that the beat note of the old meter is the same rate as the beat note of the new meter (Ex. 13–18).

Ex. 13–18

Polymeter is a term applied to two or more different meters sounded simultaneously. Ex. 13–19 shows two methods of performing polymeters by basing them on the division level.

Ex. 13–19

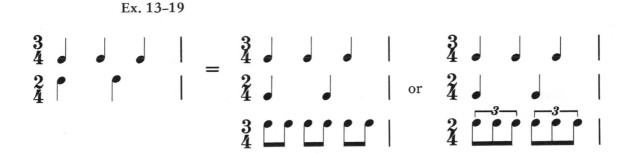

MUSIC-READING EXERCISES 13

Duets

EAR-TRAINING EXERCISES 13

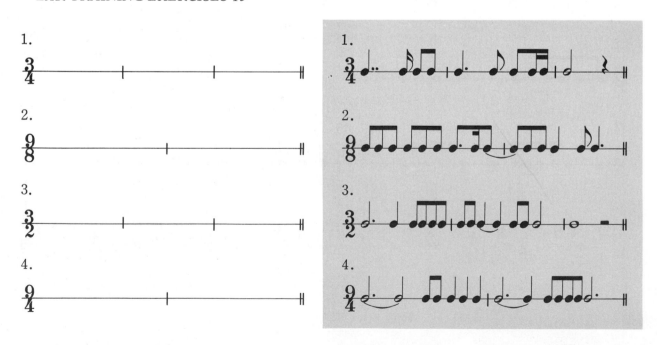

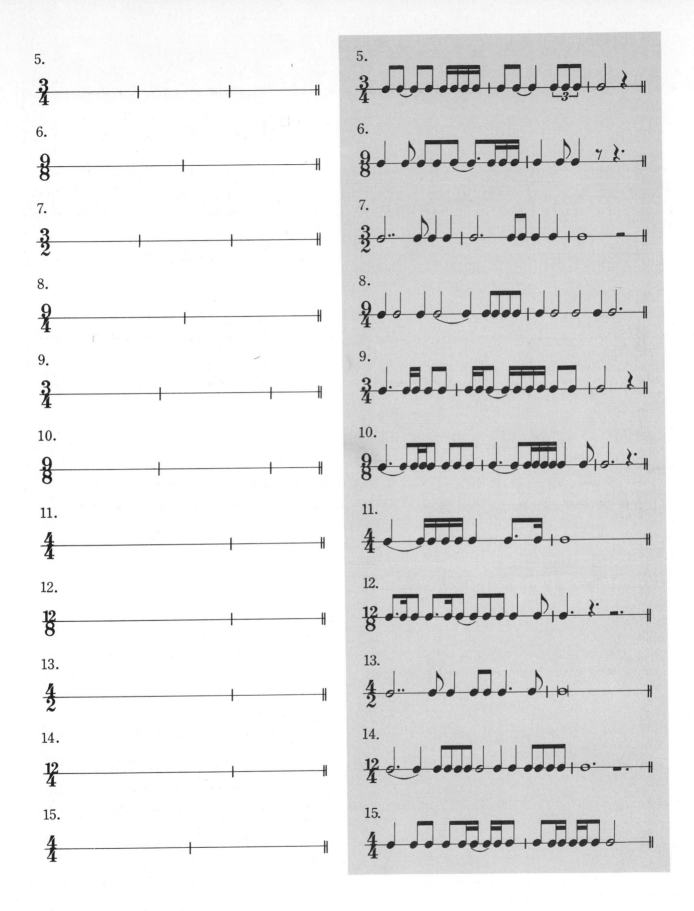

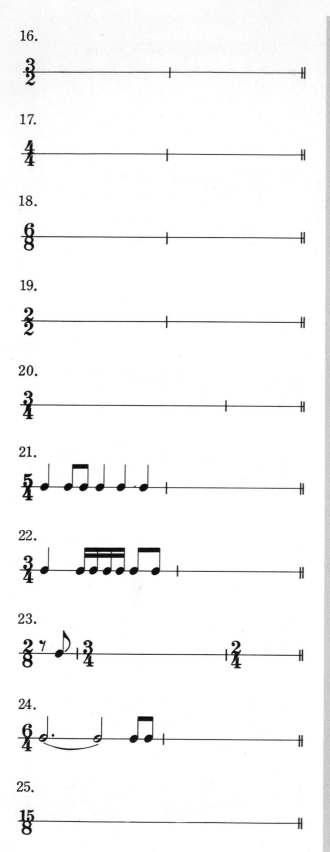

188

Duets

1.

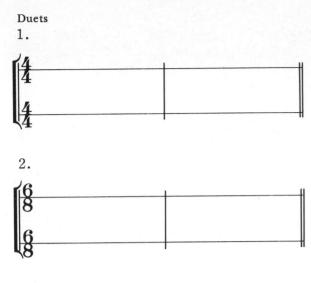

2.

MUSIC-READING EXERCISES 13A

190

EAR-TRAINING EXERCISES 13A

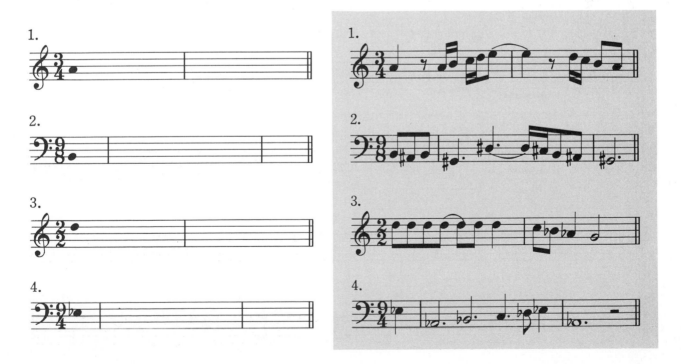

In exercises 11–15, the shaded answer is below each example.

192

EXAMPLES FROM LITERATURE

1. Schumann: Piano Concerto, first movement

2. Beethoven: Symphony No.9, fourth movement

3. Brahms: Variations and Fugue on a Theme by Handel

4. Mozart: *The Magic Flute*, Act I, No. 8 (Duet)

5. Liszt: Hungarian Rhapsody No. 14

6. Brahms: Trio, Op. 101, third movement, first theme

7. Brahms: Trio, Op. 101, third movement, second theme

8. Mozart: *Don Giovanni*

9. Brahms: Variations on a Hungarian Theme

SUPPLEMENTARY EXERCISES 13

1. Listen to live or recorded performances of standard symphonic works, and try to determine what level the conductor would use as the beat level. Try conducting on various levels as you lead class singing, and see which is the most appropriate.

2. Compose four examples similar to the ear-training exercises in this chapter, and work on them with your partner.

3. The end of a composition is the part that will most likely make the most lasting impression on your memory, and, therefore, it should be effective. Musicians refer to the end of a composition as the *cadence* or *final cadence* (Latin: *cadere*, "to fall"). Frequently, cadences are written so that the final note occurs on a strong beat, but it is also possible for the final note to occur on a weak beat or beat division.

Strong beat cadence   Weak beat cadence

Study the literature and see what different types of endings composers have used in various periods of music history. In the supplementary exercises in the following chapters, we shall see how cadences may also appear at points other than the end of a composition, and we shall consider the pitch aspects of cadences.

chapter 14

In this chapter, we shall expand our study of the pitch parameter to include scales and modes. No doubt you already have some familiarity with scales from your applied-music study; now we want to give you a theoretical understanding of them.

THE MAJOR SCALE

Sing through the familiar melody in Ex. 14–1, and study its notation.

Ex. 14–1

Traditional, "Three Blind Mice"

If we arrange the pitches of this melody from lowest to highest, the result is the *diatonic major scale* (Ex. 14-2). Notice the interval structure of this scale.

Ex. 14-2

A scale is an arrangement of pitches in consecutive ascending or descending order (Latin: *scala,* "ladder"). A diatonic scale is one that runs through seven different pitch letter names (Greek: *diatonic,* "through the tones"). The seven notes of a scale may also be called *scale degrees,* and may be numbered starting with the focal pitch as $\hat{1}$, as shown in Ex. 14-2. Notice that the last degree of the scale may be numbered either as $\hat{8}$ or as $1'$, the latter indicating that this degree is an octave above the first degree. Carets (^) are placed above the scale numbers to distinguish them from other uses of these numbers. Notice that major seconds occur between all adjacent degrees of the major scale, except for scale degrees $\hat{3}$–$\hat{4}$ and $\hat{7}$–$\hat{8}$ ($\hat{1}'$), where minor seconds occur. In writing diatonic scales, be sure to use consecutive letter names and accidentals as needed to form the proper interval structure. *Do not repeat or skip any letter names in any diatonic scale.* (See Ex. 14-3.)

Ex. 14-3

Write the major scales ascending or descending from the given notes, as indicated. Indicate the location of half steps with the sign ∨.

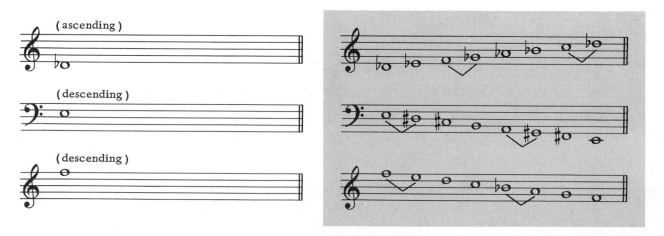

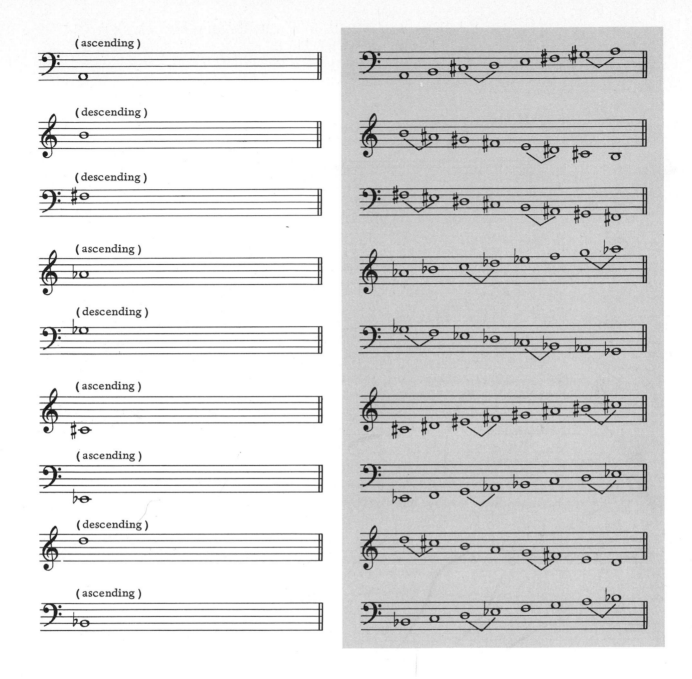

THE NATURAL MINOR SCALE

The major scale is one of the most commonly used scale forms in music. Thousands of melodies have been written with a major-scale basis, and thousands more will probably be written in the future. But other scale forms have played a significant role in the development of music, and we must also learn to write, hear, and perform them.

The next most commonly used scale form in music is the *diatonic minor scale*. This scale appears in three common forms: *natural* (or *pure*) minor, *harmonic* minor, and *melodic* minor. A study of music will show that many melodies written with a minor-scale basis actually use all three forms. For purposes of study, however, it is advisable to consider the three forms separately.

Let us begin with the natural minor.

Ex. 14–4

Study the structure of the natural minor scale in Ex. 14–4, and then complete the scales in the following exercise. Practice playing and singing the scales.

Write the indicated natural minor scales in ascending or descending order, as indicated, using accidentals (no key signatures). Cover the answers before writing the scales. Mark half steps ⌄.

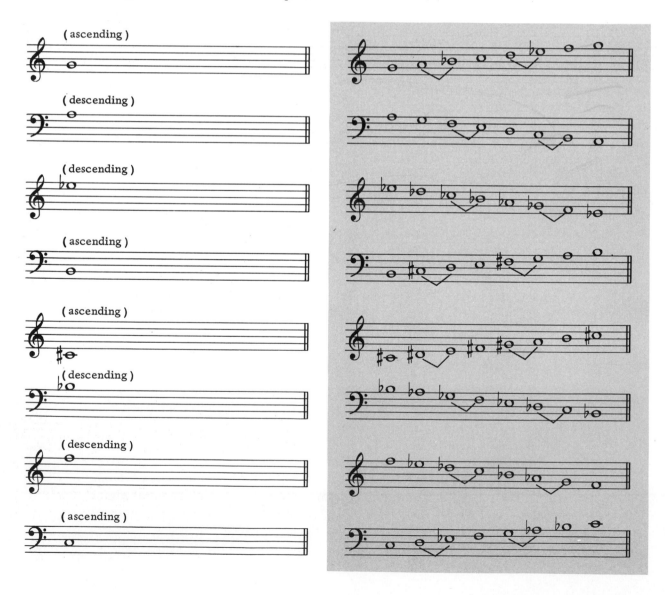

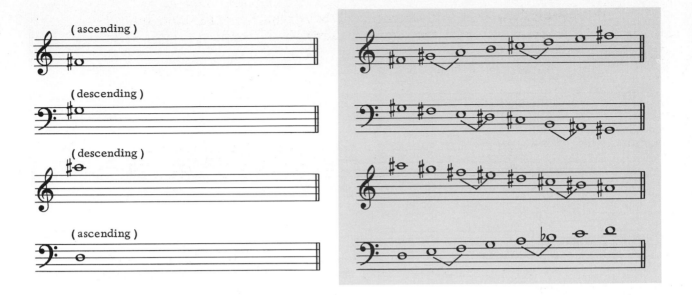

THE HARMONIC MINOR SCALE

The harmonic minor scale (Ex. 14–5) is so called because of its usefulness in harmonic writing, especially in music of the seventeenth through nineteenth centuries. Notice that it differs from the natural minor in having an augmented second between scale degrees $\hat{6}$ and $\hat{7}$.

Ex. 14–5

After you have studied the structure of this scale, practice writing, playing, and singing it. Compare its sound with that of the major and natural minor scales. Play different scales for your drill partner and see if he or she can identify them.

Write the indicated harmonic minor scales in ascending or descending order, as indicated.

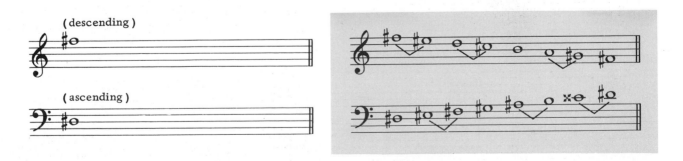

THE MELODIC MINOR SCALE

The melodic minor scale has the interval structure shown in Ex. 14–6.

Ex. 14–6

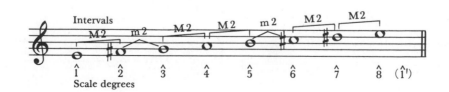

Scale degrees $\hat{1}$ through $\hat{5}$ are the same for all minor scales; scale degrees $\hat{6}$ and $\hat{7}$ are the variable ones, as shown in Ex. 14–7. Notice that the last four scale degrees ($\hat{5},\hat{6},\hat{7},\hat{8}$) of melodic minor are the same as the last four degrees of major.

Ex. 14–7

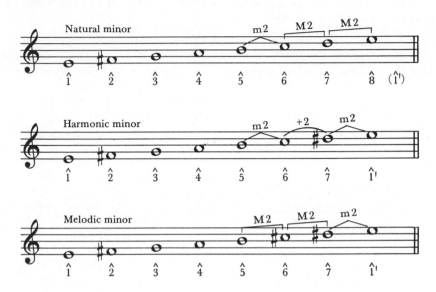

Many textbooks refer to this scale form as the "*ascending* melodic minor scale" and state that it should be used in music only for passages that ascend. For descending passages, the "*descending* melodic minor scale" is supposed to be used. This "descending melodic minor scale," however, turns out to be exactly the same as the natural minor scale, which we have already learned.

We see little value in learning two names for the same scale form. Furthermore, even though most melodies do follow the aforementioned conventions about ascending and descending forms, there are still instances where the reverse is true, as Ex. 14–8 indicates.

Ex. 14–8

Even though such instances are relatively infrequent, it is important for you to be able to handle them competently. For this reason, we encourage you to learn to use all three forms of the minor scale in ascending and descending order. Be careful that the third scale degree is low enough when you sing the melodic minor from the top down. Since the top of the scale sounds like major, there is a strong tendency to sing a major five-pitch set on the bottom. Write and practice the examples that follow, and compare the various scales studied thus far.

Write the indicated melodic minor scales in ascending or descending order, as indicated, using accidentals (no key signatures). Cover the answers before writing the scales. Mark half steps ∨.

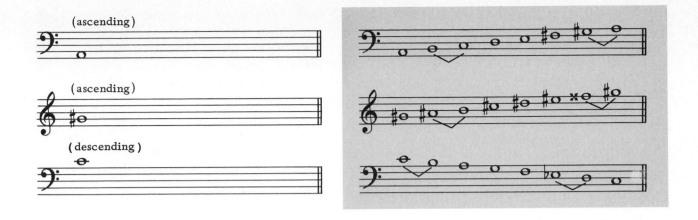

THE CHURCH MODES

The scale forms we are about to study are known collectively as the *church modes*. They formed the basis of most music written until approximately the seventeenth century.* They were generally neglected in the eighteenth and nineteenth centuries, except for some isolated instances, only to be revived in some of the music in the present century. It is especially interesting to note that many currently popular songs, including some melodies by the Beatles, make use of the church modes.

You should find the study of the church modes challenging and enjoyable. In addition, you will probably find that working with the church modes can sharpen your understanding of pitch relationships in major and minor and can prepare you for more advanced work with chromaticism.

The Dorian Mode

The Dorian mode has the interval structure shown in Ex. 14–9.

Ex. 14–9

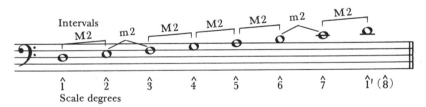

Use the following exercise to develop your ability to write, play, sing, and hear this mode. Do not proceed with any of the following modes until you are able to use this mode with ease.

Write the indicated Dorian modes in ascending or descending order, as indicated, using accidentals (no key signatures). Cover the answers before writing. Mark half steps ∨.

*Dates for significant style changes in music are difficult to determine. Do not be alarmed if you find other dates mentioned in other texts for this point.

The Phrygian Mode

The Phrygian mode has the interval structure shown in Ex. 14–10. The Phrygian scale is the only one to begin with a minor second.

Ex. 14–10

Write, play, and sing the following exercise. Compare the sound of this mode or scale form with the others we have studied so far.

Write the indicated Phrygian modes in ascending or descending order, as indicated, using accidentals (no key signatures). Cover the answers before writing. Mark half steps ∨.

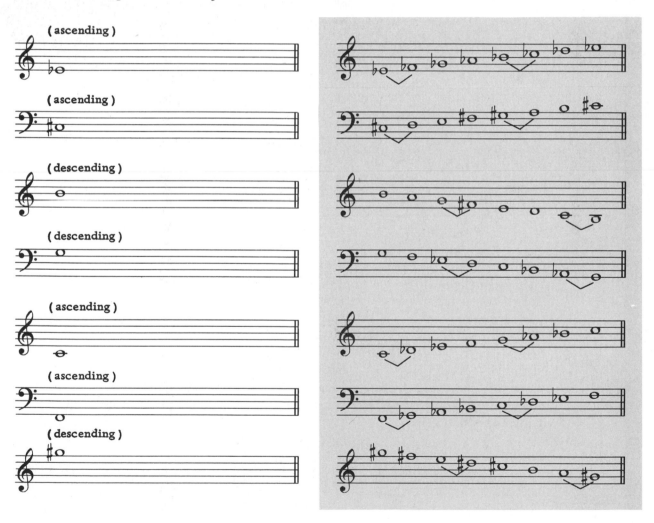

The Lydian Mode

The Lydian mode has the interval structure shown in Ex. 14–11.

Ex. 14–11

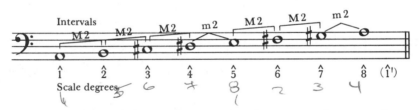

Early theorists assigned certain emotional connotations to the various modes in an elaborate system of music theory. Although we shall not recommend that you try to associate particular emotions with various scale forms, we do recommend that you attempt to recognize the characteristic sound of each scale form as you work with it.

Practice writing, playing, and singing the Lydian mode in the exercise that follows.

Write the indicated Lydian modes in ascending or descending order, as indicated, using accidentals (no key signatures). Cover the answers before writing. Mark half steps ∨.

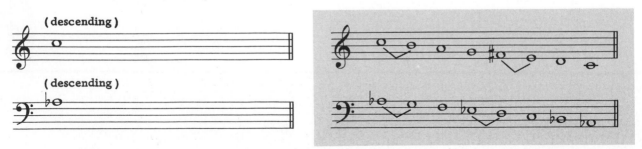

The Mixolydian Mode

The Mixolydian mode has the interval structure shown in Ex. 14–12.

Ex. 14–12

Write the indicated Mixolydian modes in ascending or descending order, as indicated, using accidentals (no key signatures). Cover the answers before writing. Mark half steps ⌄.

To conclude our introduction of the church modes, we might mention that the scale forms we now call major and natural minor are sometimes called the Ionian and Aeolian modes, respectively. The Locrian mode, which consists of natural notes extending from b to b, is sometimes cited, but it is not used in actual music. We might also mention that in some theoretical writings, five-pitch sets are referred to as *pentachords* (Greek: "five strings") and four-pitch sets are referred to as *tetrachords* (Greek: "four strings").

Write out the following scales in ascending order.

THE "PARALLEL" APPROACH TO SCALE FORMS

In addition to the interval-structure approach to scale forms, which we have just discussed, there are at least two other ways of looking at scale forms. We might call the first the "parallel" approach because it compares scale forms as they run parallel from the same starting note, taking into account ways in which the structures of the scales differ.

We shall begin this approach by recalling the structure of the major scale:

With a single alteration each time, we can derive two other scales from this one. We can produce the Lydian scale by raising the fourth degree:

We can produce the Mixolydian by lowering the seventh degree:

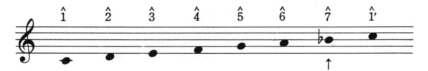

We can produce the natural minor scale by lowering the third, sixth, and seventh degrees:

From this natural minor scale we will then derive the other scale forms.

We can produce the Phrygian scale by lowering the second degree of the natural minor scale:

We can produce the Dorian scale by raising the sixth degree of the natural minor scale:

We can produce the harmonic minor scale by raising the seventh degree of the natural minor scale:

We can produce the melodic minor scale by raising the sixth and seventh degrees of the natural minor scale:

The following chart summarizes this approach:

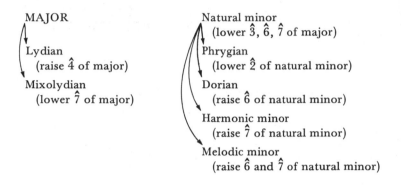

MAJOR

Lydian
(raise 4̂ of major)

Mixolydian
(lower 7̂ of major)

Natural minor
(lower 3̂, 6̂, 7̂ of major)

Phrygian
(lower 2̂ of natural minor)

Dorian
(raise 6̂ of natural minor)

Harmonic minor
(raise 7̂ of natural minor)

Melodic minor
(raise 6̂ and 7̂ of natural minor)

Using the "parallel" approach, change each of the following scales to the indicated scale.

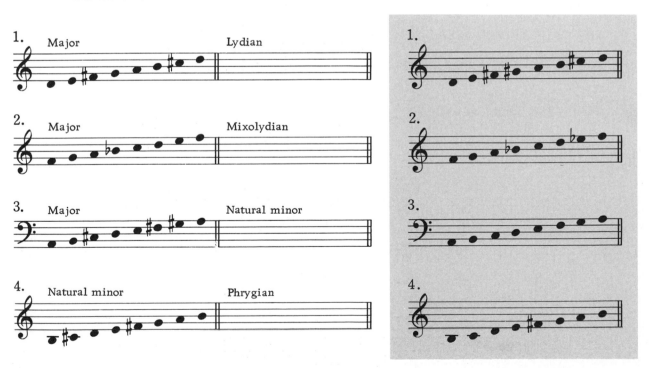

1. Major — Lydian
2. Major — Mixolydian
3. Major — Natural minor
4. Natural minor — Phrygian

213

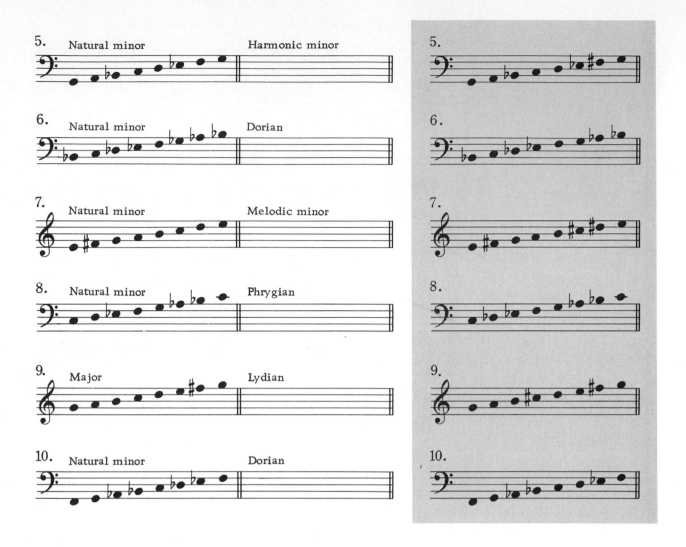

THE "RELATIVE" APPROACH TO SCALE FORMS

Another approach to an understanding of scales is to regard the scales as being based on a major scale, but beginning each scale on a different note. This might be called a "relative" approach because it relates each scale or mode to a particular note in a given major scale. This approach is illustrated in Ex. 14–13.

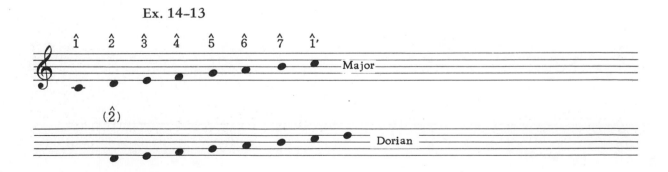

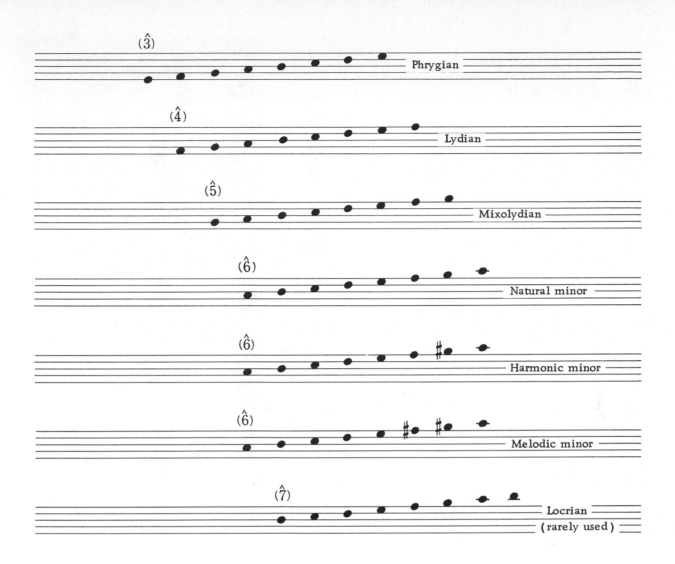

Using the "relative" approach, write the indicated scales based on the given scales, as shown in the model.

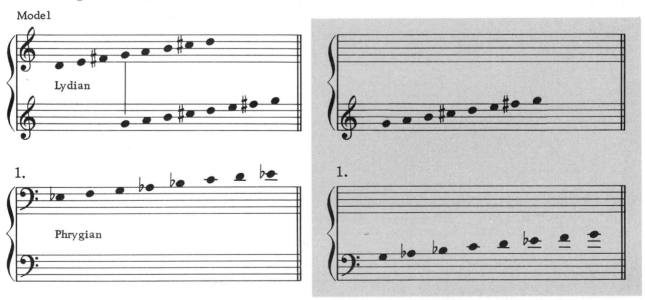

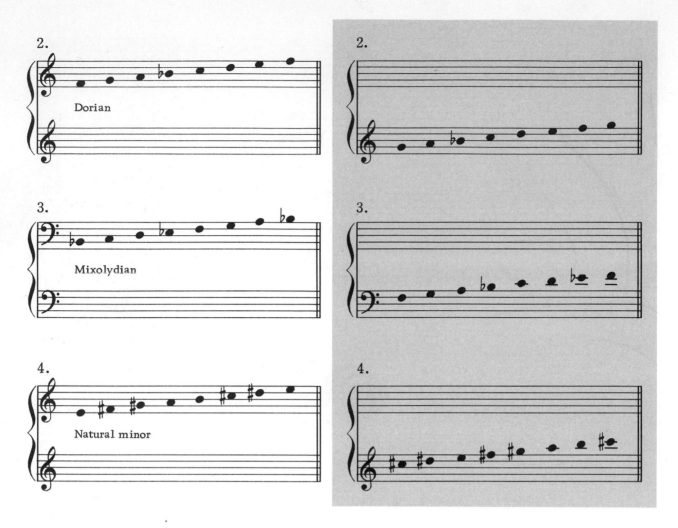

Which approach is best? The answer can only be whichever approach is more helpful to you. Ultimately, you must simply know all of these scales instantly without having to use any "approach."

SCALE DEGREE NAMES

In addition to the number names for the scale degrees, there are the following traditional terms:

Scale Degree	Name
$\hat{1}$	Tonic
$\hat{2}$	Supertonic (above the tonic)
$\hat{3}$	Mediant (midway between tonic and dominant)
$\hat{4}$	Subdominant (so called because it is a perfect fifth *below* the tonic, just as the dominant is a perfect fifth above the tonic)
$\hat{5}$	Dominant
$\hat{6}$	Submediant (midway between the tonic and the subdominant)
$\hat{7}$	Leading tone (so called because it leads to the tonic by a half step)
	Subtonic (below the tonic, applied to the seventh degree of the scale when it is a whole step below the tonic)

Complete the following statements:

1. The supertonic of G major is _____ .
2. The dominant of b minor is _____ .
3. The mediant of E major is _____ .
4. The submediant of D♭ major is _____ .
5. D is the _____ of B♭ major.
6. G is the _____ of A♭ major.
7. E♭ is the _____ of G♭ major.
8. B is the _____ of F♯ major.
9. A is the supertonic of _____ minor.
10. D♯ is the mediant of _____ major.
11. F is the leading tone of _____ major.
12. E is the tonic of _____ major.

1. A	
2. F♯	
3. G♯	
4. B♭	
5. mediant	
6. leading tone	
7. submediant	
8. subdominant	
9. g	
10. B	
11. G♭	
12. E	

The following exercises are relatively brief. If you have practiced performing and hearing scales as indicated throughout the chapter, you should have little difficulty with them. If you do have problems, review the chapter and experiment with the various approaches mentioned.

MUSIC-READING EXERCISES 14

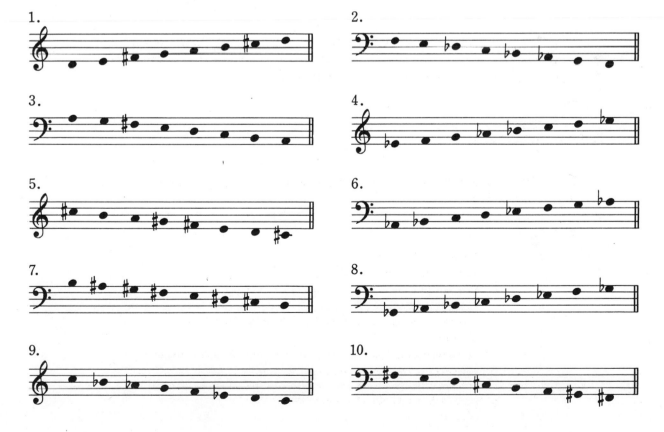

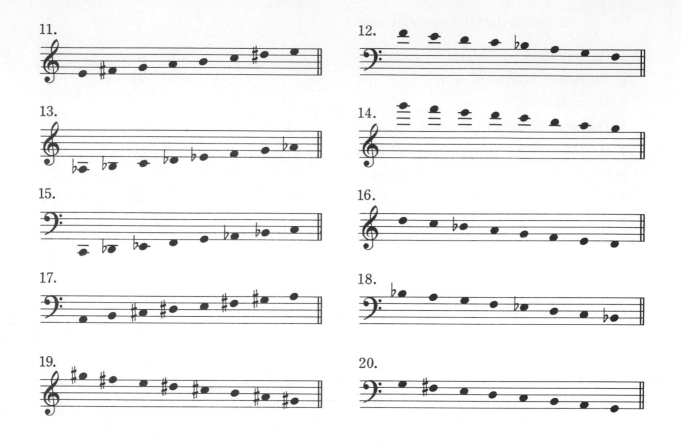

EAR-TRAINING EXERCISES 14

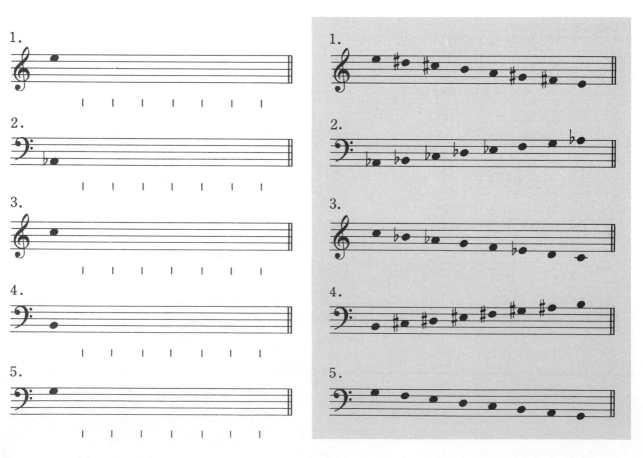

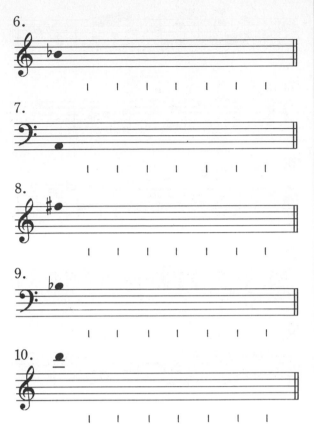

MUSIC-READING EXERCISES 14A

EAR-TRAINING EXERCISES 14A

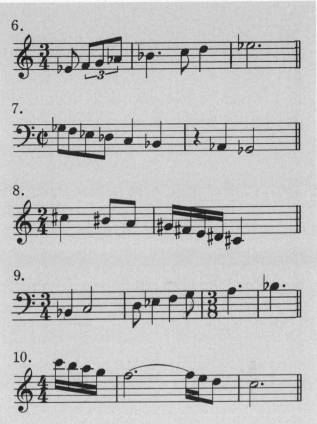

EXAMPLES FROM LITERATURE

1. Stravinsky: *Petrouchka,* "Russian Dance"

2. Wagner: *Die Meistersinger von Nürnberg*

3. Saint-Saens: *Elégie,* Op. 143

4. Bach: Chorale, "Ein feste Burg"

5. Weinberger: Variations and Fugue on an Old English Tune

6. Beethoven: Trio, Op. 97, "Archduke"

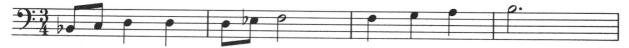

SUPPLEMENTARY EXERCISES 14

1. See how many examples from the literature you can find that are based on scale passages.

2. Compose four examples similar to the ear-training exercises in this chapter, and work on them with your partner.

3. In the previous chapter, we mentioned briefly some rhythmic aspects of cadences. In terms of pitch, it is interesting to note that the overwhelming majority of so-called common-practice compositions end on the tonic pitch. Occasionally, the other tonic triad pitches, mediant and dominant, will be used as cadence pitches.

In addition to the final cadence, it is possible to have cadences within a composition. We could compare the final cadence to a period in punctuation and the internal cadences to commas or semicolons. Usually, the internal cadences are marked by long notes or possibly by a rest, but they do not necessarily end on a pitch of the tonic triad. Indeed, it is generally advisable to avoid internal cadences on the tonic, because this might create the impression that the piece is finished.

In many simple folk songs, internal cadences occur every four bars. The span of music from the beginning of a composition to the first cadence, or from one cadence to another, is often called a *phrase*. In many ways, this phrase is similar to a phrase in English grammar. That is, it is a relatively complete utterance.

Although the four-bar phrase is common to much music literature, four bars is by no means the only possible phrase length. Phrases of three or five bars can be effective and convincing. Study examples from the literature for phrase length and for cadence pitches. Then try to compose fairly long examples made of several phrases.

To give your compositions unity as well as variety, you should include in them some contrasting phrases and some repeated phrases. It is also possible to have some phrases that are variations of previously heard phrases. You can use the following phrase plans for your compositions, or you can create your own.

AA'BA   ABAC   AAB   ABA   ABA'

Integer Notation

One of the main advantages of integer notation is that it can make interval structure instantly clear. In a major scale—for example, 0,2,4,5,7,9, 11, 0—it is obvious that there are half steps (I 1) between 4 and 5 and between 11 and the upper 0 (or 12).

The following chart shows the structure of the major and minor scales and the church modes in integer notation. Study this chart, noting the relationship of integer notation to the traditional notation of scale degrees. Note also that scale degrees 1̂ and 5̂ are the same for all scale forms, whereas all other degrees are variable.

Scale													
Major	0		2		4	5		7		9		11	0
Natural Minor	0		2	3		5		7	8		10		0
Harmonic Minor	0		2	3		5		7	8			11	0
Melodic Minor	0		2	3		5		7		9		11	0
Dorian Mode	0		2	3		5		7		9	10		0
Phrygian Mode	0	1		3		5		7	8		10		0
Lydian Mode	0		2		4		6	7		9		11	0
Mixolydian Mode	0		2		4	5		7		9	10		0'
Traditional Scale Degrees	1̂		2̂		3̂	4̂		5̂	6̂		7̂		1̂

Write out the following scales in ascending order in staff notation. Write the integer notation below.

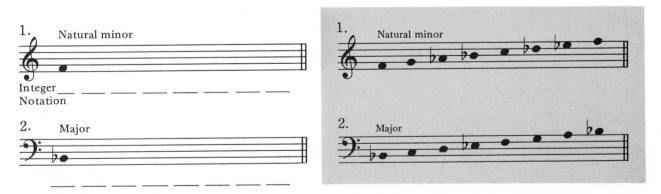

1. Natural minor

Integer Notation ___ ___ ___ ___ ___ ___ ___ ___

2. Major

___ ___ ___ ___ ___ ___ ___ ___

1. Natural minor

2. Major

3. Phrygian

4. Harmonic minor

5. Dorian

6. Mixolydian

7. Lydian

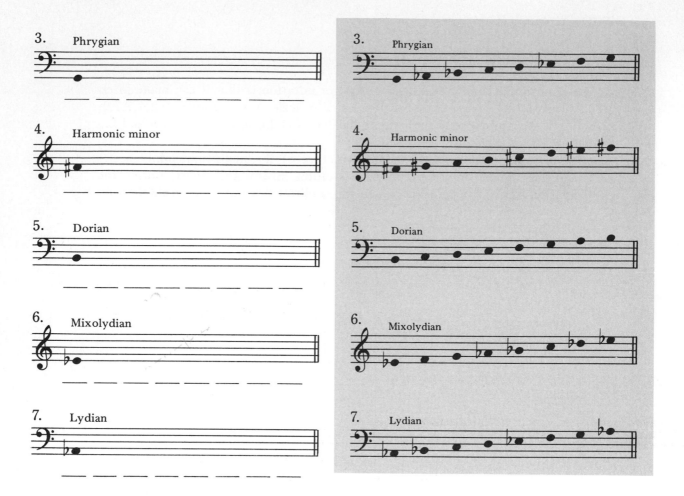

chapter 15

Until now, we have deliberately avoided the use of key signatures. In this way, you have been forced to think of the exact pitches used. Now, as we introduce key signatures in our work, you should still be conscious of the exact pitch you are hearing or performing.

KEY SIGNATURES

Key signatures are basically labor-saving devices in music writing. Rather than placing an accidental before each note as needed, we summarize the accidentals at the beginning of each line, immediately following the clef sign. Accidentals in a key signature apply to all appearances of a particular note and in all octaves. For example, the F♯ in the key signature in Ex. 15-1 applies to all of the F's, not just to the one on the fourth line.

Ex. 15-1

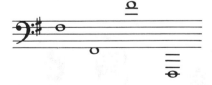

Theoretically, we could place any accidentals in a key signature, and do so in any order. In practice, the accidentals in a key signature usually appear in a certain fixed order. Our first task will be to learn this order. In Ex.

15-2, the lines show the order for placing flats in the key signature. Notice that they follow a regular pattern in both clefs. Beginning with B♭, they move up a fourth, down a fifth, and so on. Copy the signatures in each clef until you are thoroughly familiar with them.

Ex. 15-2

The sharps in bass clef follow a regular pattern, beginning with F♯ and then moving down a fourth, up a fifth, and so on. In treble clef they do not follow such a regular pattern. (See Ex. 15-3.) Study the pattern in treble clef. Then copy the signatures in both clefs until you are familiar with them.

Ex. 15-3

Now we must see how these signatures relate to the tonal organizations we have studied. If you have thoroughly learned all of the scales or modes studied thus far, it should be easy for you to extract the accidentals from the scales studied and place them in the proper position and order in a key signature, as illustrated in Ex. 15-4.

Ex. 15-4

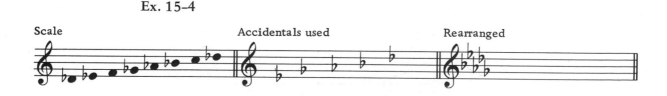

Scale   Accidentals used   Rearranged

Rather than constructing the scale first and then determining the key signature, there is another way to remember major key signatures. This is known as the *circle of fifths*. Study Ex. 15-5, and then note the following points:

1. C major has no sharps or flats.

2. Cb major has seven flats, C# major has seven sharps.

3. The sharp keys move clockwise in the circle. Each key is a perfect fifth *above* the preceding key. Each successive key adds one sharp.

4. The flat keys move counterclockwise in the circle. Each key is a perfect fifth *below* the preceding one. Each successive key adds one flat.

5. There are three pairs of enharmonic keys: Db/C#, Gb/F#, Cb/B.

6. For sharp keys, the tonic is a minor second above the last sharp.

7. For flat keys, the tonic is the same as the second last flat.

8. For keys with five or more accidentals, it may prove easier to remember what accidentals are *not* used. For example, Gb major has all flats except one (Fb).

Ex. 15–5

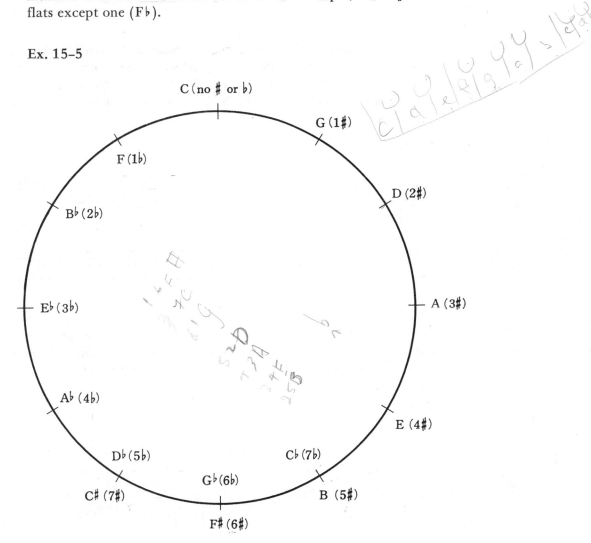

Ex. 15–6 gives the signatures for all major keys in both clefs. Study this chart, and then work the written exercises that follow. Notice that major keys are designated with capital letters.

Ex. 15–6

Identify the following major key signatures.

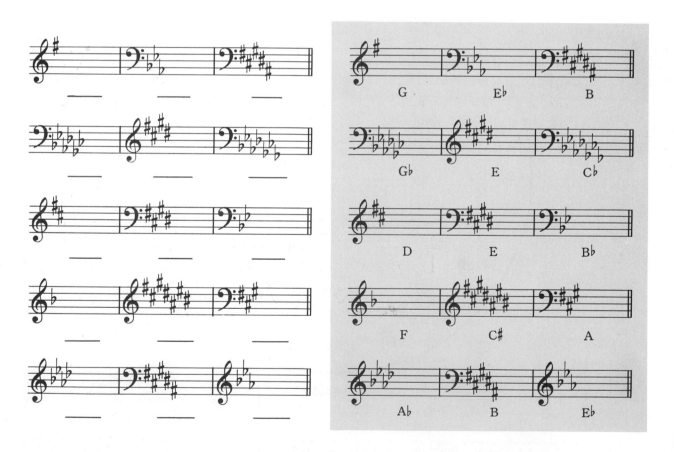

Write the following major key signatures in the clef indicated.

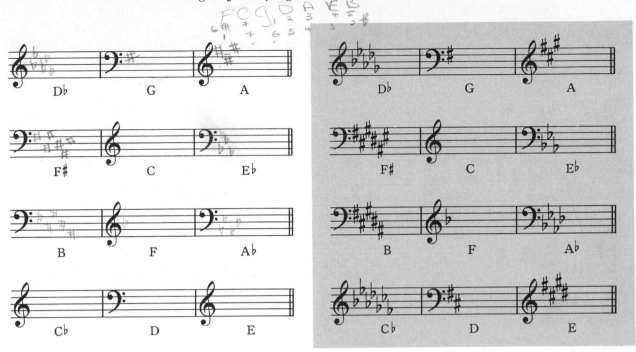

MINOR KEY SIGNATURES

The minor key signatures appear in Ex. 15-7. Key signatures for minor keys indicate only the natural minor. For harmonic and melodic minor, extra accidentals must be added in the course of the scale or composition.

Ex. 15-7

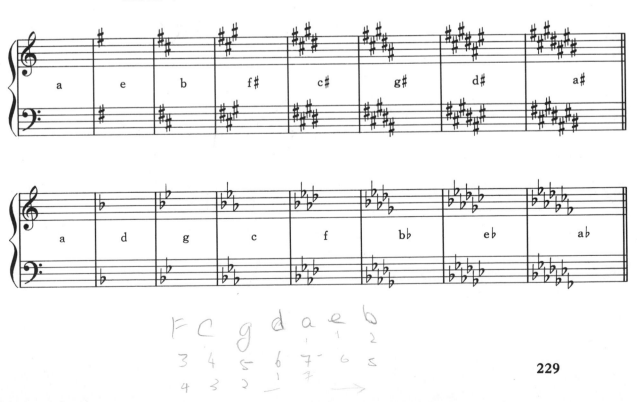

Recall from the last chapter that we learned we could form a natural minor scale from a major scale by beginning on the sixth degree of the major scale. We see now that we can use the same signature for a major scale and for the minor scale whose tonic is on the sixth degree of that major scale. If a major and a minor scale or key both use the same signature, they are said to be *relative*. For example, B♭ major and g minor both have the same signature (two flats). Therefore, g minor is the relative minor of B♭ major; B♭ major is the relative major of g minor. Many students find it easier simply to remember that the relative minor is always a minor third below the relative major. Thus, for example, c♯ minor is the relative minor of E major, e♭ minor is the relative minor of G♭ major, and so forth.

We shall again use the circle of fifths to indicate relative major and minor (Ex. 15–8). Notice that major keys are indicated with capital letters, minor keys with lower-case letters. We shall follow this practice from now on.

Ex. 15–8

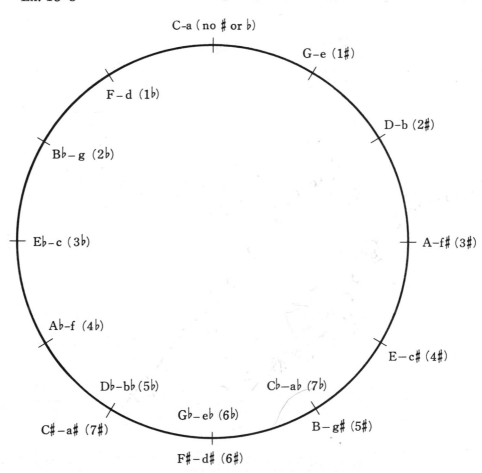

If a major and a minor scale or key both have the same tonic, they are said to be *parallel*. Thus, for example, C major is the parallel major of c minor. Ex. 15–9 lists parallel major and minor keys, again with capital letters for major and lower-case letters for minor.

Ex. 15-9

For each signature, indicate the proper major keys and the relative minor keys. Use capital letters for major keys, lower case for minor keys.

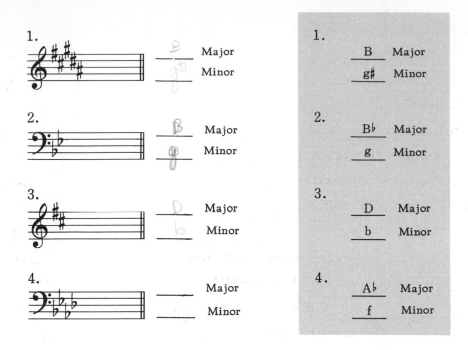

1.
_B_ Major
_g#_ Minor

2.
_Bb_ Major
_g_ Minor

3.
_D_ Major
_b_ Minor

4.
_Ab_ Major
_f_ Minor

Write the following key signatures in the clef indicated.

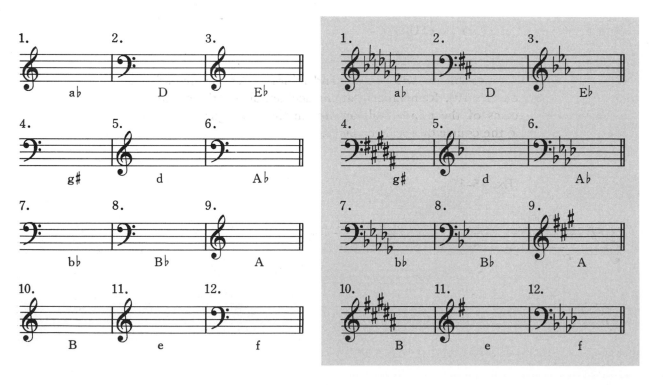

1. ab   2. D   3. Eb

4. g#   5. d   6. Ab

7. bb   8. Bb   9. A

10. B   11. e   12. f

Fill in the blanks in the following statements.

1. The parallel major of d minor is _____ .
2. The relative minor of G major is _____ .
3. The relative major of c♯ minor is _____ .
4. The relative minor of B major is _____ .
5. The parallel minor of F♯ major is _____ .
6. The relative minor of C♭ major is _____ .
7. The relative major of e minor is _____ .
8. The parallel major of a minor is _____ .
9. The relative major of e♭ minor is _____ .
10. The relative minor of E major is _____ .
11. _____ is the relative major of b minor.
12. _____ is the parallel minor of C♯ major.
13. _____ is the relative minor of E♭ major.
14. _____ is the relative minor of G♭ major.
15. _____ is the relative major of f♯ minor.

1. D major
2. e minor
3. E major
4. g♯ minor
5. f♯ minor
6. a♭ minor
7. G major
8. A major
9. G♭ major
10. c♯ minor
11. D major
12. c♯ minor
13. c minor
14. e♭ minor
15. A major

SCALES WITH KEY SIGNATURES

Now it is possible to write major and minor scales that include key signatures (Ex. 15–10). Remember that the accidentals for the harmonic and melodic forms of the minor scale are *not* in the key signature. They must be added in the course of a scale or piece.

Ex. 15–10

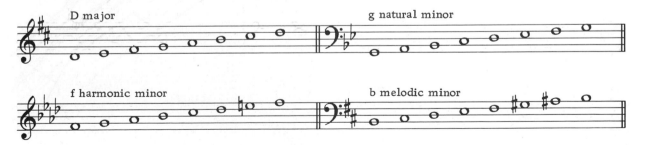

Identify the following scales.

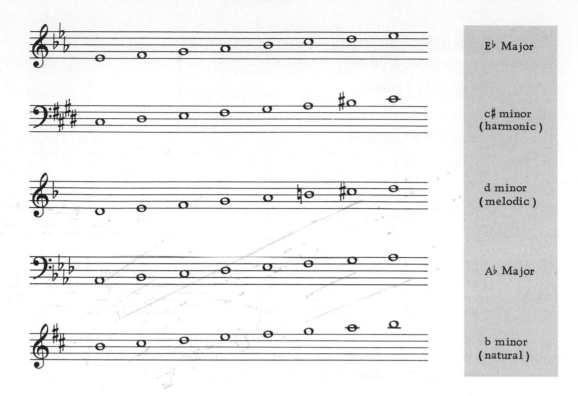

Eb Major

c# minor (harmonic)

d minor (melodic)

Ab Major

b minor (natural)

Write the following scales; include key signatures. Be sure to add the proper accidentals for harmonic and melodic minor.

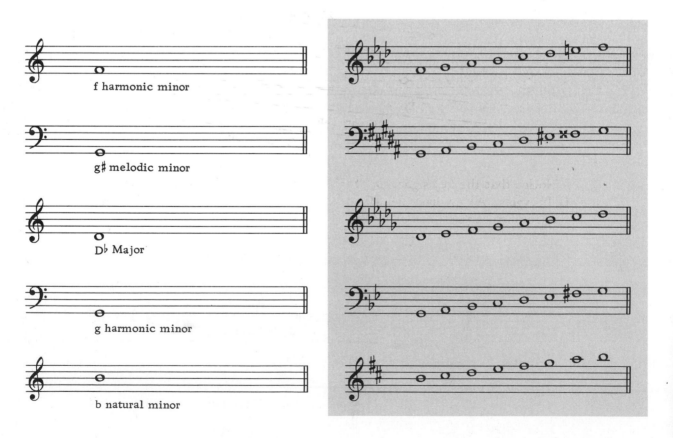

f harmonic minor

g# melodic minor

Db Major

g harmonic minor

b natural minor

234

Recall that we can obtain the various scales or modes by using the same set of pitches but beginning each mode on a different pitch. Thus, if we use only the natural notes, we would obtain the scales shown in Ex. 15–11.

Ex. 15–11

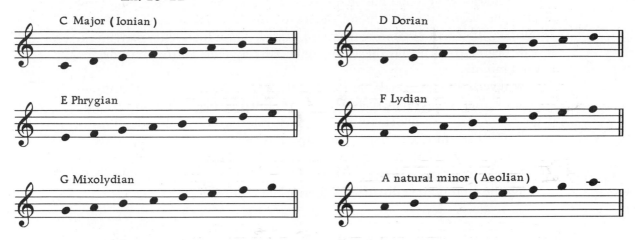

We could take any other major scale as the basis for this system. If, for example, we took the major scale of E♭, we would obtain the scales shown in Ex. 15–12.

Ex. 15–12

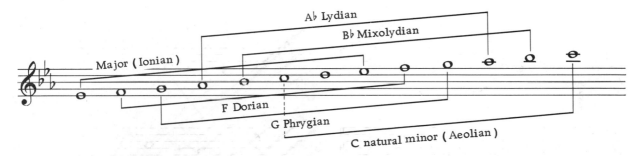

Notice that the key signature of three flats is valid for E♭ major, F Dorian, G Phrygian, A♭ Lydian, B♭ Mixolydian, and C natural minor. Remember that for any given major scale, the following rules apply.

Scale Type	Scale Degrees Spanned
Major	$\hat{1}-\hat{1}'$
Dorian	$\hat{2}-\hat{2}'$
Phrygian	$\hat{3}-\hat{3}'$
Lydian	$\hat{4}-\hat{4}'$
Mixolydian	$\hat{5}-\hat{5}'$
Natural minor	$\hat{6}-\hat{6}'$

Let us now apply this principle. What scale form or mode is represented in Ex. 15–13?

Ex. 15–13

Four sharps would be the major key signature for E major. Since the given scale *begins* on the second degree of the E major scale (f♯), it must be Dorian. If it had begun on the third degree, it would be Phrygian; on the fourth degree, Lydian; on the fifth degree, Mixolydian; on the sixth degree, natural minor.

Now reverse the process. What key signature would apply for C♯ Phrygian? We know that a Phrygian scale may be regarded as beginning on the third degree of a major scale. Therefore, we must ask ourselves, "In which major key is C♯ the third degree?" The answer is obviously A major. Since A major has a key signature of three sharps, then C♯ Phrygian would also have a key signature of three sharps.

Using the method just discussed, identify the following scales.

236

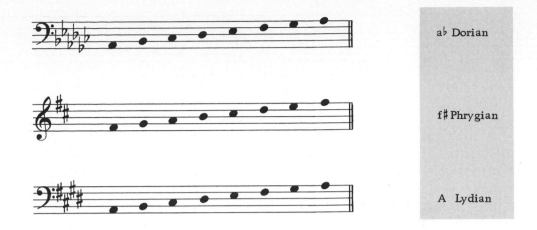

a♭ Dorian

f♯ Phrygian

A Lydian

Write the following modal scales with the proper key signatures.

d Phrygian

e Dorian

F Lydian

F♯ Mixolydian

g Dorian

D Lydian

c Phrygian

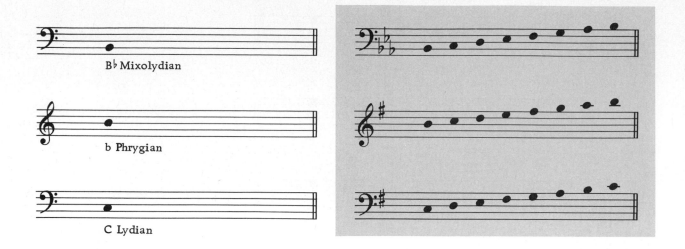

B♭ Mixolydian

b Phrygian

C Lydian

MODAL INFLECTIONS

Recall that the modal scales may be regarded as being similar to major or natural minor scales, with certain important exceptions:

1. Dorian is like natural minor with a raised sixth degree.
2. Phrygian is like natural minor with a lowered second degree.
3. Lydian is like major with a raised fourth degree.
4. Mixolydian is like major with a lowered seventh degree.

Some nineteenth- and twentieth-century composers use these principles in writing scales or compositions incorporating the church modes. For example, to write a Dorian scale or melody, they use the minor key signature and then raise the sixth degree of the natural minor scale in the course of the scale or melody. The changed or altered notes are sometimes called modal inflections. They include the Dorian sixth, the Phrygian second, the Lydian fourth, and the Mixolydian seventh. Ex. 15–14 should make this clear.

Ex. 15–14

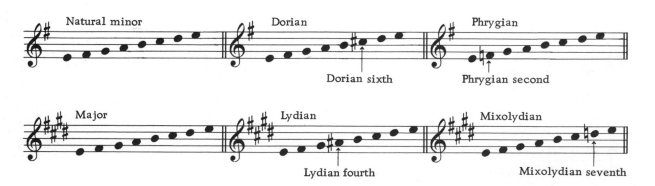

Write the following modes with appropriate major or minor key signatures
and modal inflections.

a Dorian

b♭ Lydian

d Dorian

g Lydian

c Dorian

e Phrygian

c Mixolydian

g Phrygian

a Mixolydian

In the remaining exercises in this book, we shall use both the proper modal
signatures and, occasionally, the modal inflections. In this way, you will
become familiar with both systems.

Supply proper key signatures and notes.

EXAMPLES FROM LITERATURE

1. Mahler: Symphony No. 1, first movement

2. Ravel: *Bolero*

3. Rimsky-Korsakov: *Schéhérazade*, Op. 35

4. Schönberg: *Verklärte Nacht*, Op. 4

5. J. S. Bach: Orchestral Suite No. 1, Passepied

6. Binchois: *De Plus en Plus*

7. Brahms: *Ein Deutsches Requiem*, Op. 115, No. 3

SUPPLEMENTARY EXERCISES 15

1. Compose four examples similar to the ear-training exercises in this chapter, and work on them with your partner.

2. In Supplementary Exercises 3 in Chapter 14, we discussed phrases. Often, composers will create melodies that consist of one or more *periods*. A period in music is usually

made up of two phrases. The first is called the *antecedent* phrase; the second is called the *consequent* phrase. Commonly, the antecedent phrase will end on a pitch other than the tonic, and the consequent phrase will end on the tonic.

Study examples from the literature for their use of periods, and then try to write simple melodies made up of one or more periods.

chapter 16

SCALES MOVING FROM DOMINANT TO DOMINANT

All the scales and modes we have presented to this point move from tonic to tonic. It is also possible for scales to move from dominant to dominant. (See Ex. 16–1.)

Ex. 16–1

Many familiar folk songs, hymns, and popular tunes, as well as melodies by serious composers, may be analyzed as being based upon a scale moving from dominant to dominant. Two such songs are illustrated in Ex. 16–2.

Ex. 16–2

SCALE, MODE, KEY, TONALITY

We have been devoting so much of our attention to scales in recent chapters that it is important to recall that scales are in reality nothing but theoretical or pedagogical abstractions. It is essential for you as a musician to understand the basic principles of scales and to be able to hear and perform them. But it is just as essential that you realize that melodies were created before scales were formulated. It is just as wrong to assume that Beethoven took a c minor scale and then wrote the opening of his Fifth Symphony from it as it would be to assume that Shakespeare took the alphabet and then fashioned the opening of *Hamlet* from it.

We can say, as we have in the last section, that a piece is based upon a particular scale form, as long as we are fully aware that this does not imply anything about the way in which the melody was created by the composer. Knowing that a melody is based on a particular scale form can help us in our perception and performance of it for we can relate the melody to a previously understood concept.

We have defined a *scale* as a ladderlike succession of ascending or descending pitches, and we have indicated that in some cases "mode" can be used as a synonym for "scale." *Mode* has a broader meaning. It refers to the scale basis of a melody without any connotation of pitches ascending or descending in a stepwise order, as in a scale.

Musicians also use "mode" in a more restricted sense to refer to the Dorian, Phrygian, Lydian, and Mixolydian scale forms (the so-called church modes), as distinct from the major and minor scale forms. Thus, we could say that some recent popular music shows frequent use of the modes, or that it is modal, and we would be implying that it uses the church modes, rather than major or minor. This is true even though it is proper to refer to the major mode or the minor mode. Just remember that the word mode, used alone, often refers to the church modes.

Key refers to the particular scale form of a piece, and also to the tonic. It is usually used only for major and minor. We say, for example, that a piece is "in the key of G major," "in the key of c minor," and so on. It is not customary to say that a piece is "in the key of d Dorian."

Tonality is a broader term. It encompasses the idea of mode and key, and also includes other tonal organizations. The simplest definition of tonality is that it is a form of pitch organization in which one pitch, the tonic, is heard as the central or most important pitch. We can say that a melody is in the key of D major or that it is in the tonality of D major. We can say that a melody is in the tonality of G Mixolydian. We can say that a melody such as Ex. 16–3 is in the tonality of E or that it has a tonal center of E. Notice that Ex. 16–3 is not based on any of the scale forms we have discussed; yet E is heard as the most important pitch because of its duration, frequency, and position in the melody.

Ex. 16–3

As you can see from this brief discussion, there is some ambiguity about such terms as mode, key, and tonality. As you progress in your study of music and read other books and articles, you will encounter even more debate about the proper meaning and use of these terms, but this should not distress you. In any area of learning, there is always considerable discussion and disagreement regarding the meaning of important terms.

PITCH HIERARCHY

One of the characteristics of music written in a major or minor mode or in one of the church modes is that the various pitches are usually not treated equally but rather in a hierarchy ranging from the most important pitches to pitches of lesser importance.

We have already noted that the tonic pitch is the most important pitch; that is, it is usually heard for longer durations, more frequently, and at significant positions in the melody, especially as the last pitch or as the first accented pitch. The dominant is usually heard as the second most important pitch. The mediant may also be an important pitch, not necessarily because it is emphasized by duration, frequency, and position, but because it is crucial in determining the characteristic difference between major and minor, or between the major-based church modes (Lydian and Mixolydian) and the minor-based church modes (Dorian and Phrygian). We have seen in our study of five-pitch sets that these three pitches—tonic, mediant, and dominant—form one of the most characteristic patterns in music, the triad, and this also accounts for the relative importance of the mediant.

The remaining pitches may be regarded as secondary or satellite pitches gravitating around the tonic and dominant or, to a degree, the mediant. Ex. 16–4 symbolizes this relationship with variously weighted note values.

Ex. 16–4

Various writers on music theory use different terms to refer to these two classes of pitches—the tonic, mediant, and dominant in one class and the leading tone, supertonic, subdominant, and submediant in the other class. They may call them *rest* tones and *active* tones, in that the tonic, mediant, and dominant seem more suitable for points of repose, and the other tones seem to have more of a feeling of motion or a need for resolution. They may refer to them as *strong* pitches and *weak* pitches, somewhat as pulses or beats are called strong or weak. To avoid any unnecessary and perhaps inaccurate connotations that terms such as these might suggest, we shall refer to these two classes of pitches as *triad* tones or pitches and *nontriad* tones or pitches.

For the present, we shall always use these terms in reference to the *tonic triad*—that is, the triad built on the first degree of the scale, key, or tonality. Later, we shall extend the use of the terms to apply them to other triads in a tonality. For now, the term *triad pitches* will refer to degrees $\hat{1}$, $\hat{3}$, and $\hat{5}$ of a tonality; the term *nontriad pitches* will refer to degrees $\hat{2}$, $\hat{4}$, $\hat{6}$, and $\hat{7}$ of a tonality.

Many simple melodies are characterized by a clear emphasis on triad tones and a secondary use of nontriad tones. Study, for example, "Three Blind Mice" (Ex. 14–1) for its use of triad tones and nontriad tones.

SCALAR AND NEIGHBOR TONE PATTERNS

Throughout this book we have emphasized the importance of seeing and hearing patterns rather than individual notes. We shall now consider two types of pitch patterns that involve only stepwise motion—scalar patterns and neighbor tone patterns. *Scalar patterns* involve stepwise motion in one direction, ascending or descending. These patterns may consist of three or more pitches, as illustrated in Ex. 16–5.

Ex. 16–5

Mendelssohn: Overture to a Midsummer Night's Dream
1.

Bach: "Ein' Feste Burg Ist Unser Gott"
2.

Beethoven: Symphony No. 2, third movement
3.

Neighbor tone patterns, as the name suggests, involve the sounding of one pitch, then the sounding of the pitch directly above (upper neighbor, or UN) or directly below (lower neighbor, or LN), and then a return to the original pitch. Neighbor-tone patterns are illustrated in Ex. 16–6.

Ex. 16–6

Before you begin the music-reading and ear-training exercises in this chapter, practice performing scalar and neighbor tone patterns in various scales or modes, using exercises such as the following:

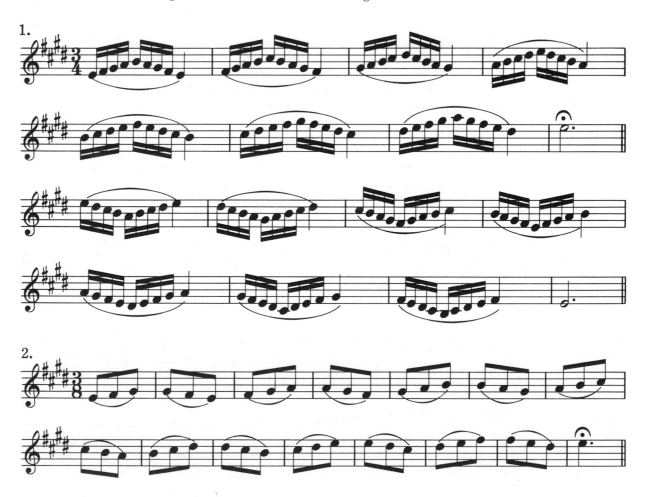

From this point on, you should always determine the tonality and scale basis of each exercise and drill on these before beginning the exercise.

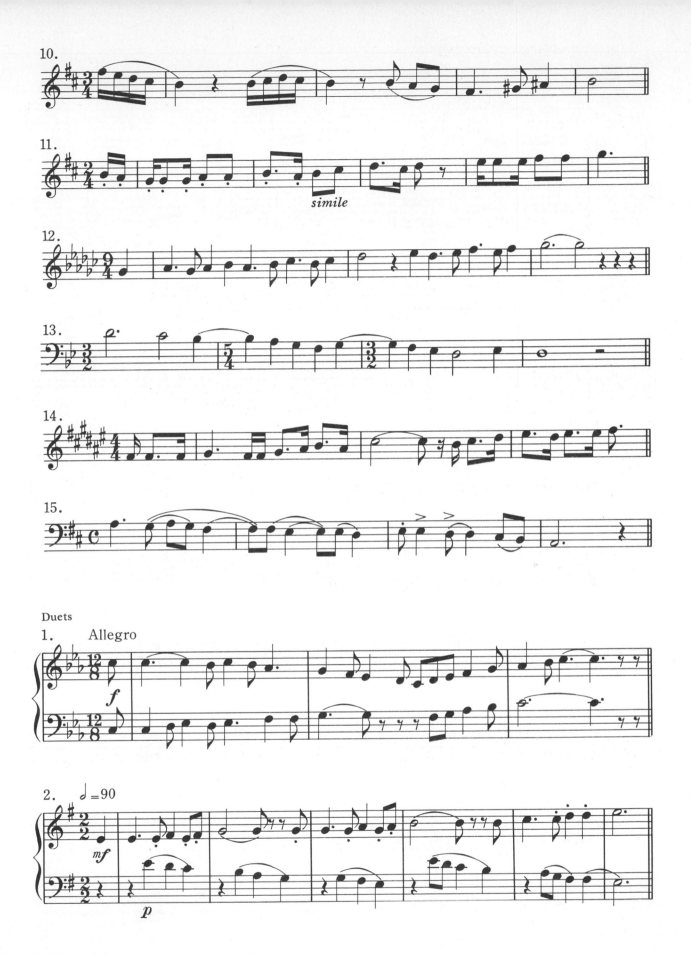

Fill in the missing measures. Answers appear below each exercise.

Complete both parts.

Duets

EXAMPLES FROM LITERATURE

1. Tchaikovsky: Symphony No. 4, third movement

2. Mendelssohn: Symphony No. 3, second movement

3. Mozart: Symphony No. 41, fourth movement

4. Sibelius: Symphony No. 2, first movement

5. J.S.Bach: "Christ lag in Todesbanden"

6. Tchaikovsky: Symphony No. 4, third movement

7. Tchaikovsky: Symphony No. 5, second movement

254

1. Analyze examples from the literature aurally and visually, and see how they differ from one another in terms of pitch hierarchy. For example, listen to the opening of Ravel's String Quartet in F Major and to the opening of Mozart's Sonata for Piano in C Major, K. 545, and see which piece emphasizes more clearly the triad tones over the nontriad tones.

2. Compose four examples similar to the ear-training exercises in this chapter, and work on them with your partner.

3. Use phrase marks to analyze musical gestures in various exercises from this chapter and preceding chapters.

4. Until now, all of our supplementary work has been with single lines. You might find it interesting now to compose, hear, and sing examples that have a melodic line accompanied by rhythms. Two such examples are given below. Perform them and then create similar examples. Notice that it is effective to have contrasting rhythms in the two parts. You may perform the rhythmic accompaniment by clapping, by tapping, or by playing a percussion instrument.

chapter 17

This chapter focuses primarily upon the melodic as well as the harmonic use of the tonic triad (major or minor). It is as important for musicians to master these uses as it is for them to master the various scale forms. Though many contemporary composers deliberately avoid using scale and triad passages, there is still an enormous body of literature in which these are the essential musical materials.

TRIADS

We have discussed the triad as a musical configuration formed by the tonic, mediant, and dominant pitches. A broader and more accurate definition of a triad is that it is any collection of three tones sounding successively (melodically) or simultaneously (harmonically). A triad that is formed with the interval of a third (major or minor) between tones is called a *tertian triad* (Latin: *tertius,* "third"). Other triads are called *nontertian.* A major triad consists of a major third followed by a minor third; a minor triad consists of a minor third followed by a major third. In both cases, there is a perfect fifth between the outer tones.

By now, you should be able to write triads quickly because of your familiarity with scales. There is another way to learn to write or recognize major triads, which can be used for all triads, even those that cannot be easily related to a scale. According to this system, major triads may be organized into three categories. We shall refer to the three notes constituting the triad as 1, 3, and 5.

CATEGORY A: *1, 3, and 5 all have the same sign.* Triads based on C, F, and G or on any altered version of these tones fall into this category. (See Ex. 17-1.)

Ex. 17-1

Using this rule, write major triads above the following tones.

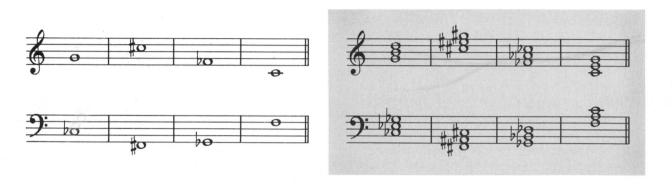

CATEGORY B: *1 and 5 have the same sign, 3 is one accidental higher.* Triads based on d, e, and a or on any altered version of these tones fall into this category. (See Ex. 17-2.)

Ex. 17-2

Using this rule, write major triads based on the following tones.

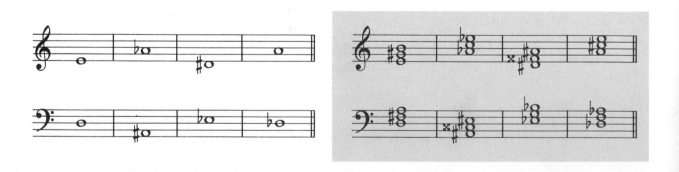

CATEGORY C: *3 and 5 are both one accidental higher than 1.* Triads based on b or on any altered version of this tone fall into this category. (See Ex. 17-3.)

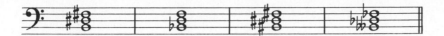

Write major triads based on the following tones.

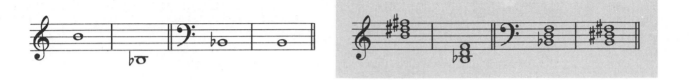

Using these three categories, write triads based on the following tones. Try to write the triads as quickly as possible. Play and sing each triad.

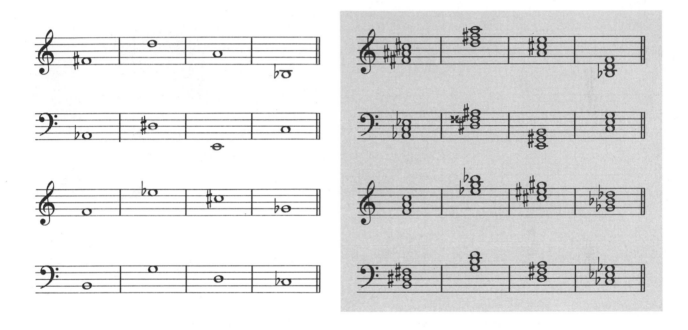

Once you have gained speed and accuracy in writing major triads, it is easy to change them to minor triads simply by lowering the mediant ($\hat{3}$) a chromatic half step.

Change the following major triads to minor triads.

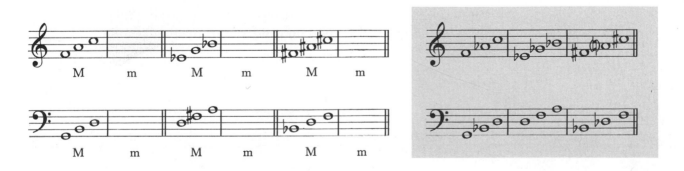

Write the indicated minor triads above the given tones.

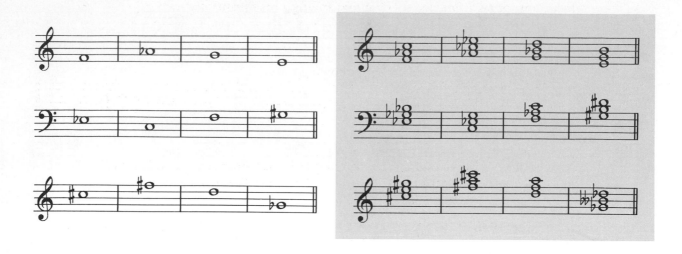

Identify the following as major ls or minor triads (M = major, m = minor).

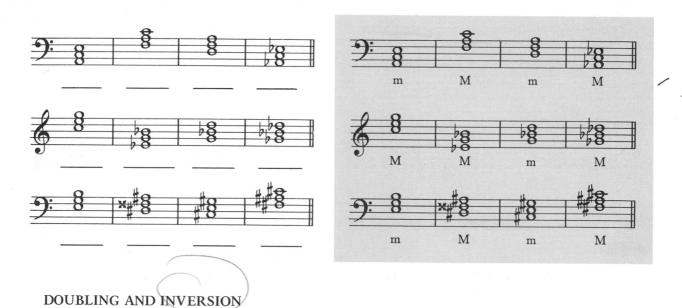

DOUBLING AND INVERSION

The bottom or "1" note of a triad is called the root of the triad; the other tones are called the third and fifth, respectively. It is possible to double or to replace any note of a triad with notes one or more octaves above or below. Thus, the triads in Ex. 17–4 are all versions of the F major triad. Play them on the piano, and notice that despite some difference in sound, they all have a basic similarity.

Ex. 17–4

As long as the root of the triad is the lowest sounding note, the triad is said to be in *root position.* Ex. 17–5 shows triads in root position.

Ex. 17–5

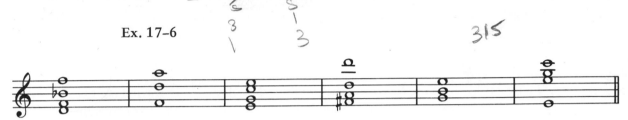

If the third of the triad is sounded as the lowest note, the triad is said to be in *first inversion.* All the triads in Ex. 17–6 are in first inversion.

Ex. 17–6

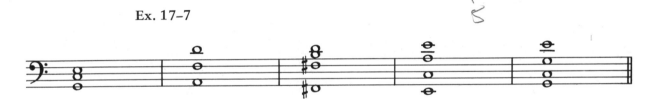

If the fifth of the triad is sounded as the lowest note, the triad is said to be in *second inversion.* All the triads in Ex. 17–7 are in second inversion.

Ex. 17–7

To find the root of a triad, regardless of doubling or inversion, you must rearrange the pitches so that they are in consecutive thirds. The root is then the lowest tone. A quick way to find the root is to look for the perfect fifth or the perfect fourth. The root will be the top of the perfect fourth or the bottom of the perfect fifth. (See Ex. 17–8.)

Ex. 17–8

Determine the root of the following triads, and indicate whether the triad is major (M) or minor (m). To indicate the root, use a small arrow, as in the following example.

261

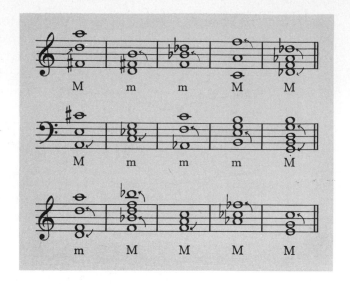

Once you have learned to recognize easily what the root of a triad is, it is easy to determine whether the triad is in root position, first inversion, or second inversion by seeing which note is the lowest sounded—the root, the third, or the fifth.

Indicate the root (↗) of the following triads, the type of triad (M or m), and whether the triad is in root position (R), first inversion (1st), or second inversion (2nd).

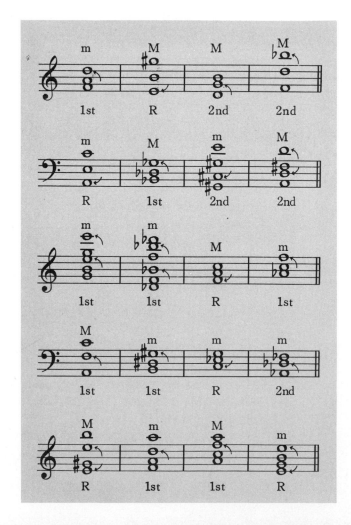

MELODIC TRIAD PATTERNS

We have been dealing with triads as harmonic entities. Now we must learn to deal with them as melodic entities. Study and practice the patterns in Ex. 17–9, first by sounding the triad harmonically on the piano and then by singing the various patterns that follow. Ex. 17–9 does not illustrate all of the possible melodic patterns based upon triads, but if you learn to master the patterns that are illustrated, other patterns may easily be derived from them.

Ex. 17–9

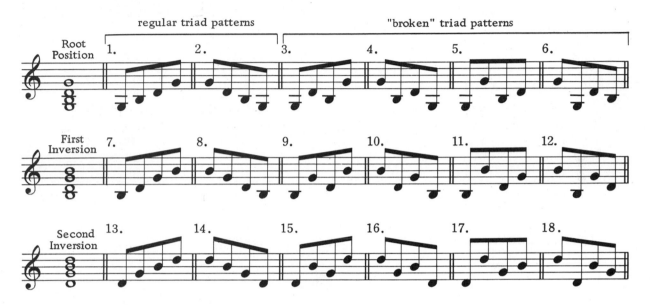

Repeat this exercise, using other major and minor triads.

The aural exercises that follow include triad patterns as well as the scalar and neighbor-tone patterns studied in the previous chapter.

MUSIC-READING EXERCISES 17

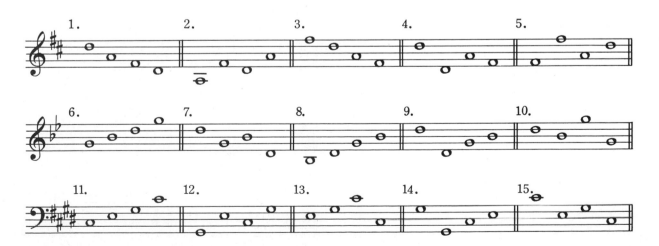

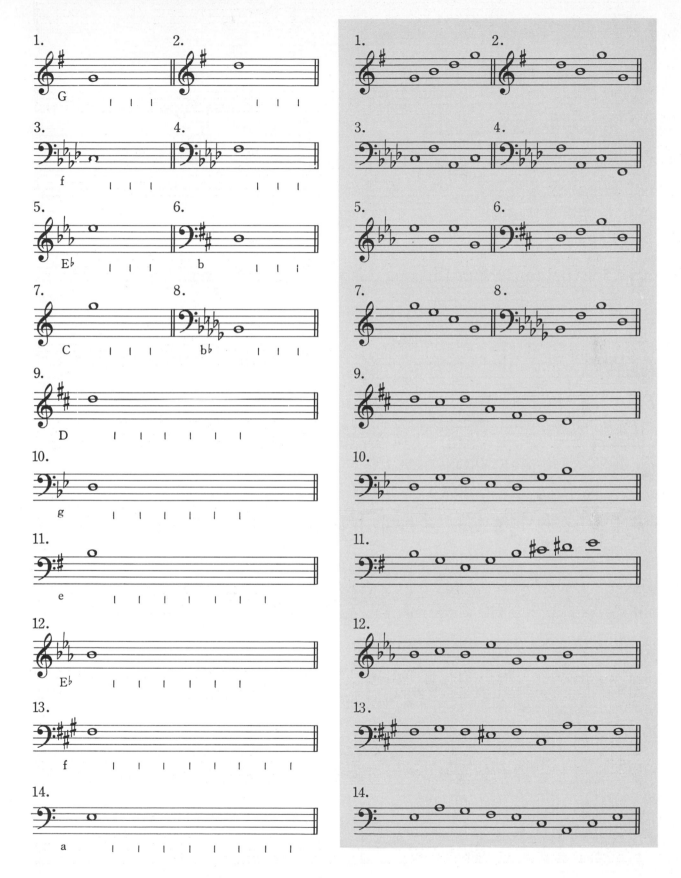

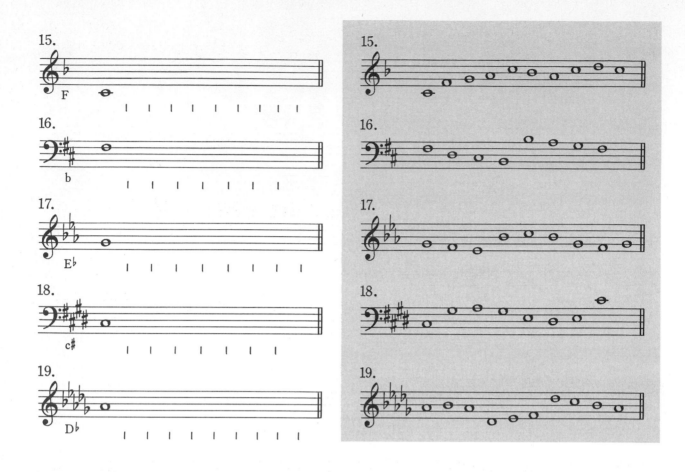

MUSIC-READING EXERCISES 17A

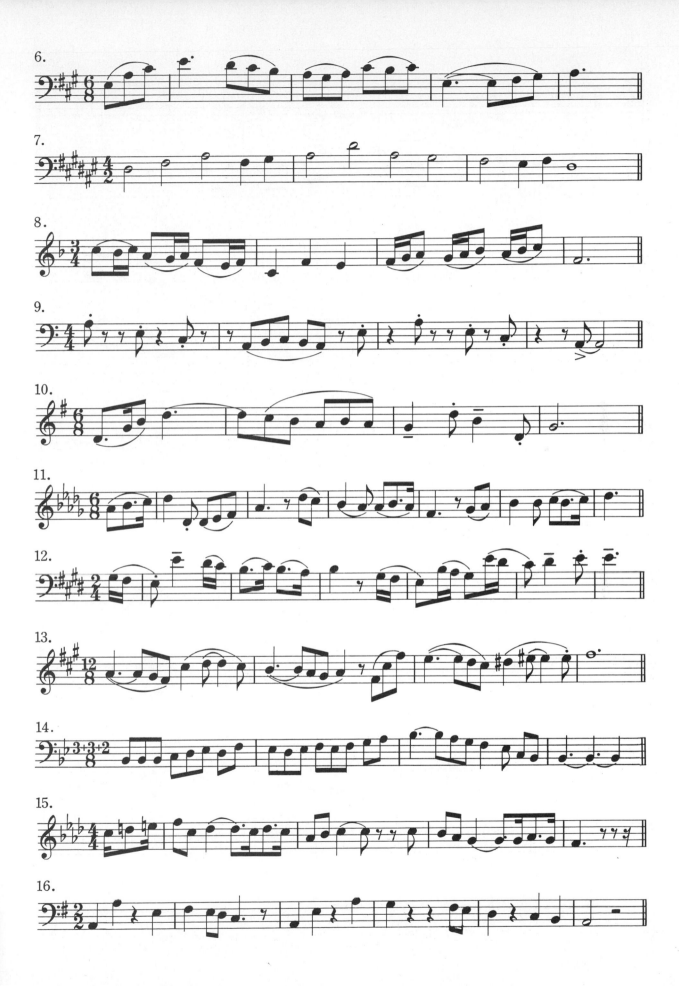

Duets

1. Andante

2. Allegro

3. Moderato

4. Vivace

5. ♩=120

Fill in the empty bars. Answers appear below the exercises.

Answers are on the facing page.

Duets

1.
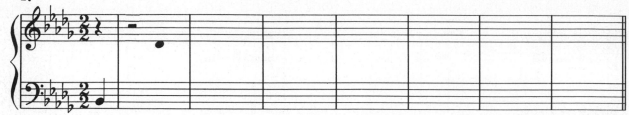

2.

3.

4.
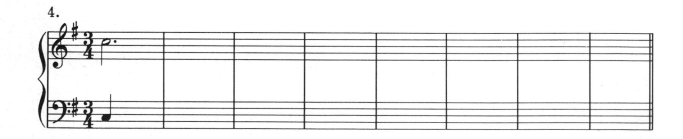

270

Identify the following chords as Major (M) or minor (m).

1._____   2._____   3._____

4._____   5._____   6._____

7._____   8._____   9._____

10._____   11._____   12._____

13._____   14._____   15._____

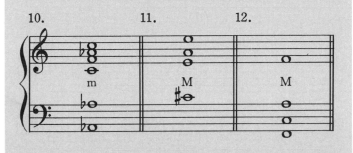

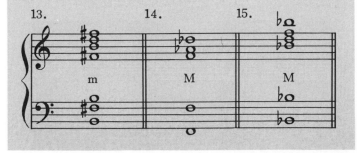

EXAMPLES FROM LITERATURE

1. Wagner: *Die Meistersinger von Nürnberg*

2. Tchaikovsky: Symphony No. 5, first movement

3. Smetana: *The Bartered Bride*

4. Saint-saëns: *Sampson and Delila*

5. Beethoven: Symphony No. 1, first movement

6. Beethoven: Symphony No. 2, first movement

7. Beethoven: Symphony no. 3, first movement

8. Beethoven: Symphony No. 4, first movement

9. Beethoven: Symphony No. 5, third movement

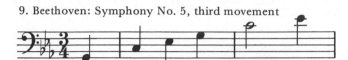

10. Beethoven: Symphony No. 6, third movement

11. Beethoven: Symphony No. 7, third movement

12. Beethoven: Symphony No. 9, first movement

SUPPLEMENTARY EXERCISES 17

1. Compose four examples similar to the ear-training exercises in this chapter, and work on them as ear-training material with your partner.

2. Experiment with playing triads in all inversions and spacings on the piano.

3. Analyze examples from the literature both visually and aurally for their use of triad sonorities.

4. You may now wish to experiment with adding a simple block chord or repeated chord accompaniment to some of your examples, using the tonic chord only as shown below.

OPTIONAL MATERIAL

The Overtone Series

You may be interested in one of the classic experiments of music theory. Go to a piano, depress (without sounding) the notes g, c^1, e^1, and g^1, and hold them down. Then strike the note C_1 as loudly as you can, release it, and let it ring. Listen carefully and you will hear the notes g, c^1, e^1, and g^1 also ringing, but somewhat fainter.

These upper notes were set into sympathetic vibration by the *overtones* of the low C_1. Whenever a string or other vibrating body is set in motion, it vibrates not only as a whole but also in proportional parts. The vibrations of the whole string produce the fundamental sound—that is, the one we hear most prominently. The faster vibrations of the proportional parts of the string produce higher pitches, or overtones. Overtones are much softer than the fundamental and are not usually heard as separate pitches unless we reinforce them, as we did in our experiment. Instead, overtones impart to the fundamental pitch its particular tone quality, or timbre.

The overtones of any given note follow a certain order, as indicated in Ex. 17–10.

Ex. 17–10

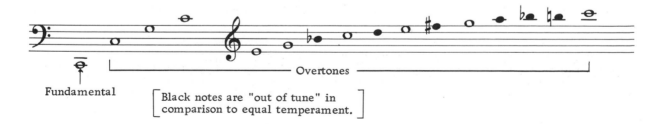

Notice that the major triad appears as a part of the overtone series. It could be said, therefore, that the major triad is in effect "given to us by nature." Because of this, many music theorists of the eighteenth and nineteenth centuries, and indeed some of the twentieth century, have claimed that the major triad is the very basis of music. According to these theorists, music begins with the natural perfection of the major triad, and everything else is derived from it.

In this book, we have not taken such a position. Although we recognize the major triad as a potent force in much music, we are not willing to give it the central role that natural-law theorists would. We urge you to become familiar with it to the same degree that you become familiar with other pitch patterns.

chapter 18

By now, you should have gained facility in singing tonal or modal melodies that involve scalar patterns, neighbor-tone patterns, and tonic-triad patterns. The only leaps we have had in the last few chapters have been leaps between triad pitches.

LEAPS INVOLVING NONTRIAD PITCHES

Although some examples from music literature are limited to these types of pitch motion, many examples, such as those in Ex. 18–1, have leaps to or from pitches that are not members of the tonic triad. These are bracketed in Ex. 18–1.

Ex. 18–1

How shall we perform these? One obvious way is to sing from note to note, using our sense of pitch distance or interval recognition (Ex. 18–2).

However, there is another, more efficient way of singing such passages in a tonal or modal context. Notice that in every passage in Ex. 18–2 the nontriad pitch is an upper or lower neighbor of a triad pitch; that is, it lies a half or a whole step above or below a triad pitch. If you have the triad pitches clearly in mind, you should be able to hear or perform leaps to or from nontriad pitches by relating them to a tonic-triad pitch. Ex. 18–3 shows how this technique could be applied to the passage in Ex. 18–2.

Ex. 18–3

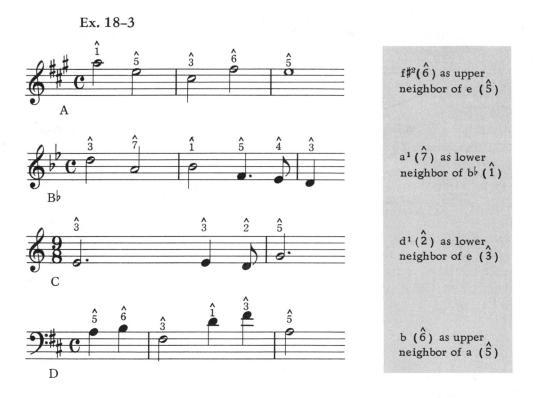

Although this technique may seem somewhat complicated at first, with practice you will find that it becomes more natural and helpful. The patterns in Ex. 18–4 are designed to help you master these relationships. Notice that you first establish two triad pitches (given in parentheses) and then sing patterns in which a nontriad pitch (scale degrees $\hat{2}$, $\hat{4}$, $\hat{6}$, or $\hat{7}$) is inserted between the two triad pitches (scale degrees $\hat{1}$, $\hat{3}$, or $\hat{5}$). Practice this exercise in various keys and modes and in various rhythms. Concentrate on the first fifty-two patterns because they are used more frequently in music. This exercise is written in C major. Practice it in other tonalities as well.

Ex. 18-4

OTHER PITCH PATTERNS

Two other patterns that appear frequently in music are the *broken-third pattern* and the *turn pattern*. Broken-third patterns may appear in several forms, as illustrated in Ex. 18–5. Practice these patterns in various keys and modes.

Ex. 18–5

Turn patterns are essentially derived from neighbor-tone patterns, as can be seen from Ex. 18–6.

Ex. 18–6

3.

4.

MELODIC EMBELLISHMENTS

Some stereotyped pitch patterns have been used so frequently that composers use special signs or abbreviations to represent them rather than writing them out. These stereotyped patterns consist of a main note and one or more embellishing or decorative notes. Some of the more common embellishments, together with translations into regular notation, are illustrated in Ex. 18–7.

Ex. 18–7

HEARING ANY PITCH IN A TONALITY

By now, you should have developed a sense of the function of each note or degree in a tonality as a result of having worked with the various pitch patterns. The following exercises may be helpful in further developing your ability to identify or produce quickly any pitch or degree in a given tonality.

First sing a scale, and then sing the appropriate triad. Sing slowly enough so that you can remember the sound and functional importance of each pitch. Then think of any pitch in the tonality, try to imagine how it would sound, sing it, and, finally, play that pitch on the piano in order to check your accuracy. After a little practice, you should find that you can do this accurately and quickly.

Next, repeat the same process with a drill partner. Warm up by singing scales, triads, and isolated pitches in the tonality. Then play pitches in the tonality at random, and have your partner name them.

A variation of the last learning technique is to play several notes in a tonality rapidly, stop on a particular note, and have your partner name this pitch (Ex. 18–8).

Ex. 18–8

Eventually, you should move from playing and identifying single pitches to playing two, three, four, or more pitches, which your partner should be able to identify immediately. In developing your ability to hear pitches, you will probably be using some combination of the various skills we have discussed throughout this text—that is, pitch memory, and recognition of pitch function and pitch distance.

The aural exercises that follow incorporate the techniques discussed in this chapter. Notice that no longer do only triad notes appear in important places, such as the beginnings of measures or the ends of phrases.

Before singing these exercises, quickly establish the tonality by singing a scale and the tonic triad. Occasionally, as your skill improves, try to sing without this preparation.

MUSIC-READING EXERCISES 18

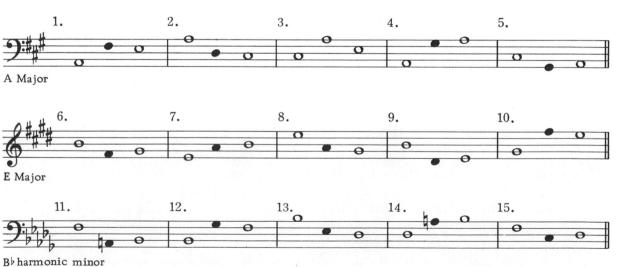

B Major

C Phrygian

D Lydian

eb minor (various forms)

Eb Major

b minor (harmonic)

Gb Major

e Phrygian

f minor (melodic)

A Major

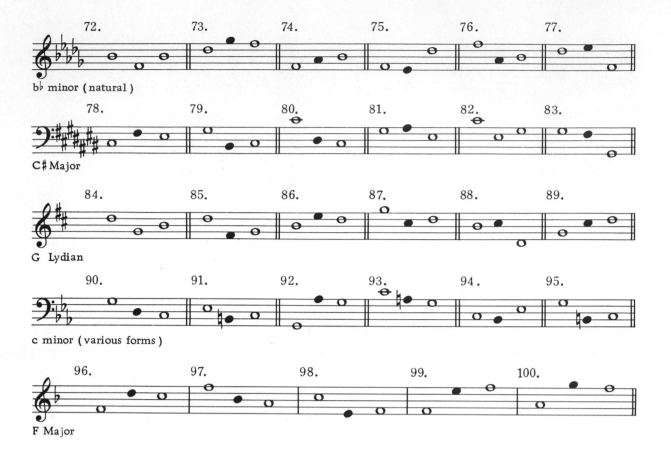

b♭ minor (natural)

C# Major

G Lydian

c minor (various forms)

F Major

EAR-TRAINING EXERCISES 18

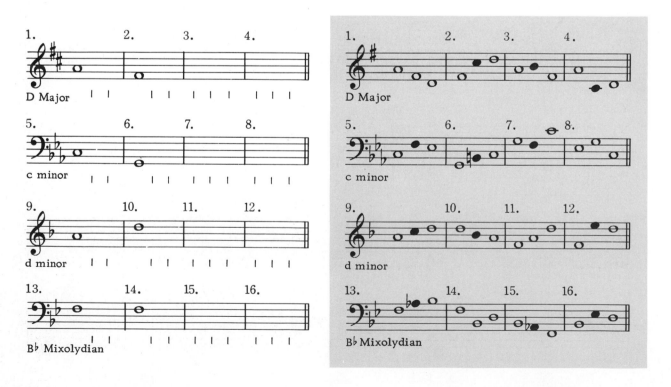

D Major

c minor

d minor

B♭ Mixolydian

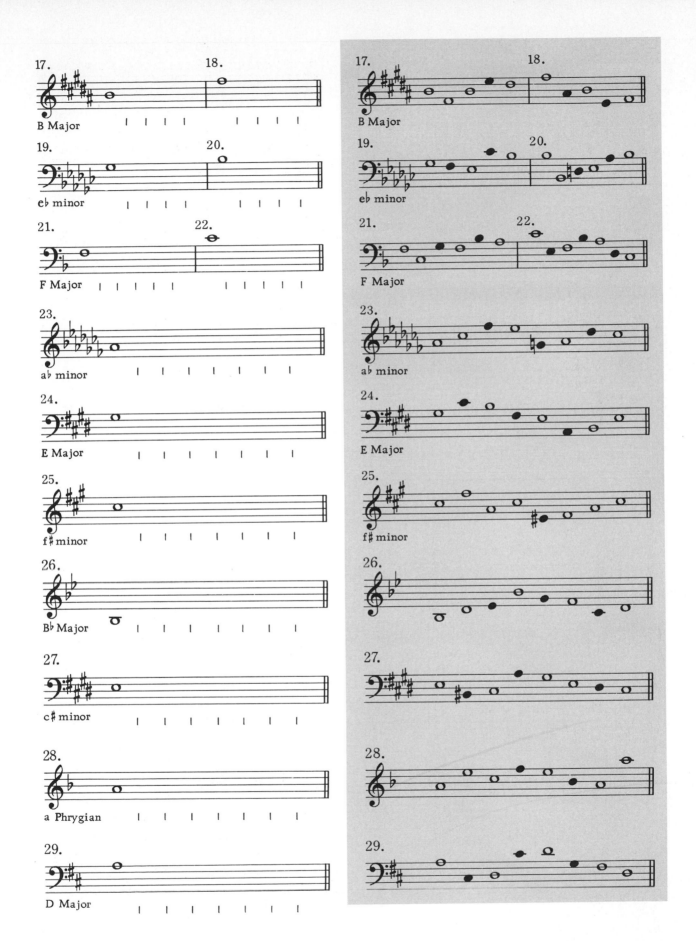

285

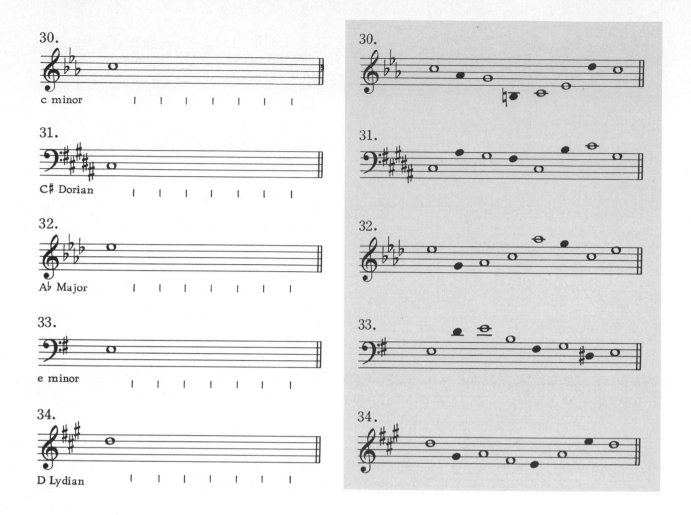

30. c minor

31. C# Dorian

32. A♭ Major

33. e minor

34. D Lydian

MUSIC-READING EXERCISES 18A

1.

2.

3.

4.

1. Andante

2. Grave

3. Moderato

EAR-TRAINING EXERCISES 18A

Complete the blank bars. Answers are given below the exercises.

1.

Eb Major

2.

Ab Major

3.

C Major

4.

e Phrygian

5.

d minor

Duets

1.

2.

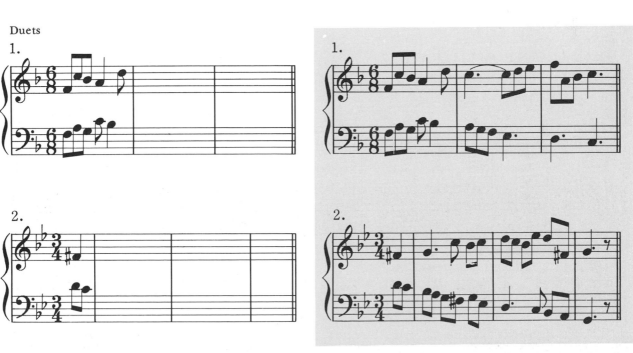

1.

2.

EXAMPLES FROM LITERATURE

1. Purcell: "To All Lovers of Music"

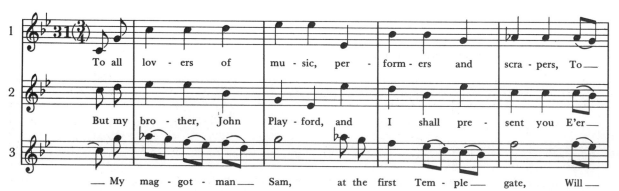

those that love—— catch - es, play—— tunes and cut ca - pers, With a

long with a book I pre - sume will con - tent you, 'Tis

fur - ther—— in - form you, If not, my wife—— Kate; From be -

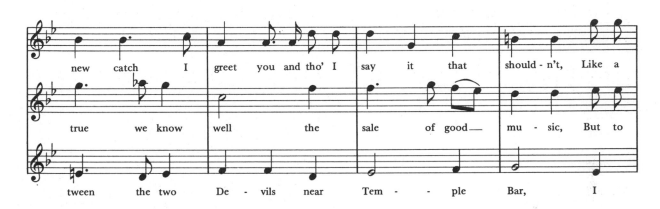

new catch I greet you and tho' I say it that should - n't, Like a

true we know well the sale of good—— mu - sic, But to

tween the two De - vils near Tem - ple Bar, I

fid - dle, 'tis mu - sic,—— tho' the words—— are but wood - en.

hear us—— per - form would make—— him sick—— or —— you sick.

rest, your friend and ser - vant John Carr.

2. Purcell: "Of All the Instruments That Are"

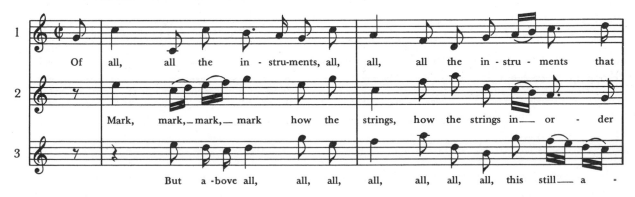

Of all, all the in - stru-ments, all, all, all the in - stru - ments that

Mark, mark,—— mark,—— mark how the strings, how the strings in - or - der

But a - bove all, all, all, all, all, all, all, this still—— a -

291

are None, none, none, none, none, none, none, none, none, none, none,_____ with the

keep, With a whet, whet, whet, whet, whet, whet, whet, whet, whet, whet, whet, whet, whet and a

bounds, With a zin-gle, zin-gle, zin-gle, zin-gle, zin-gle, zin-gle, zin-gle, zin-gle zing and a

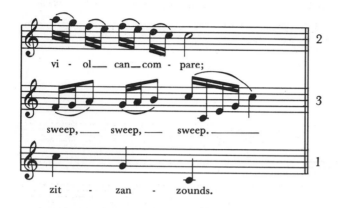

vi - ol___ can___ com - pare; **2**

sweep,___ sweep,___ sweep.___ **3**

zit - zan - zounds. **1**

3. Purcell: "Fie, Nay Prithee, John"

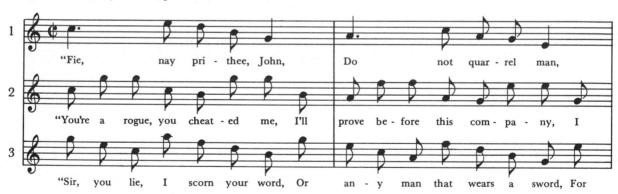

1 "Fie, nay pri - thee, John, Do not quar-rel man,

2 "You're a rogue, you cheat-ed me, I'll prove be - fore this com - pa - ny, I

3 "Sir, you lie, I scorn your word, Or an - y man that wears a sword, For

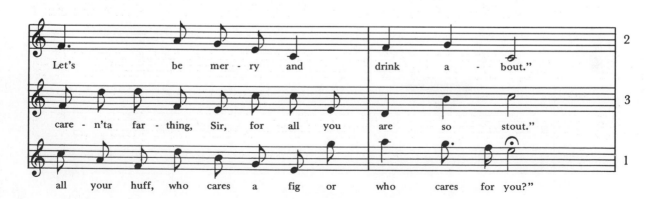

Let's be mer - ry and drink a - bout." **2**

care - n'ta far - thing, Sir, for all you are so stout." **3**

all your huff, who cares a fig or who cares for you?" **1**

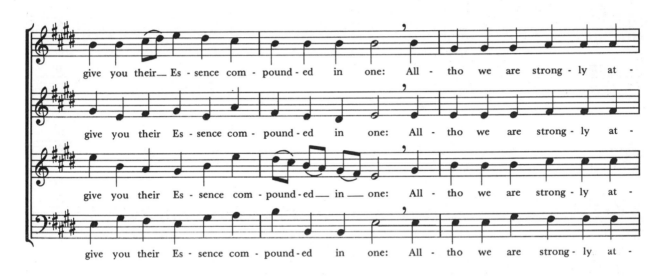

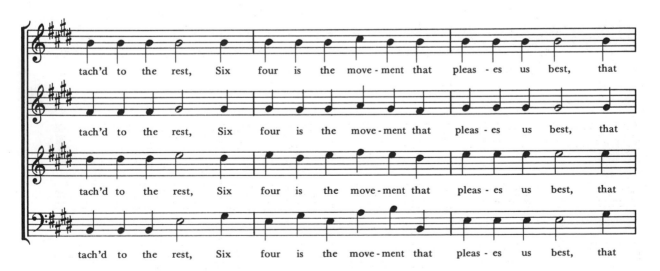

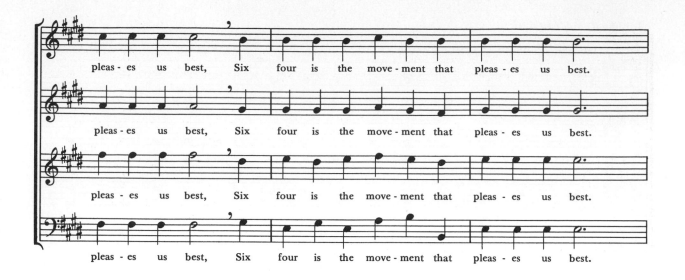

pleas - es us best, Six four is the move - ment that pleas - es us best.

pleas - es us best, Six four is the move - ment that pleas - es us best.

pleas - es us best, Six four is the move - ment that pleas - es us best.

pleas - es us best, Six four is the move - ment that pleas - es us best.

And now we ad - dress you as Friends to the cause (Per -

And now we ad - dress you as Friends to the cause (Per -

And now we ad - dress you as Friends to the cause (Per -

And now we ad - dress you as Friends to the cause (Per -

form - ers are mod - est and write their own laws): Al - tho we are san - guine and

form - ers are mod - est and write their own laws): Al - tho we are san - guine and

form - ers are mod - est and write their own laws): Al - tho we are san - guine and

form - ers are mod - est and write their own laws): Al - tho we are san - guine and

294

clap at the Bars, 'tis the part of the Hear-ers to clap their Ap-plause, to___

clap at the Bars, 'tis the part of the Hear-ers to clap their Ap-plause, to

clap at the Bars, 'tis the part of the Hear-ers to clap their Ap-plause, to

clap at the Bars, 'tis the part of the Hear-ers to clap their Ap-plause, to

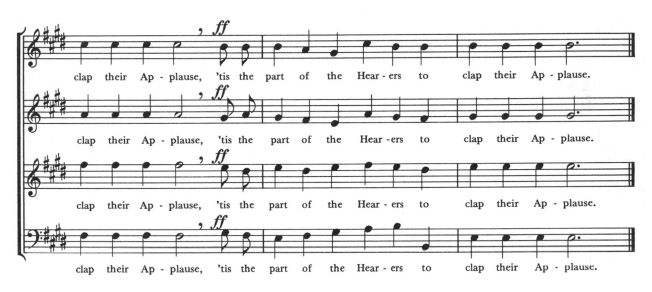

clap their Ap-plause, 'tis the part of the Hear-ers to clap their Ap-plause.

clap their Ap-plause, 'tis the part of the Hear-ers to clap their Ap-plause.

clap their Ap-plause, 'tis the part of the Hear-ers to clap their Ap-plause.

clap their Ap-plause, 'tis the part of the Hear-ers to clap their Ap-plause.

5. J. S. Bach: "Jesu, Meine Freude"

6. Monteverdi: *Zefiro torna,* Ciaccona

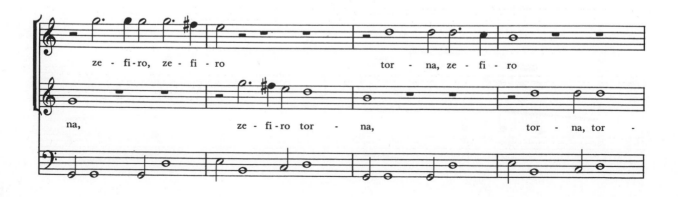

SUPPLEMENTARY EXERCISES 18

1. Compose four examples similar to the ear-training exercises in this chapter, and work on them with your partner.

2. Study the literature for examples of patterns studied in this chapter.

3. Experiment with other accompaniment types, still basing them on the tonic triad only. Some possibilities are shown below.

chapter 19

In this chapter, we shall complete our study of intervals and also discuss other clefs used in music.

SIXTHS, SEVENTHS, AND OCTAVES

You have actually been hearing and performing sixths, sevenths, and octaves in the last few chapters, but we have not studied their nomenclature. Study the following table.

Descriptive Name	Numerical Name	Abbreviations	Half Steps	Whole Steps	Examples
Diminished	sixth	°6	7	$3\frac{1}{2}$	c–a$\flat\flat$, d$\sharp$–b$\flat$, e$\sharp$–c^1
Minor	sixth	m6	8	4	c–a$\flat$, d$\sharp$–b, f$\sharp$–d^1
Major	sixth	M6	9	$4\frac{1}{2}$	c–a, d$\sharp$–b$\sharp$, g$\flat$–e$\flat^1$
Augmented	sixth	+6	10	5	c–a$\sharp$, d$\flat$–b, f$\sharp$–d$\times^1$
Diminished	seventh	°7	9	$4\frac{1}{2}$	c–b$\flat\flat$, d$\sharp$–c^1, g–f$\flat^1$
Minor	seventh	m7	10	5	c–b$\flat$, d$\sharp$–c$\sharp^1$, g–f^1
Major	seventh	M7	11	$5\frac{1}{2}$	c–b, e–d$\sharp^1$, g$\flat$–f^1
Augmented	seventh	+7	12	6	c–b$\sharp$, e–d$\times^1$, g$\flat$–f$\sharp^1$
Diminished	octave	°8	11	$5\frac{1}{2}$	c–c$\flat^1$, e$\sharp$–e^1, g$\flat$–g$\flat\flat$ ^{1}
Perfect	octave	P8	12	6	c–c^1, d$\sharp$–d$\sharp^1$, f$\flat$–f$\flat^1$
Augmented	octave	+8	13	$6\frac{1}{2}$	c–c$\sharp^1$, d$\flat$–d^1, f$\sharp$–$\times^1$

An easier way to remember sixths and sevenths is to relate them to fifths and octaves, respectively:

1. A minor sixth is a diatonic half step above a perfect fifth.

2. A major sixth is a diatonic whole step above a perfect fifth.

3. A minor seventh is a diatonic whole step below a perfect octave.

4. A major seventh is a diatonic half step below a perfect octave.

Diminished and augmented sixths and sevenths may then be easily derived from the minor and major sixths and sevenths.

Identify the following intervals.

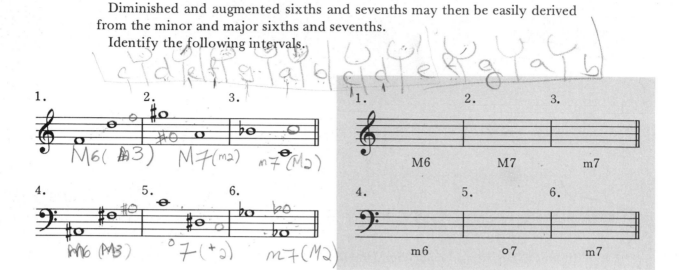

Write the indicated intervals above the given notes.

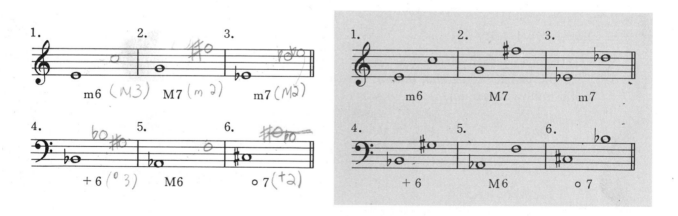

Write the indicated intervals below the given notes.

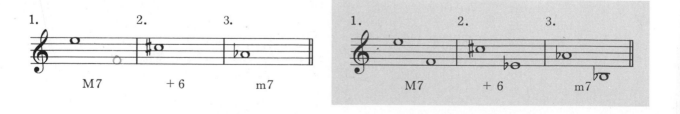

302

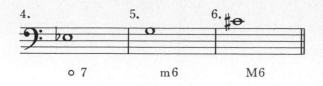 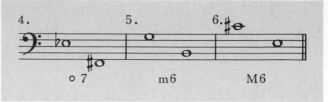

INTERVALS BASED ON THE MAJOR SCALE

If we move from the first degree of a major scale up to a note in the scale, the interval will always be major for seconds, thirds, sixths, and sevenths, and will always be perfect for unisons, fourths, fifths, and octaves. This knowledge can provide you with an easy way to identify or write intervals. You can find the major or perfect intervals from the scale; you can find minor, diminished, or augmented intervals by relating them to major or perfect intervals. The following examples show how this approach may be used:

Problem	*Solution*
Write a major sixth above D.	Regard D as the tonic of a major scale and move up to the sixth degree of this scale—that is, to B.
Write an augmented fourth above E.	Regard E as the tonic of a major scale and move up to the fourth degree of this scale—that is, to A. This is a perfect fourth; an augmented fourth, therefore, would be A♯.
Write a perfect fifth below A♭.	Regard A♭ as the fifth degree of a major scale and move down to the tonic—that is, to D♭.
Write a minor seventh above C.	Regard C as the tonic of a major scale and move up to the seventh degree of this scale—that is, to B. This is a major seventh; a minor seventh would be B♭.

Another approach that some people use in calculating intervals is to know all of the "white-key" intervals from memory and to relate other intervals to them. As with scales, the question of which is the best approach to intervals depends upon the individual and upon the situation. The ultimate goal in any case is instant recognition. In solving the following interval problems, experiment with various methods.

Identify the following intervals.

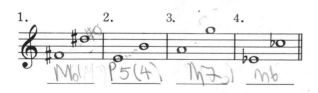 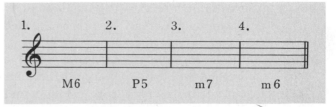

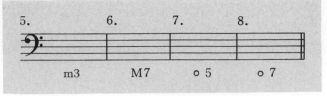

Write the indicated intervals above the given notes.

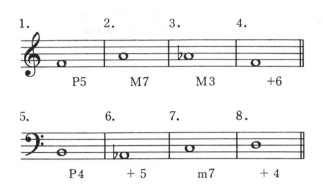

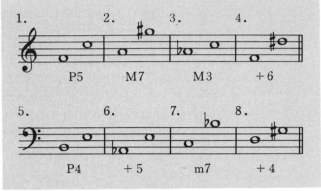

Write the indicated intervals below the given notes.

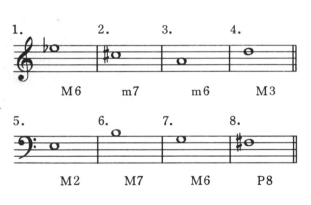

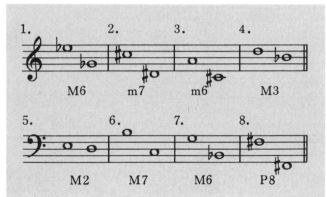

HARMONIC INTERVALS

We have been discussing only melodic intervals to this point, but it is also important for a musician to become acquainted with the characteristics of harmonic intervals (the simultaneous sounding of two pitches). Traditionally, harmonic intervals have been divided into three categories—*perfect consonances, imperfect consonances,* and *dissonances.* To discuss the rationale underlying this classification would lead us into one of the oldest and most vexing problems of music theory. Instead, we shall merely list the intervals that fall into each category and indicate some generally (though not universally) accepted characteristics of each classification. These characteristics may help you, but in the long run the best plan is to listen to the quality of the intervals and find your own characteristics.

Category	Intervals	Characteristics
Perfect consonances	Perfect octave, fourth, fifth, unison	Unisons and octaves sound like replications of the original pitch. Fourths and fifths may have a hollow or oriental sound.
Imperfect consonances	Major and minor thirds and sixths	These have a sweet, euphonious sound.
Dissonances	Major and minor seconds and sevenths, tritone	The sound of these intervals may be described as tense, not euphonious, unpleasant, unstable, and so on. In modern music, however, they may lose these characteristics.

Identify the following intervals as perfect consonances (perf. cons.), imperfect consonances (imp. cons.), or dissonances (diss.).

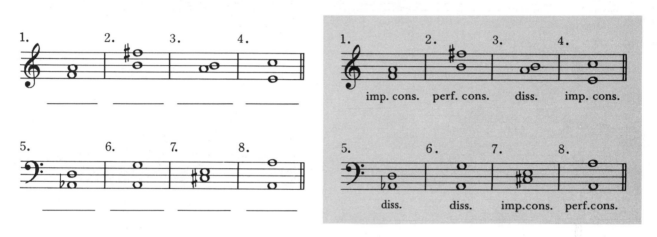

It is possible to relate both melodic and harmonic intervals to the major or minor triad. Thus, a major third could be heard as the root to third of a major triad or third to fifth of a minor triad. A perfect fifth could be heard as the root to fifth of a major or minor triad.

COMPOUND INTERVALS

Harmonic or melodic intervals larger than an octave are called *compound intervals*. These intervals are named in a manner similar to the equivalent intervals within the octave. Thus, ninths and tenths, like seconds and thirds, are called major or minor; elevenths and twelfths, like fourths and fifths, are called perfect; and so forth. Compound harmonic intervals generally have the same characteristics as the equivalent intervals within the octave. Thus, ninths, like seconds, are dissonances; tenths, like thirds, are imperfect consonances; and so on. This does not apply to compound melodic intervals, however. A melodic ninth sounds quite different from a melodic second.

Identify the following compound intervals.

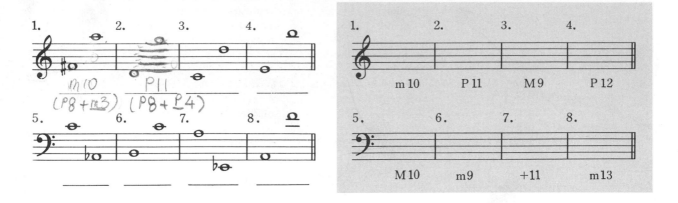

Write the indicated intervals above the given notes.

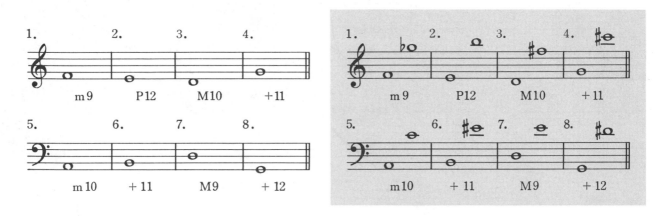

Write the indicated intervals below the given notes.

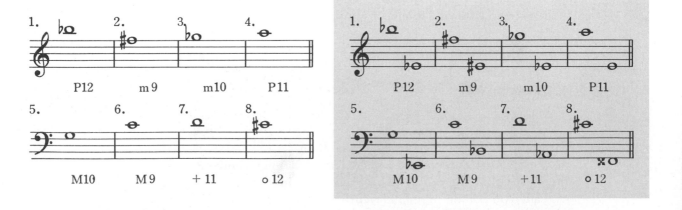

Any interval may be inverted by sounding the bottom tone one octave higher or the upper tone one octave lower (Ex. 19–1).

Ex. 19–1

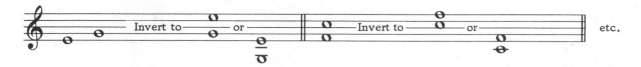

Invert the following intervals by writing the bottom note one octave higher. Identify the newly formed interval.

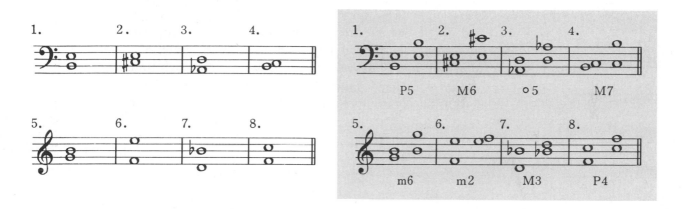

Invert the following intervals by writing the top note one octave lower. Identify the newly formed interval.

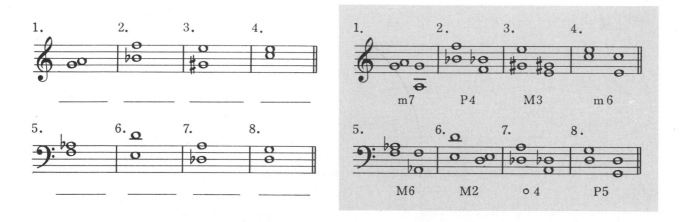

By now, you may have begun to develop some of a theorist's approach to musical materials. Look over the work you have just done, and see if you can formulate some general principles governing the inversion of intervals. Then complete the following statements.

1. Major intervals invert to ___minor___ intervals.
2. Minor intervals invert to ___major___ intervals.
3. Perfect intervals invert to ___perfect___ intervals.
4. Augmented intervals invert to ___diminished___ intervals.
5. Diminished intervals invert to ___augmented___ intervals.
6. The sum of the numerical designations of an interval and its inversion is always ___9___ .
7. In terms of interval category (perfect consonance, imperfect consonance, dissonance), an interval and its inversion are in the _____same_____ category.
(same or different)

If you answered all of the questions above correctly, you are beginning to develop a thoughtful, theoretical approach to musical materials. This does not mean that you must minimize your instinctive approach to music; you still need this if you are to be a complete musician. In the long run, however, developing an intellectual approach to music can make your instinctive responses more effective and reliable.

OTHER CLEFS

In addition to treble and bass clefs, musicians use other clefs. The most common of these are illustrated in Ex. 19–2, together with an indication of the *clef note*—that is, the note whose location is shown by the clef itself.

Ex. 19–2

Alto clef   Tenor clef

These clefs are used for certain instruments, such as the viola, trombone, and cello, and their use makes it possible to write passages within the staff that otherwise would have to be written with many ledger lines (Ex. 19–3).

Ex. 19–3

It is beyond the scope of this introductory text to explain how you can develop facility in the use of these clefs, but you should at least gain some familiarity with the two most common C clefs, the alto and the tenor clefs. We suggest that in working the following exercises, you find notes by relating them to the given clef note—that is, C—and not by relating these clefs to treble or bass clef. In other words, regard the clef on its own terms, not as a transposition of treble or bass clef. To facilitate this approach, the exercises begin with the clef note and gradually work away from it.

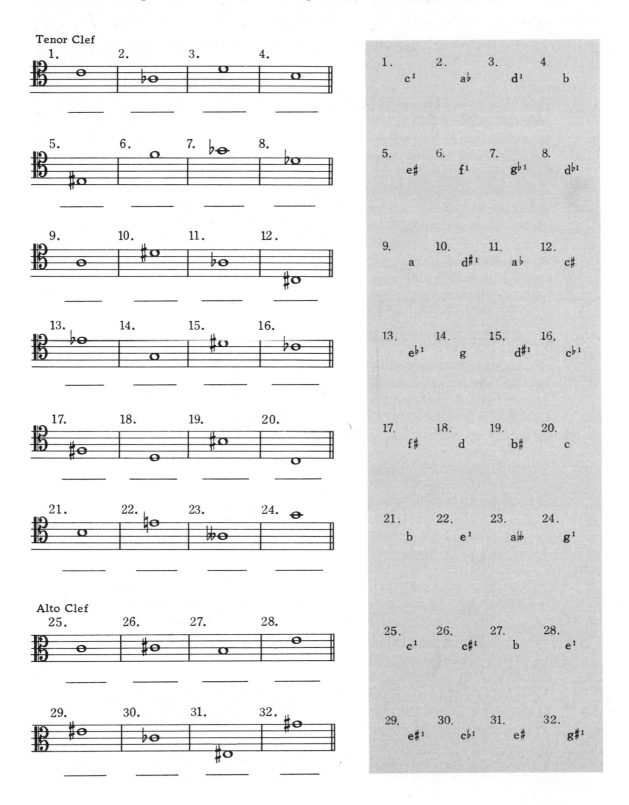

Tenor Clef

1.	2.	3.	4.
c¹	a♭	d¹	b

5.	6.	7.	8.
e♯	f¹	g♭¹	d♭¹

9.	10.	11.	12.
a	d♯¹	a♭	c♯

13.	14.	15.	16.
e♭¹	g	d♯¹	c♭¹

17.	18.	19.	20.
f♯	d	b♯	c

21.	22.	23.	24.
b	e¹	a♭♭	g¹

Alto Clef

25.	26.	27.	28.
c¹	c♯¹	b	e¹

29.	30.	31.	32.
e♯¹	c♭¹	e♯	g♯¹

Alto and Tenor Clef

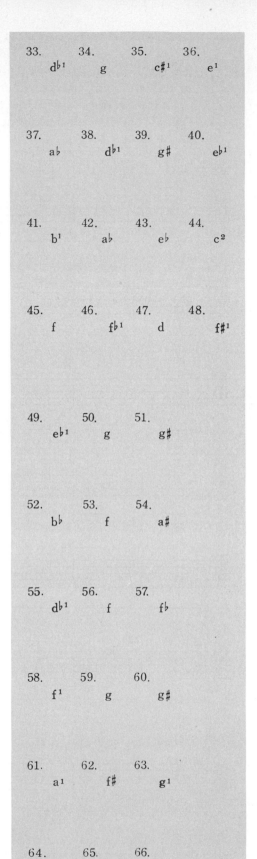

33.	34.	35.	36.
d♭¹	g	c♯¹	e¹

37.	38.	39.	40.
a♭	d♭¹	g♯	e♭¹

41.	42.	43.	44.
b¹	a♭	e♭	c²

45.	46.	47.	48.
f	f♭¹	d	f♯¹

49.	50.	51.
e♭¹	g	g♯

52.	53.	54.
b♭	f	a♯

55.	56.	57.
d♭¹	f	f♭

58.	59.	60.
f¹	g	g♯

61.	62.	63.
a¹	f♯	g¹

64.	65.	66.
f♯¹	e¹	d

310

Ex. 19-4 shows the correct placement of sharps and flats in key signatures in the alto and tenor clefs.

Ex. 19-4

Alto clef

Tenor clef

The music-reading exercises that follow stress the larger intervals and should be practiced very slowly and deliberately. At first, you may find it helpful to think of these larger leaps in terms of a major or minor scale, as indicated in Ex. 19-5.

Ex. 19-5

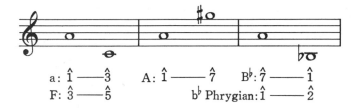

a: $\hat{1}$ —— $\hat{3}$ A: $\hat{1}$ —— $\hat{7}$ B♭: $\hat{7}$ —— $\hat{1}$

F: $\hat{3}$ —— $\hat{5}$ b♭ Phrygian: $\hat{1}$ —— $\hat{2}$

MUSIC-READING EXERCISES 19

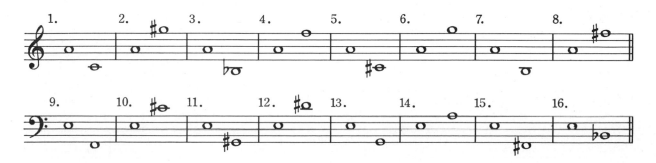

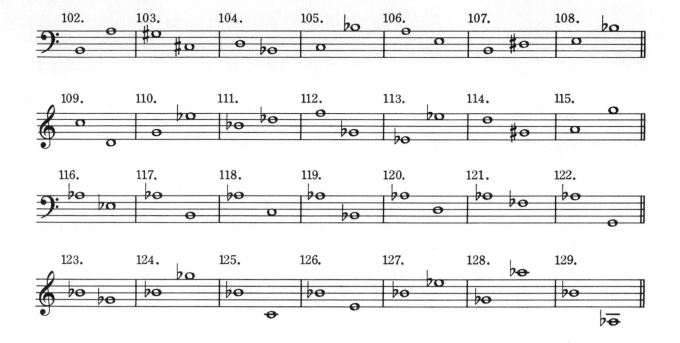

EAR-TRAINING EXERCISES 19

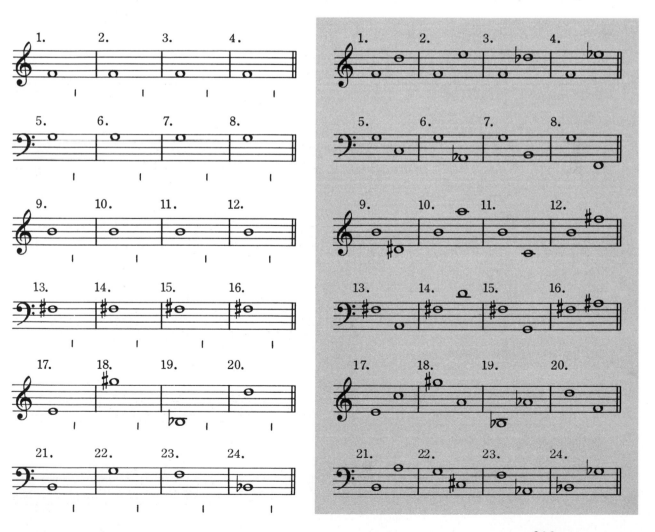

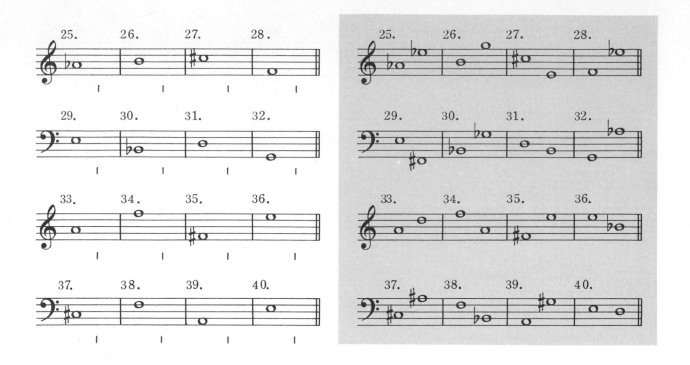

Multiple choice. Select the correct harmonic interval.

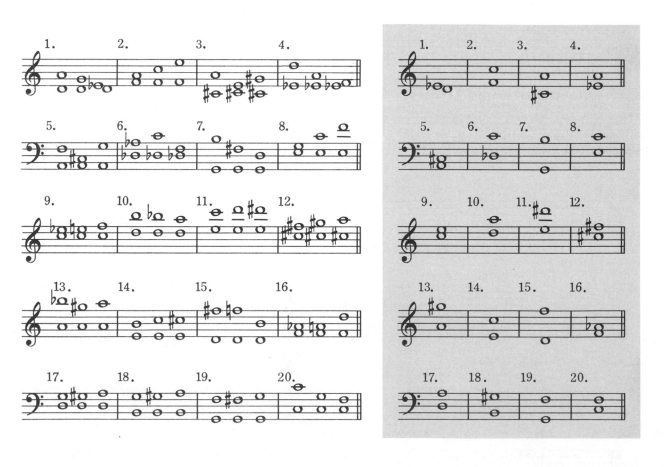

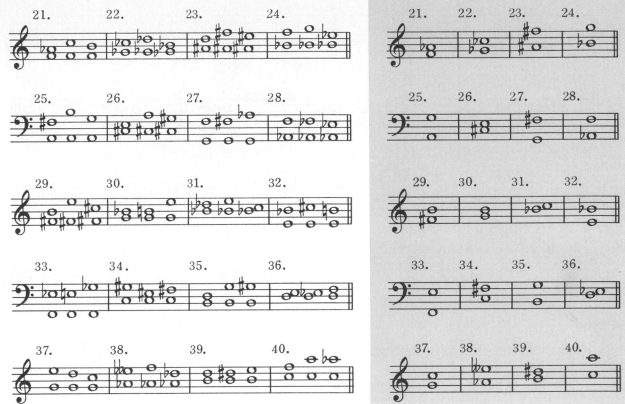
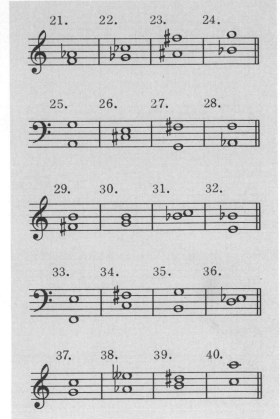

MUSIC-READING EXERCISES 19A

316

1. J. S. Bach: Cantata No. 140

mit Har - fen und mit Cym - beln schon,
whilst har - pers harp and trum - pets sound,

mit Har - fen und mit Cym - beln schon,
whilst har - pers harp and trum - pets sound,

mit Har - fen und mit Cym - beln schon,
whilst har - pers harp and trum - pets sound,

mit Har - fen und mit Cym - beln schon,
whilst har - pers harp and trum - pets sound,

Von zwölf Per - len sind die Pfor - ten
gates all pearl and streets all gol - den

Von zwölf Per - len sind die Pfor - ten
gates all pearl and streets all gol - den

Von zwölf Per - len sind die Pfor - ten
gates all pearl and streets all gol - den

Von zwölf Per - len sind die Pfor - ten
gates all pearl and streets all gol - den

an dei - ner Stadt; wir sind Con - sor - ten
in Si - on's ci - ty are be - hol - - den

an dei - ner Stadt; wir sind Con - sor - ten
in Si - on's ci - ty are be - hol - - den

an dei - ner Stadt; wir sind Con - sor - ten
in Si - on's ci - ty are be - hol - - den

an dei - ner Stadt; Wir sind Con - sor - ten
in Si - on's ci - ty are be - hol - - den

der En - gel hoch um dei - nen Thron.
by hap - py saints who en - ter in.

der En - gel hoch um dei - nen Thron.
by hap - py saints who en - ter in.

der En - gel hoch um dei - nen Thron.
by hap - py saints who en - ter in.

der En - gel hoch um dei - ner Thron.
by hap - py saints who en - ter in.

322

Dess sind wir froh, i - o! i -
Such end - less bliss; Our song be

Dess sind wir froh, i - o! i -
Such end - less bliss; Our song be

Dess sind wir froh, i - o! i -
Such end - less bliss; Our song be

Dess sind wir froh, i - o! i -
Such - end - less bliss; Our - song be

o! e - wig in dul - ci ju - bi - lo.
this: sem - per in dul - ci ju - bi - lo.

o! e - wig in dul - ci ju - bi - lo.
this: sem - per in dul - ci ju - bi - lo.

o! e - wig in dul - ci ju - bi - lo.
this: sem - per in dul - ci ju - bi - lo.

o! e - wig in dul - ci ju - bi - lo.
this: sem - per in dul - ci ju - bi - lo.

2. Handel: *Israel in Egypt,* No. 4 (chorus)

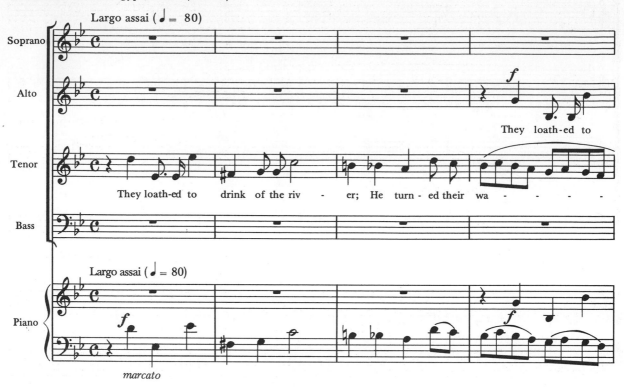

turn - ed their wa - ters in - to blood; they loath - - - -
- - ed to drink of the riv - er, they loath - ed, they loath - -
- ed, they loath - ed to drink of the
they loath - ed to drink of the riv - -

- - ed to drink of the riv - ver, they loath - ed, they loath - ed to drink of the
- - ed to drink of the riv - er, they loath - ed, they
riv - er,
er; He turn - ed their wa - ters in - to blood; they

river, they loath-ed, they loath-ed, they loath-ed to drink of the riv - er.

loath - ed to drink of the riv - er, they loath-ed to drink of the riv - er.

they loath - ed to drink of the riv - er.

loath - - - - - ed, they loath-ed to drink of the riv - er.

3. Haydn: Quartet Op. 76, No. 3, second movement

Poco adagio cantabile

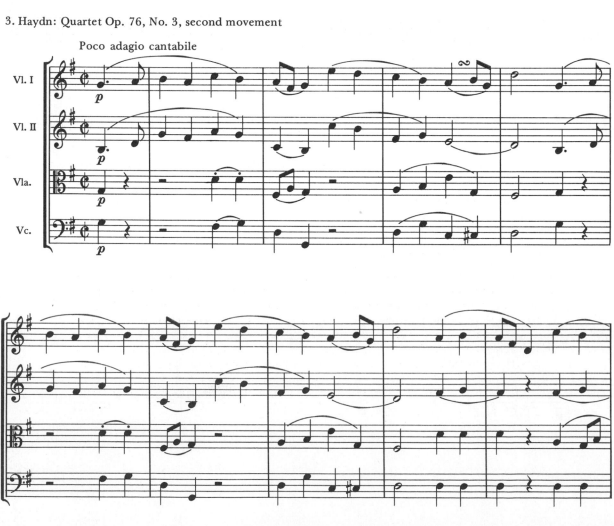

SUPPLEMENTARY EXERCISES 19

1. Listen to the second movement of Bartók's *Concerto for Orchestra,* and try to determine which harmonic intervals are featured.

2. Compose four examples similar to the ear-training exercises in this chapter, and work on them with your partner.

3. Experiment with writing, performing, and taking by dictation melodies written in other clefs, especially alto and tenor.

4. Experiment with writing two melodies together. The technique of writing two or more simultaneously sounding melodies is part of the study of counterpoint, and this will be a significant aspect of your advanced work in music theory. Although we cannot hope to convey to you all the necessary procedures for writing counterpoint at this time, we would recommend that you gain some introductory experience with this fascinating technique at this point. The results may not sound like Bach, Beethoven, or Bartók, but the exercise will give you some notion of the problems that these and other composers faced in trying to combine two or more melodies in a musical texture.

   At this point, we shall just give you three general principles (not rules) to think about as you write:

a. Try to write two melodies that are relatively independent in the pitch and duration parameters, such that they can be heard clearly as two melodies, not as one melody with a musical shadow. You thereby avoid having the two parts move too often in the same rhythmic patterns or pitch patterns. In particular, avoid writing parallel octaves or fifths.

Parallel Octaves

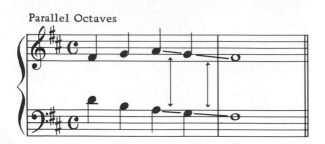

Parallel Fifths

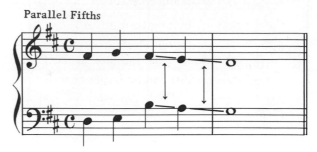

b. Pay attention to the harmonic intervals formed between the two parts. If you want your composition to sound more conventional, use more consonances between the parts, especially at the beginning and end and on most of the first beats of the measures. If you want your composition to sound somewhat less conventional, use a higher proportion of dissonances.

c. Judge the final result by how it sounds, not by how it looks. As you write, try to hear the composition in your "mind's ear." Sing it through with your drill partner. Play it on the piano. Modify and change it in places where it does not satisfy you.

OPTIONAL MATERIAL

Inversion in Integer Notation; Interval Class

Inversion in integer notation may be accomplished easily by simply subtracting the number of the original interval from 12. Thus, the inversion of **I** 4 is **I** 8 (12 – 4 = 8); the inversion of **I** 1 is **I** 11 (12 – 1 = 11); the inversion of **I** 6 is **I** 6 (12 – 6 = 6).

An interval and its inversion share many of the same aural characteristics. Therefore, it has become customary in recent writings to refer to an interval and its inversion as belonging to the same *interval class* (IC). There are six interval classes, as follows:

Interval Class	*Interval and Inversion*		*Example in Pitch Notation*	
IC 1	I 1	I 11	c–c♯	c–b
IC 2	I 2	I 10	c–d	c–b♭
IC 3	I 3	I 9	c–e♭	c–a
IC 4	I 4	I 8	c–e	c–a♭
IC 5	I 5	I 7	c–f	c–g
IC 6	I 6	I 6	c–f♯	c–g♭

Test your comprehension of these concepts by completing the following exercise.

1. The inversion of **I** 2 is _____ .

2. The inversion of **I** 5 is _____ .

3. The inversion of **I** 3 is _____ .

4. **I** 4 and **I** 8 belong to interval class _____ .

5. **I** 1 and **I** 11 belong to interval class _____ .

6. Indicate the interval class to which the following intervals belong. Remember, no interval class can be larger than 6.

$\overline{\text{d–f♯}}$ $\overline{\text{b–g♭}}$ $\overline{\text{c♯–g}}$ $\overline{\text{d–a♯}}$

Compound Intervals

Compound intervals may be represented in integer notation in terms of the total number of half steps in the interval (**I** 14, **I** 18, **I** 33, and so on). Or they may be reduced by subtracting 12 or a multiple thereof, in which case **I** 14 would become **I** 2 (14 - 2 = 2); **I** 18 would become **I** 6 (18 - 12 = 6); and **I** 33 would become **I** 9 (33 - 24 = 9). Compound intervals belong to the same interval class as their "reduced" versions. Thus, **I** 14 and **I** 22 both belong to IC 2, and **I** 33 and **I** 27 both belong to IC 3.

Indicate the interval class for each of the following. Remember that no interval class may be larger than 6.

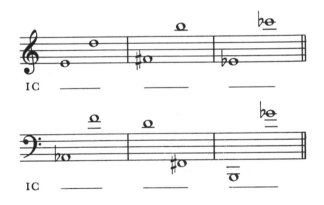

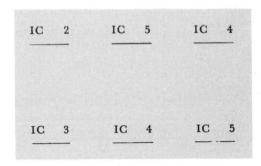

IC   2   IC   5   IC   4

IC   3   IC   4   IC   5

Operations with Sets

Inversion may be accomplished by subtracting the pitch-class integers in turn from 12. If you desire to have the same pitch class at the beginning of both the original set and the inverted set, then you should subtract the integers in turn from a number that is twice the first number in the set. Thus, the inversion of the set (7,8,1,2) would be (7,6,1,0) (2 × 7 = 14; 14 - 7 = 7, 14 - 8 = 6, 14 - 1 = 1 [mod 12], and 14 - 2 = 0 [mod 12]).

Transposition may be accomplished simply by adding a constant to each member of the set. To transpose the set (0,4,5) a perfect fourth (**I** 5), simply add 5 to each member; the result is (5,9,10).

A subset may be derived from a set simply by extracting some members of the set. For example, (0,4,5) is a subset of (0,2,4,5,7).

chapter 20

In our final chapter, we further expand the pitch parameter to include other triads in a tonality, chromaticism, mutation, and modulation.

OTHER TRIADS IN A TONALITY

Triads can be built upon all degrees of any scale, as shown in Ex. 20-1.*

Ex. 20-1

Major

Major	minor	minor	Major	Major	minor	diminished
I	ii	iii	IV	V	vi	vii°

Natural minor

minor	diminished	Major	minor	minor	Major	Major
i	ii	III	iv	v	VI	VII

*We are using Roman numerals to indicate the scale degree of the roots and the quality of the triads. Further explanation of these symbols can be found in *Materials and Structures in Music*, Christ et al., Prentice-Hall, N.J., 1973.

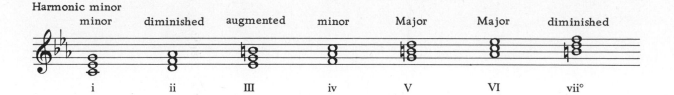

Most of the triads so constructed will be major or minor triads such as we have already encountered. However, two new triadic types appear here, and we should look at them more closely before we proceed. The *diminished triad* consists of two minor thirds. The *augmented triad* consists of two major thirds. Over any given root, we can now construct the four triads shown in Ex. 20–2.

Ex. 20–2

Identify the following triads as major, minor, augmented, or diminished, using the standard abbreviations M, m, +, and °.

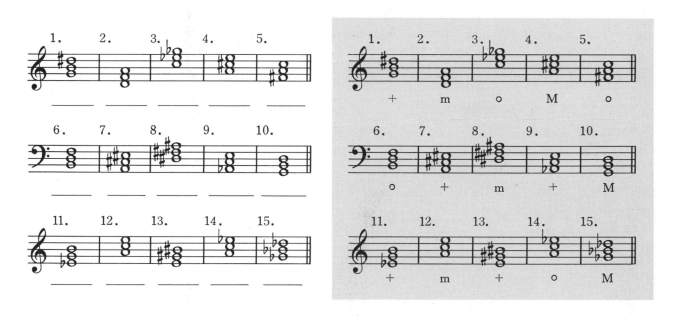

Write the following harmonic triads.

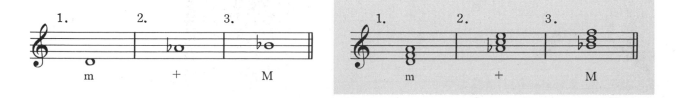

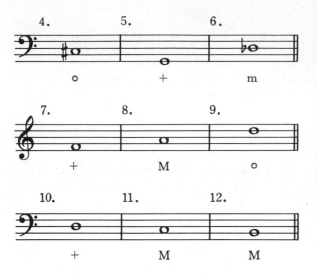

SEVENTH CHORDS

We can create *seventh chords* by adding another major or minor third to any triad. Seventh chords are so called because the added tone forms an interval of a seventh with the root. Ex. 20–3 shows seven possible seventh-chord types. Notice that they are named according to the type of triad and the type of seventh. Thus, a major-minor seventh chord includes a major triad and a minor seventh. Notice also that some of these seventh chords have special names.

Ex. 20–3

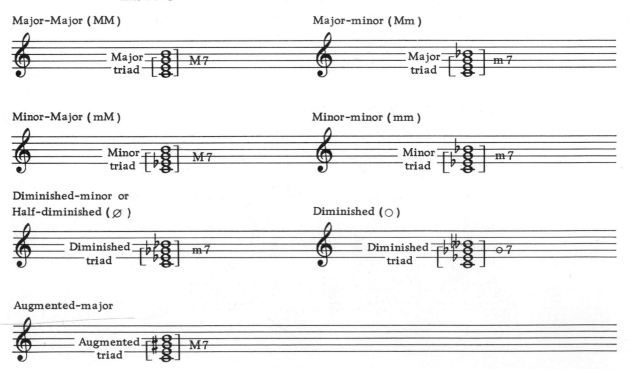

336

It is beyond the scope of this introductory text to explore all of the seventh chords, but we are introducing them now because one of them—the major-minor, or dominant, seventh chord—plays such an important role even in relatively simple music. This chord is called the *dominant seventh* because it can be found on the dominant degree of the major or harmonic minor scales.

Build a dominant seventh on each of the following roots.

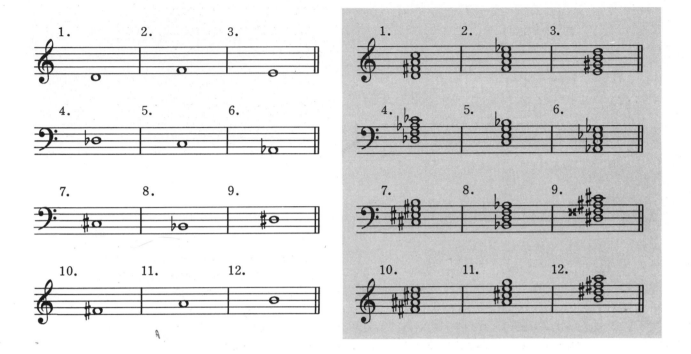

Now that we have discussed these other triads and the dominant seventh chord in a harmonic sense, let us see how they can apply to melodic analysis and how they can help us in hearing and performing melodies. Ex. 20-4 shows how melodies may use patterns based not only upon the tonic triad but also upon other triads and the dominant seventh chord.

Ex. 20-4

Haydn: Symphony No. 94, "Surprise"

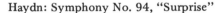

C: C_____ G7_____

Mozart: Sonata for Piano and Violin, K. 303

C: C_____ d_____

337

Analyze the following melodies in a similar manner.

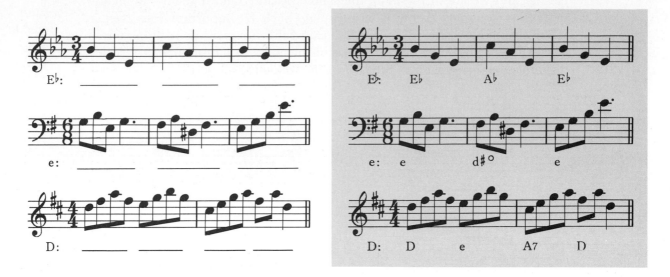

Not only do melodies employ simple triad patterns based on triads other than tonic, they also frequently embellish these nontonic triads. Ex. 20–5 demonstrates this with neighbor tones.

Ex. 20–5

Handel: Royal Fireworks Music

Notice that it would be possible to analyze this melody completely in terms of patterns based on the tonic triad. Such an analysis, however, does not make nearly as much musical sense as the one in Ex. 20–5.

In this chapter, we have given you a very brief preview of certain aspects of harmony. Much of your advanced study in music theory will be devoted to analyzing, writing, hearing, and performing harmonic materials. You will learn how harmony functions as one of the shaping forces of music, and you will discuss such principles as harmonic progression, harmonic rhythm, and voice leading.

For our present purposes, we shall concentrate on a limited area of this extensive subject. Simply stated, our objectives now are that you learn to recognize, write, hear, and perform the four triads we have discussed (major, minor, diminished, and augmented) and the major-minor or dominant seventh chord. You should be able to do this with isolated examples presented melodically and harmonically and with examples of these sonorities that appear in the context of a melody.

Previous chapters have provided drill material for major and minor triads.

The drills below deal with diminished and augmented triads and the dominant seventh chord. Practice them in all keys before beginning the music-reading and ear-training exercises in this chapter.

1.

Continue the pattern and repeat the entire pattern on successive half steps higher.

2.

Continue the pattern and repeat the entire pattern on successive half steps higher.

3.

Continue the pattern and repeat the entire pattern on successive half steps higher.

In the beginning of our study of pitch, we learned that a half step written with two consecutive letter names was a diatonic half step; a half step written with the same letter name but with different accidentals was a chromatic half step. (See Ex. 20–6.)

Ex. 20–6

Diatonic half steps   Chromatic half steps

All of the scales and modes we have studied thus far are written with seven different letter names; none of them contains any chromatic half steps. These scales are called diatonic scales, and the notes that they comprise are called diatonic notes. A composition using only the given notes of a particular scale or mode is said to be a diatonic composition.

However, it is also possible in the course of a composition to use tones that are not in the basic scale or mode of the composition. These tones will always be related to one of the diatonic tones by a chromatic half step. In other words, they will represent an alteration of one of the diatonic tones by a change of accidental. These tones are called *chromatic tones* or simply *chromatics*. A composition that uses chromatic tones extensively is said to be a chromatic composition. We shall examine some of the ways in which chromaticism may be used, and we shall observe how it is possible to hear and perform passages involving chromaticism, but first we shall study the chromatic scale.

THE CHROMATIC SCALE

The chromatic scale comprises twelve notes, each a half step apart. It is customary to write the ascending scale with sharps and the descending scale with flats (Ex. 20–7). Though it is possible to begin a chromatic scale on any pitch, there is really only one chromatic scale, since each chromatic scale uses the same set of twelve pitches.

Ex. 20–7

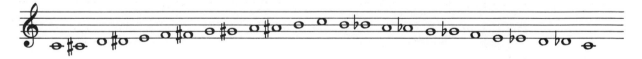

Practice playing and singing chromatic scales beginning on various pitches. In singing, you may find it helpful to think of the scale as a major scale with chromatic notes inserted between degrees $\hat{1}$ and $\hat{2}$, $\hat{2}$ and $\hat{3}$, $\hat{4}$ and $\hat{5}$, $\hat{5}$ and $\hat{6}$, and $\hat{6}$ and $\hat{7}$. Chromatic pitches cannot be inserted between degrees $\hat{3}$ and $\hat{4}$ or $\hat{7}$ and $\hat{1}$ because the interval between these scale degrees is already the smallest we are using—the half step. (See Ex. 20-8.)

Ex. 20-8

INCIDENTAL CHROMATICISM

One of the simplest and most frequent uses of chromatic notes is in an incidental or embellishing role as a neighbor tone to a diatonic note. Usually, chromatic tones are used to change what would normally be a whole-step neighbor-tone relationship to a half-step relationship (Ex. 20-9).

Ex. 20-9

Diatonic neighbor tones · · · · · · · Chromatic neighbor tones

G Major

Ex. 20-10 illustrates the use of incidental chromaticism. Sing and play these two excerpts, and you will notice that the use of incidental chromaticism often contributes to a smoother, easier melodic flow. Compare the chromatic versions on the left to the equivalent diatonic versions on the right.

Ex. 20-10

Beethoven: Minuet in G

"Mexican Hat Dance"

MUTATION

If one or more chromatic notes are used with fairly great frequency and significance, they may create the effect of a change of mode, or a *mutation*. Notice in Ex. 20–11, that the tonic remains the same but the mode or scale form is changed. Sometimes this change is temporary and the original mode returns; sometimes it is more permanent and the composition ends in the new mode.

Ex. 20–11

Schubert: "Die Winterreise"

MODULATION

All of the music studied to this point has been characterized by the clear establishment of one tone as tonic throughout the piece or exercise. Except for very simple folk songs, hymns, and tunes, most music does not display such unswerving loyalty to a single tonic.

The process of moving from one pitch as tonic to another pitch as tonic is usually called *modulation,* or change of tonality.

In your advanced studies, you will consider many aspects of this fascinating topic. Now, we only want to alert you to the possibility of a change of tonality, especially in longer examples. The same factors of placement, frequency, length, and pitch configuration that are used to establish an initial tonic can be used to establish a new tonic within the course of the piece. When the new tonic has been established, you should adapt your sense of pitch function. In tonally unstable sections, between two tonalities, you will probably have to rely on your sense of pitch distance and pitch memory.

THE IMPORTANCE OF AN ECLECTIC APPROACH

We have given you many different things to think about when dealing with the pitch problems of a melody. You have been working to build up your sense of pitch memory so that you can remember perhaps as many as seven or more different pitches and sing a melody merely by moving from one remembered sound to another. You have been building up your sense of pitch distance or intervals so that you can sing a melody merely by singing one interval after the next. You have been building up a sense of pitch function so that you can sing a melody by moving from one scale degree to the next. Finally, you have been building up a repertoire of pitch patterns so that you can sing a melody merely by singing one pattern after the next.

As we have indicated frequently in this book, it is your responsibility to work out for yourself some combination of all of these methods that will best suit you and will best suit the music. Some music will be so simple and so clearly in a major or minor tonality that it would be inefficient to think of intervals; instead, tonal function and tonal patterns would best help you. In some more complex melodies, tonal function and patterns may be of less assistance, and you will have to rely more upon interval sense. The important thing is to master each skill to the fullest. In this way, you have an arsenal of techniques at your disposal to meet any musical demand.

MUSIC-READING EXERCISES 20

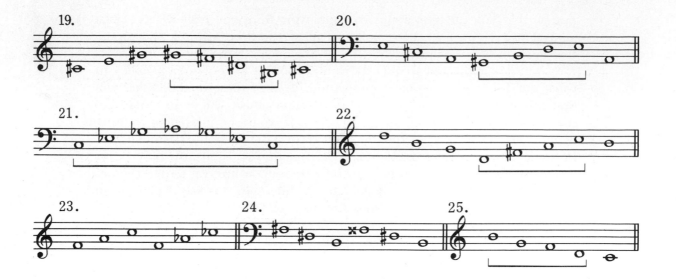

EAR-TRAINING EXERCISES 20

Identify the following chords as major (M), minor (m), augmented (+), diminished (°), or major-minor seventh (Mm 7). If a chord is none of these, write "other."

1. _____

2. _____

3. _____

4. _____

5. _____

6. _____

1. minor triad

2. major-minor 7th

3. other

4. major triad

5. diminished triad

6. minor triad

7. _____

8. _____

9. _____

10. _____

11. _____

12. _____

13. _____

14. _____

15. _____

16. _____

7.

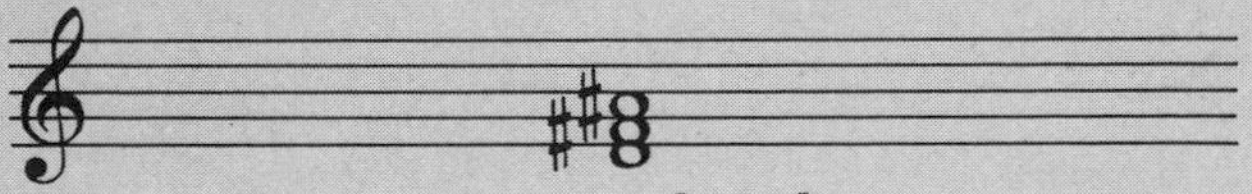

augmented triad

8.

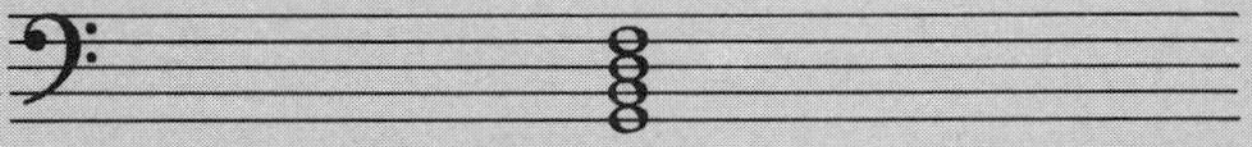

major-minor 7th

9.

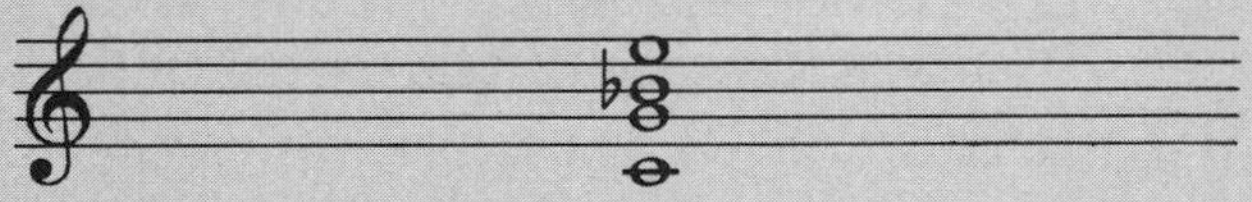

major-minor 7th

10.

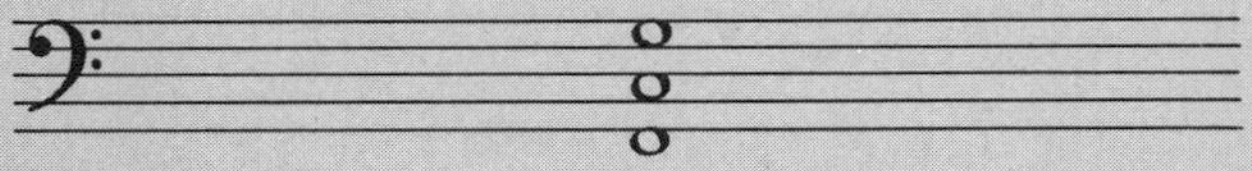

other

11.

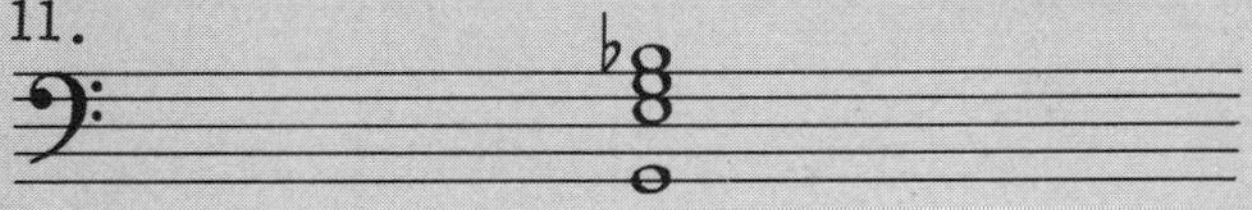

diminished triad

12.

augmented triad

13.

minor triad

14.

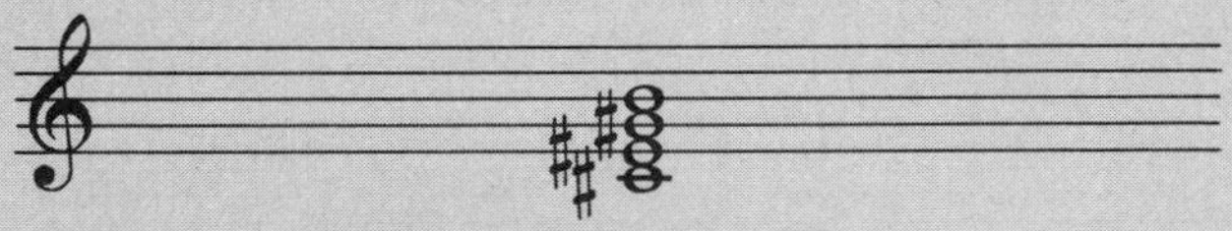

major-minor 7th

15.

augmented triad

16.

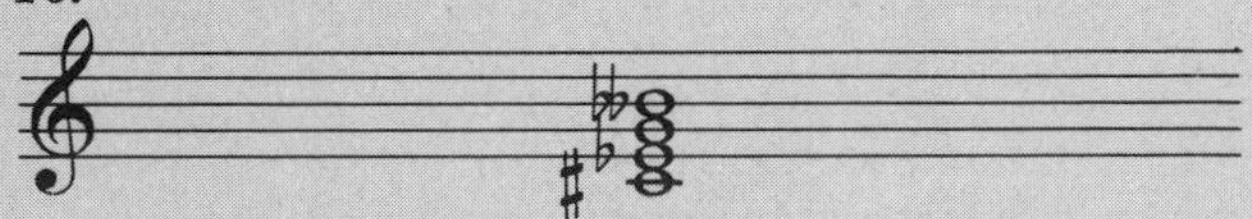

other

345

Supply the missing notes.

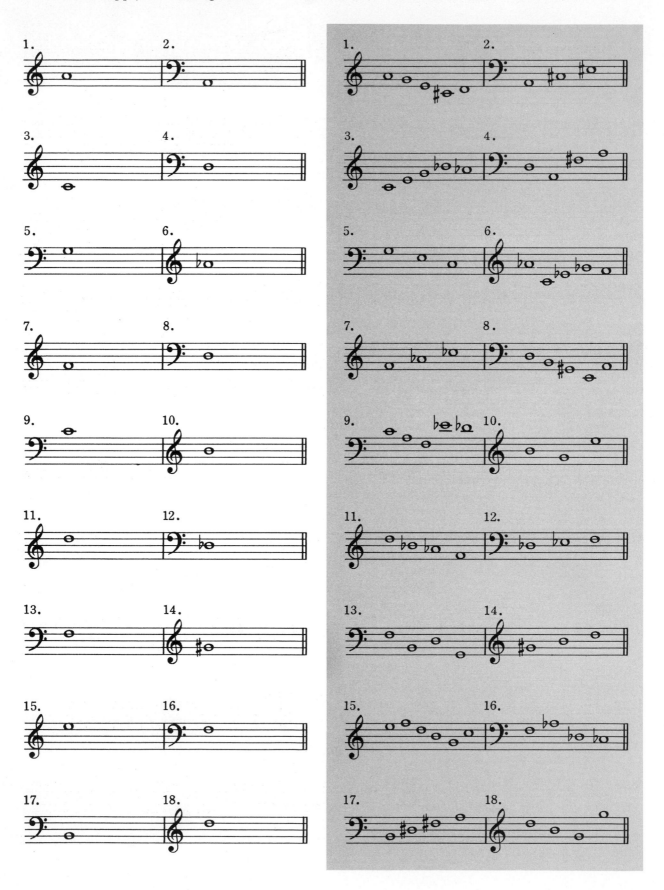

348

1. Gesualdo: "Non é, questa la mano"

SUPPLEMENTARY EXERCISES 20

1. See how many examples of diminished or augmented chords you can find in the literature. How many melodies can you find with clearly outlined dominant seventh chords?

2. Compose examples similar to the ear-training exercises in this chapter, and work on them with your drill partner.

3. Take several melodies from the literature or from sight-singing books and indicate what techniques would be most helpful in singing the pitches for each measure.

4. Experiment on the piano with moving from one chord to another. Do not be concerned with any rules for voice leading or spacing; merely listen to the different sonorities and the different effects that you can create by moving, for example, from C to F, C to e, and C to Ab.

5. In earlier supplementary exercises, we suggested that you write simple melodies accompanied only by the tonic triad. You may now wish to extend this technique to writing melodies with accompaniments that involve other chords. A significant part of your advanced study in music theory will consist of the analysis and writing of melody with a harmonic accompaniment. Obviously, it would be impossible for us to summarize all the various harmonic procedures at this point. Instead, we shall simply make some brief suggestions.

You might wish to try two different approaches to this problem. The first approach would be to first write a series of chords in a definite durational pattern—for example, a change of chord per measure, a change of chord per beat, or some combination of the two. Then, play the chord progression several times and listen carefully to it. Finally, try to sing an improvised melody that "fits" with this chord progression. This is somewhat the same technique that jazz players use when they improvise a solo. For the melody to "fit" the chords, you will find that it should generally be built around the notes of the chords. For the sake of variety, however, it should also use other notes, especially in unaccented parts of the measure and especially in stepwise motion.

The second approach would be to first write a melody and then try to find a series of chords that fit well with it. In either approach, you can experiment with different accompanimental types.

If you find it difficult to get started on an exercise such as this, you might begin by basing your composition on an already existing composition. The following shows how you might write "Silent Night" with the two approaches mentioned above.

6. From listening only, describe the differences and similarities of two works from different periods of music literature.

7. From visual study of the score, describe as many aspects as possible of a short work from the literature.

8. Write a composition of fairly extended length for a varied instrumental ensemble. The following brief information can help you in this project:

   a. Flutes, oboes, and violins are written in treble clef. They are *concert-pitch* instruments; that is, the notes sound as written.
   b. Bassoons, trombones, and cellos are concert-pitch instruments. They are usually written in bass clef, occasionally in tenor clef. For higher parts, alto clef is used for trombones and treble clef for cellos.
   c. Violas are concert-pitch instruments. They are usually written in alto clef, occasionally in treble clef.
   d. Other instruments are *transposing* instruments; that is, the notes sound a given interval lower or higher than written. With the exception of the string bass, they are all written in treble clef. The string bass is written in bass clef, and occasionally in tenor clef.

To compensate for transposition, you should write the parts as follows:

   a. B-flat clarinets and trumpets: write notes a major second higher than you want them to sound. Key signatures must also be a major second higher.
   b. French horns in F: write notes a P5 higher than you want them to sound. French horn parts are generally written without key signatures.
   c. String bass: write notes a P8 higher than you want them to sound.

For detailed information on ranges and characteristics, see Chapter 2. For more information, see Walter Piston, *Orchestration* (New York: W.W. Norton and Company, Inc., 1955), or Kennan, *The Technique of Orchestration*, 2nd ed. (Englewood Cliffs, N.J.: Prentice-Hall, Inc., 1970, 1952).

In writing a more extended composition, it might be helpful to have in mind some general principles governing the organization of music. In your later study, you will discuss these principles in detail in classes devoted to form and analysis. At this point, we can present some brief concepts and ideas. You should also review the points made in Chapter 1 concerning the organization of music.

Perhaps the simplest procedure would be to adopt one of the more or less standard formal plans that have appeared in music in various periods. These are summarized below. The letters represent short sections of music that could range in length from a four-measure phrase to a sixteen-measure double period or longer. As before, exact repetition or return is indicated by the use of the same letter, variation is indicated by the use of the same letter with a superscript, and contrast is indicated by the use of successive letters.

Theme and variations: $AA^1 A^2 A^3$ etc.
Binary form: AB *or* AA *or* AA^1
Ternary form: ABA *or* ABA^1
Rondo form: ABACA *or* ABACABA etc.

Before you begin, it would probably be most helpful for you to study one or more examples of the form as used in works from the literature. You will see that composers frequently write connecting sections, or *transitions*, between the main thematic sections.

In this brief summary it has, of course, been impossible to discuss the important conventions of various forms or even to mention such significant forms as sonata-allegro form and other larger forms. All we can hope to do is stimulate your interest in this aspect of music theory so that you will be ready to consider it in your advanced study. We do, however, want to guard against one possible misconception that many students have about form in music—namely, that forms, such as those listed above, are rigid molds into which composers simply pour their musical material. Though this may be true of some banal composers of popular music, it is not true for the majority of composers of serious music or even for the more creative composers of present-day popular music. Instead, for these composers composition is an organic or evolutionary process with highly complex and effective interactions and relationships between the various parts of the composition.

For more information on form in music, see Wallace Berry, *Form in Music* (Englewood Cliffs, N.J.: Prentice-Hall, 1966); Paul Fontaine, *Basic Formal Structures in Music* (New York: Appleton-Century-Crofts, 1967).

OPTIONAL MATERIAL

Integer Notation

Triads and other chords may be represented very clearly with the integer notation shown in the following chart.

Triads

M	0				4			7				
m	0			3				7				
o	0			3			6					
+	0				4				8			

Seventh Chords

Mm7	0				4			7			10	
mm7	0			3				7			10	
ϕ_7	0			3			6				10	
o_7	0			3			6			9		
MM7	0				4			7				11
mM7	0			3				7				11
+M7	0				4				8			11

Review some of the materials in this chapter, applying concepts of integer notation.

index

PRONUNCIATION GUIDE

Foreign words and proper names have approximate pronunciations indicated in parentheses after the main entry. A key to the sounds employed is given below. It is impossible to indicate all the various nuances of vowel sound and length without employing a system such as the International Phonetic Transcription. To use this, however, would probably be confusing and cumbersome for most readers. Ideally the best way, if not the only way, to learn proper pronunciation is to hear the words spoken by a good native speaker of the language. The conscientious reader can, however, achieve an adequate comprehension and command of the terms used in this book by studying carefully the pronunciations given in the index.

Vowels:
a—as in *sat*
ah—as in *father*
ai—as in *raid* (but as a single vowel, not as a diphthong)
e—as in *get* (like the *ai* sound, but shorter. In concluding syllables in German it should be pronounced almost like the *a* in *along*)
ee—as in *see*
i—as in *hit* (like the *ee* sound, but shorter)
o—as in *hot*
oh—as in *go* (for concluding syllables in Italian it should be pronounced very short)
oo—as in *too*

Diphthongs:
ie—as in *lie*

oi—as in *ointment*
ou—as in *house*

Foreign vowels:
The following vowels have no equivalent sounds in English, but they may be approximated as indicated.
ö—*ai* (as in *raid*) through closely rounded lips
ü—*ee* (as in *see*) through closely rounded lips

Diphthongs:
The following consonants are to be pronounced according to normal English usage:
b, d, f, h, j, k, m, n, p, t, v, w, y, z.
g—hard as in *go*
l—generally brighter and more *"palatized"* (with the tongue closer to the roof of the mouth)
r—generally to be "rolled," especially at the beginning of syllables.
s—always sibilant as in *so*.

Foreign consonants:
The following consonants have no equivalent sounds in English, but may be approximated as indicated.
kh—like the guttural Scotch *ch* in *loch*
nh—the nasal French *n*
xh—place the tongue as for the vowel *ee* (as in *see*) and emit a strong current of breath.
zh—like the *s* in *measure*.

Accent is indicated by capital letters. As a general rule vowels are long for accented syllables, short for unaccented syllables. The glottal stop is indicated with a diagonal line (/).

A

370